Push You Pay
5 Alive

In This Game
If You
Gamble, It'll
Be With Your
Life

The Dice Series

By Kalub Shipman

This is a work of fiction. All incidents and dialogue, and all characters, are products of the author's imagination and are not to be construed as real. Any resemblance to persons living or dead is entirely coincidental.

Learn more from UMG Writers Block LLC by following @ UMGWritersBlock on Instagram.

3

Bea and her best friend Meme have been living a life of secrecy since they were teenagers, only depending on each other and no one else! Risking their lives and freedom, all in the name of the come up. But after stumbling into a serious situation, the sisters can't deny they need help. So, the best friends take a chance by rolling the dice and putting their fate in the hands of Boolaid; a person they never met but only talked to through a single text message. Everything is well until Boolaids' problems become their problems. But at the same time, Bea and Meme's secrets become his secrets. The three seem to be at a stalemate, but the game they're playing isn't chess—because in this game, if "You Push, You Pay."

Acknowledgements

This being my first book there are so many people I would love to acknowledge. If I don't mention you, I promise you are not forgotten. Even in my lowest point I stand tall on the tip of the highest pyramid. I am here because I have been lifted onto the shoulders of my family and friends. I would not be here if it were not for their sweat, their attention, their hearts, and their love! To my mother, my true heart and the only woman I know that will never leave my side, I love you Booba! To my sister Kaina and my two children Khiah and Khaileah, you three are my Queens and make things so much more hopeful for me because I know there's royalty inside my DNA! Every man has a breaking point, but you held me down when others couldn't, so for that you get a special thank you. Akaila, and to my twin brother from another mother, Manny Pacman, I give a special thanks, you stood by my side since childhood, you fought with me through thick and thin literally in some cases. Just know we are forever. To my cousin Drama and his wife Patty Mayo, I've watched you grow from a boy to a man. You stand tall where others fall short, you two are a man and woman of your word. When others are just people with mouths. To Gutter and Sabrina, my power couple when I think back on your journey it gives me strength, you've endured so much pain but as the saying goes "no pain, no gain", you make hard seem easy, the impossible possible you inspire me to grow. My baby cousin Rita, for if it were not for you my novel would still be just words on paper complete yet soooo incomplete. My cousin RJ Richie Rich, thank you for always coming through in the times where it matters the most, truly a brother's keeper.

UMG, we the union and the G stands for greatness. I couldn't ask for a better group of guys. Can't forget the "Ugh's". To all my day ones I don't have to mention because what's understood doesn't need to be explained.

Dedication

This book is dedicated to family and whatever that means to you.

"Sharing the same DNA with a person does not make you family, family is when two or more individuals can depend on each other, provide for one another at all costs, always standing back-to-back no matter the good, the bad, and the ugly." - Big Ugly-

"Make loyalty override your everyday lifestyle, all family no friends." -AFNF –Ti-

Prologue

"The street life is like a dice game—one big gamble, and we're talking C-lo not craps. Everybody is liable to catch a point one time or another. You can four, five, six or you can ace out. Especially if you're in the game for the long haul. Keep shaking and rolling the dice in the name of the almighty dollar, power, and respect, because when they stop it's only three outcomes. Alone at the Top, the prison yard, or the graveyard, because if you push you pay with your life. No cap."

-- Pimp God –

Kalub Shipman
PUSH YOU PAY

Chapter 1

"I told you for the hundredth time, stop doing that!" she barks with fury in her voice. "What did I do baby?" asked the john. The couple were parked on a dark street called Randolph. Randolph Street was connected to the main road called Martin Luther King Drive, also known as MLK for short. MLK in Greensboro, North Carolina, is a well-known area for prostitution. The john sat in the driver's seat with the chair leaned back as far as it would go. His pants and boxers were at ankle level, his penis was hard. The hooker was sitting on her knees on the passenger side, leaning over the middle console with her face in his lap. "I told you to stop grabbing the back of my head, I don't like when you do that," she explained.

The John was a big, muscular man who looked like he worked out 24 hours a day. At least 270 pounds, he could overpower her with ease, and she knew it. She weighed 115 pounds and was only 16, but that didn't stop her from speaking her mind. "OK baby, now put that dick back in that warm sweet mouth of yours and get me right," the John pleaded as he waved his penis back and forth. *I hate yo nasty ass*, she thought to herself. "I promise I won't do it again," said the john, putting his hands in the air as if the police told him to freeze. The two sat for a long moment, having an intense staring contest. She said nothing, she had a gut feeling she couldn't trust him. But she was hungry, she hadn't eaten in two days and needed the money desperately. She grilled him with an evil eye. Unsure of his trust, but slowly began to go back down on him. "Umm, ummm, huh right there. Just like that, nice and slow," the john whispered as the young woman's head moved up and down at a steady pace. Suddenly he grabbed the back of her head with both hands and rammed himself violently into her mouth. She choked and gagged, then vomit filled her throat. "Ahh, my fuckin eye!" the john yelled, letting her head go. She had clawed his face and poked him in the eye.

"What the fuck is wrong with yo stupid ass!" she screamed out, still fighting for air. This nigga is crazy, and the money he got is not worth my life, she said to herself as she reached for the door handle to get out. But the door wouldn't open. He had put the child safety lock on, which meant her door could only be opened from the outside. Panic filled her heart and mind. "Please let me out of the car," she asked. "You not going nowhere until you finish your job. I gave you $25 you little thot and I want my money's worth", the Creep growled. She couldn't win a fist fight with this grown ass man. She was helpless and needed to think fast. Fearing for her own life, she reached into her pocket and pulled out her cell phone. The phone had been off for a couple weeks because she couldn't afford to pay the bill. "I'm calling 911 you're going to jail!", she threatened. She hoped he would fall for her bluff, but just like the card game poker, he called.

Whoop! Whoop! Whoop! The echoes from the punches he delivered were like small explosions to the side of her head and face. Her small body fell out of the seat and folded onto the floor, knocking open the glove compartment on her way down. She was seeing stars and was trapped in a car with a maniac. She could only see out of one eye because his combo instantly shut the other. She was going to die that night. "See what you made me do?" the john said. "You hear me, get your little ass up off that floor." She shook her head no. "I'm not playing girl wake up."

Bea snapped open her eyes and sighed. Just a nightmare, Bea whispered to herself. This wasn't just any nightmare, but the same one she'd been having every night for the past 10 years.

Boom, boom, "Bea? Wake up girl," Meme said while she knocked. Meme was Bea's roommate and childhood friend, really her only friend. "Giiirlll if you don't stop banging on my damn door," Bea answered. "Bitch whatever! Don't catch no 'tude wit me, you asked me to wake you up and that's what I'm doing, period. Now get up because you know it takes you forever to get dressed," Meme said. Bea laughed to herself because Meme wasn't lying, she did take forever to get dressed. "OK girl, I'm up," she said through a long yawn. Bea got out of bed and walked to the bathroom that connected to her bedroom. After allowing the water to warm up, Bea jumped in the tub and took a long hot shower. She always did, trying to wash away the filthy memories of her long ago past. The thoughts never really left, but the showers did help. Bea stepped out of the shower and wrapped a towel around her body. The bathroom had filled up with hot steam, making the mirror fog up. She swiped her hand across the glass a few times, then gazed into her own eyes.

Sometimes Bea didn't recognize the person looking back at her." One who has a specified quality," Bea said out loud talking to the stranger in the mirror. She waited for her reflection to answer back. She shook her head at even entertaining such a thought. Specified quality is what her name meant. Her father would tell her what her name meant every day while he was alive.

Bea's father was a well-known pimp that had been murdered in a drug deal gone bad, Bea's mother was one of his hoes, and not just any hoe—she was the bottom bitch. The bottom bitch was the one who made the most cash. If the pimp was to ever stop pimping, his bottom bitch would become his wife. Her name was Rochelle, and she was so beautiful it was as if God made her out of clay with his bare hands. Rochelle also met her demise—she had gotten strangled to death by one of her John's. Somebody dumped her body in a dumpster behind Food Lion off of the corner of Alamance Church Road and MLK Drive. A worker found the body taking boxes to the trash one early morning. At the time of Rochelle's death,
Bea was still a baby—she was three years old.

The memories of her mother were fuzzy to her, sometimes Bea would have these images of a young woman just pop up in her mind. The thoughts were empty, they had no emotional connection. Her father went by the name Pimp God, but everybody that knew him called him PG for short. When Rochelle died, PG raised Bea. He was with his daughter every day of her life until the day he died.

Pimp God taught Bea everything there was to know about pimps and hoes. PG was hard on Bea. As a pimp he could be very verbally abusive. But there were two things he never did to Bea— smack her to the ground or make her sell her body like he did and made his hoes do. He even shot a man dead for asking for Bea instead of his hoes. Most of the hookers became jealous and envious because of their relationship. Bea was small but the shape of her body was unbelievable. By the time she was 12, her body looked more developed than most 21-year-olds. Know your quality, no need to sell your body, PG would tell the young child, hoping she understood his words. He treated her like a Queen and gave her all the lessons on the art of seduction. Pimp God was a master manipulator, so he tried to teach Bea how to make men and women bow down to her very will without opening her legs, but by using her mind to manipulate. When PG got murdered Bea was only 13, too young to understand everything he told her. Even though she didn't understand everything he said, she never forgot one word that came out of his mouth. His knowledge would forever be locked into her subconscious.

So, for the past 10 years, Bea made many mistakes, but over time with trial and error the seeds that PG planted began to grow. Now at the age of 26 she was well trained, a pro at what she did for a living. On the outside she looked soft as cotton, but on the inside, she was as solid as concrete. She walked on in the day and then slept on at night because she had nowhere to go. "It ain't your beauty, it's your booty," Bea said looking into the mirror while brushing her teeth. She rinsed her mouth out and smiled at the thought of her father, she missed him, and he was the only family member she knew.

"Bea, get yo slow ass out that mirror daydreaming and shit. I told you, you take forever," Meme said from the other side of the bathroom. Bea opened the door to face Meme. The two looked at each other with sisterly love and embraced each other with a hug. "Bitch, how you get in my room?" Bea asked Meme with raised eyebrows. "Girl, I got the keys to the city!," Meme said, showing the clothes hanger she bent straight so she could pop the lock to the door. Bea shook her head and laughed. "I don't see nothing funny, you know we gotta go to work tonight", Meme said seriously. Bea sighed, "I know sis, my clothes are already laid out, give me 30 minutes", Bea replied. "No, I'ma give yo slow ass an hour, but after that I'm on your wig" — meaning she was going to be all over Bea. Meme looked at her bestie with arms folded across her chest, a stern look in her eyes but a silly smile on her face. "OK, one hour," Bea answered. Without another word, Meme turned and walked away. Bea watched Meme's ass open and clap with each step she took. She admired beautiful women and Meme was all that and then some.

Meme had a dark chocolate complexion; her skin was smooth and flawless. Her eyes were dark honey brown that could pierce any man's soul and could look straight through you to see all bullshit. You would have thought she spoke Spanish at first glance, because she had a Dominican look. But she was Black, a Southern bell from Georgia. 5 '1 and 137 pounds, damn you got a phat ass Meme, Bea said to herself. Meme's lips were round and luscious, she always talked about getting a tummy tuck and a breast lift even though there was nothing wrong with her body. She was a dime and belonged in someone's magazine as the next top model. Meme had a natural gift for doing hair since she was 12, so she kept Bea's and hers on point. Today, she wore her hair in a style called soft dread. They fell down her back and stopped where her plump ass began. Bea walked to her closet and opened it. Tonight, was a work night, so she pulled her clean uniform. "This outfit is perfect," she said out loud. I love my job.

****

Mekka held onto the back of Kesha's head and cried out a soft moan. Kesha's face laid in between Mekka's warm thighs. "Yesss, yesss, ohh I love the way you eat my pussy," Mekka whispered while biting down on her bottom lip. Kesha held Mekka's pussy lips spread apart to expose her pink clit. She finger fucked the pussy and asshole at the same time with her pointer finger and thumb. In the mix of that she put her mouth around her clit and gently sucked. Mekka's body began to shake uncontrollably, like she had been hit with a tease gun. "I'm-m-m-m-m c-c-c-um-n-n-n", Mekka stuttered. She arched her back into the air and back down repeatedly, Kesha never letting up, her tongue glided across Mekka's clit like ice skates. Mekka's body flopped like a fish on dry land. Kesha finally came up for air and climbed on top of her lover. They were face to face, breast to breast, Mekka still taking heavy breaths from her orgasm, making the couples' nipples rub against each other and they became super hard. They stared in each other's eyes, both seeing sisterly love. "I love you," Kesha whispered. "I love you more," Mekka said back. "Are you ready?" Kesha asked her lover. Mekka just nodded to answer Kesha's question. They kissed passionately, then turned their heads in the same direction. John stared back with lust in his eyes. He had been patiently watching them have sex for the past 30 minutes. The girls were hot and ready and wet. He was hard. John gave them a round of applause. "That was quite a show, but if you two don't mind, I would love to join," he stated as a matter of fact.

Bea and Meme were at John's private condo. The women had met John at a swinger's party. They had tricked him into thinking they were a lesbian couple that wanted to have their first threesome. John told them he was the perfect man for the job, and he was because after a few weeks of careful observation the girls found out he kept large amounts of money stashed at his condo, and he had just invited them to stay for the whole weekend. "John, why don't you come and join us," Meme said, then rolled her eyes in ecstasy when Bea sat up and kissed the side of her neck. John quickly undressed.

He was a small, framed man. He stood at 5'6, 150 pounds, with a bald head and a little goatee. John was in his late 40s and he sold cocaine even though he was far from a street nigga. All his customers were white people. They thought he was gangsta, but Bea only saw a goofy, straight lame. He climbed into bed with hunger on his mind. He brought his hand down and smacked Meme on the ass. In response, she made her ass clap in slow motion while looking back at it. Meme's ass wobbled and made waves like the ocean. John palmed both of her butt cheeks and spread them apart. Her asshole was clean and tight, and Meme's pussy looked like a sacred rose that dripped wet from a light drizzle of rain. John leaned in and used his tongue as a straw to taste her Aquafina. "Uhmm," Meme moaned. "Slow down baby, you gotta remember this is our first time. We not going anywhere," Meme told him. "We got all night," Bea joined in. Meme rolled off of Bea onto her back. Then both ladies patted the empty space between them. "Come here and lay in the middle of us, you've waited long enough. Let us please you," Bea spoke again. John happily obliged, he felt like a king with two bad bitches, one on each side.

The girls simultaneously went to work on him. Rubbing his chest, kissing, licking, and sucking his neck then ears. Chills flowed through his body. "Oh, hell yea," John said, closing his eyes because of the pleasure. "No baby, I want you to see this," Bea said, looking him in the eyes. Bea and Meme began going down, slowly, and gently touching his midsection. Bea took his dick into her hand; he was big and hard. She felt his penis throb as she gripped him. *Damn, I might gotta see what that dick like for real for real*, she thought. One look at Meme, she knew she was thinking the same thing. In their line of work, you could mix pleasure and business. *If you catch my girl's legs open better smash that, but don't be surprised if she asks where the cash at,* Bea sang *Lil Wayne* in her head. Meme opened her mouth and a glob of spit oozed down and spilled all over John's dick head. She worked her hand, jacking him. Bea placed her mouth around the rim of his penis, blowing hot heat. "Oh my god girl stop playing and eat that dick", John cried out. John grabbed the back of Bea's head. She immediately pulled her head away. Both Meme and John saw aggravation in her facial expression.

"Please don't grab the back of my head," she warned him. "Damn, I been waiting all night for this, are y'all bitches gone pop that pussy or just tease a nigga? Because if that's what type time y'all on, you two should find another nigga to play with". John looked at them and waited for an answer. Meme took one look into Bea's slanted eyes and knew no more words were needed to be said. Meme mounted on top of John in the 69 position and sat her perfectly waxed pussy on his chin. "We're sorry baby," Meme told John as she took him into her mouth and slurped. John pushed his tongue into Meme's warm wetness and Bea held John's pole in place while Meme performed like a porn star. "Yeah, that's it girl, suck that dick", John tells Meme. John palms the back of Bea's head once again. "Help your girlfriend," he moans. Bea allowed him to guide her face to his penis, she put his head into her mouth and sucked. Meme jacked him with both hands as the room became quiet and the only sounds you heard were moans and slurps from the girls' taking turns.

Meme's fat apple shaped ass blocked John's view; he was so caught up in the moment that he didn't care about sight. All he cared about was feeling, and it felt oh so good to him. Meme went down on John, gagged, then came up for air. She looked at her bestie with excitement. Bea went down and deep throated all 10 inches. She cupped his balls and attempted to swallow them as well. Her mouth made squishing sounds with every try. She felt his penis swell heading for climax, when she came up off of him a trail of saliva followed. Even though her mouth no longer touched his dick, they were still connected from the spit. She stroked him very slowly. "Ohh shit I'm about to bust," John sang. Bea grabbed John's dick and squeezed tightly to stop cum from ejecting. With her free hand, she reached into her mouth and pulled out a hidden razor from under her tongue. In one quick motion, she sliced, removing John's dick head from the penis. His mouth opened wide, trying to let out a scream, but the sound had been muffled when Meme rose up and sat on his face. Her legs locked around the inside of his armpits, holding him down. Bea stood on the bed and applied pressure to Meme's shoulders. His face was trapped, being suffocated by a fat ass. Blood and semen sprayed out of John's private part into the air, covering his chest and painting Meme's stomach up her titties. Bea's feet stood in a puddle of blood on the bed. The couple's adrenaline was pumping at an all-time high as John fought for his life. He clawed at Meme's breast but couldn't grip anything because he slipped in his own blood.

"Girl, I know you not doing what it looks like you doing", Bea said, looking down at Meme's scrunched up face. Meme hugged Bea's thighs and palmed her ass with a death grip. "Oh, oh god," she moaned as she grinded back and forth on the dying man's face. At first hard and slow grinds but then they became violent. Bea held her friends' arm because she knew what was coming next. "I-I-I-I'm-m-m sorryyyy, I'm cumming," Meme yelled out as she looked up into Bea's eyes. Cum sprayed then gushed out of Meme's kitty cat. You would have thought she was pissing on herself. It was so much liquid. It took ten whole minutes before she caught her breath. That's the same amount of time it took for John's body to stop moving. "Woo girl that was a crazy nut," Meme said as she climbed off John's face. The girls got out of bed to get a closer look.

John's eyes were still open, frozen with fear. His face looked like it had been dipped into *Krispy*

Kreme glaze. "Now that's how you drown a nigga in pussy," Meme said with her hands on her hips, amusement danced in her eyes. "Bitch really?," Bea said with her head cocked to the side. She held her hand out to John with the *bitch is you crazy* face. "What girl, don't look at me like that, live by the pussy, die by the pussy," Meme answered back. "And bitch don't act like you not mental health, you all like don't touch my big ass head," Meme joked. Both the girls laughed out loud. "Whatever, touch my head and I take yours," Bea said. Seriously. "Come on sis, let's clean up this mess and get our money, ain't nobody gone be looking for him for a couple days. Enough time to make a solid alibi just in case we need one." The girls got dressed and began their search for John's stash. "We killed the trick, so take the treat."

Chapter 2

"Ok baby, I love you," Meme said to the person she was on the phone with. "I'ma send you some money later, I just gotta load it to my cashapp card first." Meme blushed from the words the man spoke into her ear. "You know I got you daddy. I can't wait until you get out of the hell hole and come home to me", Meme said and then listened. "I know daddy all we gotta do is keep faith, make sure you call me tonight when you come off of lock down at seven." She ended the call and stared off in space with a dreamy smile.

She had just hung up with her boyfriend. He was in prison serving a life sentence. He had been down for six years. They had met each other through a mutual friend and became as thick as thieves ever since. She helped him get a lawyer to get an appeal. Meme was a loyal woman, so she held him down at all costs. He had his own bag, he supported her whenever he could. He knew she was in the streets and still never judged her; that's what really made their relationship one of a kind. They were soul mates. "Hello? Earth to Meme!," Bea said, snapping back and forth. Meme stared at her bestie with googly eyes. "What bitch! Yeah, I'm in love, so what?", she fired back with a quick finger snap along with a roll of the neck, only joking with her friend. "Hey to each their own," Bea shrugged her shoulders. "I just don't see how a nigga that's locked up got yo ass all whipped. I don't know girl, it's just these niggas out here ain't hittin' on shit. You know," Meme pointed, "we deal with all types of niggas in our line of work. He different, I swear he is. I might give a nigga some pussy, but he got all of me, mind, body, soul. He got my heart," Meme explained with both hands laid flat on her chest where her heartbeat. Meme looked at her friend and sighed. "You wouldn't understand Bea, you ain't never loved nothing, it's an icebox where your heart used to be ". *That is not true*, was the only thing Bea could think of saying.

The fact of the matter was she didn't love anything but her father, and he was dead. She loved Meme but that didn't count in this case. She never stayed in a relationship for long, all she thought men were good for was sex and giving her money, and she felt like not wasting time on milking him. She would just take it from you. Her and Meme had been robbing for over ten years, and they realized that a lot of niggas were really bitches. *That's why I can't keep a man, because they all hoes*, Bea thought to herself. "Bea!" Meme said this time Bea had been snapped out of a daydream. "I hate it when you do that," Meme told her with a look of concern. "What did I do?" Bea asked Meme. "Sometimes you be staring off into outer space looking all silly and shit. Like somebody narrating our lives—this ain't no book bitch," Meme voiced her opinion.

They were parked in a brand new I8 BMW, this was a $150,000 vehicle. They went in half on the car after they hit the lick on a John. These two beautiful women had men just throwing money and gifts at them, but sometimes that wasn't enough. So, they would rob men from out of state. They didn't mean to kill John, but his death put them in a great position. They had found a trash bag with $300,000. The car was metallic smoke gray outlined with black. It was hot outside. The sunroof was pulled back so the whole world could see that the occupants were two bad bitches. They were eating lunch at the *Bojangles* off of Summit and Bessemer Ave. That was the east side of Greensboro near *A&T University*, a historical black university. This area was filled with different shopping centers that had many stores and restaurants. Meme bit down into her cajun filet chicken biscuit. She always added egg and cheese, a Bo-Berry biscuit with strawberry jelly. Bea had her favorite, chicken supreme combo with extra seasoned fries and honey mustard sauce. Both girls drank large, sweet tea and extra ice.

Bea tapped the push start and the luxury car hummed to life. Bea tossed a French fry into her mouth as she spoke. "I know this ain't no book bitch, all we do is make movies." She hit the gas, the engine roared and shot out of their parking spot. Bea whipped the steering left then right; the car swerved then fishtailed. The girls flew into oncoming traffic at 35 miles an hour, people swerved out of the way and honked their horns as the sisters came their way. The car straightened, Bea hit the gas once more, the speedometer shot to 80 miles per hour, and the girls balled down Bessemer Ave. leaving nothing but dark tire marks and their asses to kiss.

****

"Hey Chinks!", he hollered over the loud music. They were in his strip club called Cabaret. This place was located off Gate City and Coliseum Blvd., the beginning of the west side. The owner's name was Diddy. He had known Bea's father back in the day. Diddy used to be in the streets heavy but got into club ownership and went legit. He wanted Bea to dance in his club because her body was amazing, she was popular to certain street niggas for getting money without poppin' the pussy. So, her dancing would bring lots of attention. She refused, not because she felt like she was better than strippers, because she didn't. Bea respected the hustle; she just knew she could get niggas to drop that bag without shaking her ass. It was easy to her; she was like the Michael Jordan of finesse. Diddy offered her a job as a bottle girl, she was reluctant at first but finally agreed. It really was the perfect job for Bea, she could provide proof of income when needed. Plus, the club was like an office, and all the trick niggas were her employees. She enjoyed the music and enjoyed dressing up even more. Tonight, she wore a *Gucci* sweatsuit that hugged her hips and ass, it looked like somebody painted it on her. She did a lot of walking, so she settled for some *Yeezy* foam runners. Diddy called over the music and waved his hands in the air to get Bea's attention. She noticed him and began to make her way through the crowded club.

"She fat as hell, what's yo name?" She was used to all the catcalls and comments. She politely said "thank you's and hello's and hi's." She waved and smiled. Bea's top half of her *Gucci* shirt was zipped down, showing off her cleavage. Her breasts were B cups, nice and perky, so she didn't need a bra. Around her neck she sported a ten-karat rope chain with matching earrings and a bracelet. "Damn you looking good girl", Diddy said, looking her up and down. Her hair was a braid that fell down the length of her body and stopped at her waist. Her bangs had been brushed down perfectly giving her the baby hair effect. Her eyes had deep slants that gave her an Asian descent. Her skin tone was like a cup of hot chocolate with a half cup of milk added. She looked so creamy. I feel like *"I'm Gucci in 2006"*, Bea sang *Young Boy* back to Diddy as she moved her hips in a sexual manner. He licked his lips and watched as she moved her body from side to side. He wanted her and she knew it. He never came onto her out of respect for her father, PG. Diddy was one of the good ones, she thought to herself, but she still couldn't help teasing him. "Table six wants two bottles of Henny, and table ten."

It was a couple sitting there, a very well-dressed man and an attractive, dark-skinned woman. They saw Bea looking and threw their cups in the air, saluting her. She smiled and waved. "Aye aye captain," she saluted Diddy then headed to the bar to fill her orders. Once the drinks were given to her, she made her way through the club with the bottles held high in the air, sparks shooting into the air for all to see. That's what the dope boys, ballers, hustlers, and clout chasers did. Order bottle after bottle showing off, basically trying to prove who had it. "Boys will be boys," she said to herself, baring a smile. "Thank you, pretty lady," the gentleman said once she sat the bottle down on his table. "You're welcome ugly," she replied. "What I tell you about calling me ugly?," he said with a frown. I'm sorry, she apologized. "You're welcome big fucking ugly," she corrected herself. He smiled at her, revealing a mouth full of diamonds, $100,000 that glittered in the night. "Now that's more like it pretty lady". Bea wondered why they called him ugly because she thought he was handsome. Brown skin, long healthy locks; people said he looked like Bigs from the movie Shottas.

"What I owe you Chinks?," asked Ugly. "$300", she replied. He reached into his pocket and pulled out a wad of cash, he gave her the money without counting. She counted what he handed her very quickly. There were fifty $20 bills. One thousand dollars, Ugly paid attention to the dancers on stage, letting Bea know he wasn't interested in his change. She dropped $700 into a small Fendi tip bag she kept tied around her wrist, then headed towards the bar to take the rest to the cashier. Ugly was a regular to the club, he was the reason why everybody called her Chinks. Every time he saw her, he tried to holler, he would call her Chinks. After a while, the name just stuck. Even though Ugly tried to bag her, she knew he was a good nigga, not the trick lame type of man. Just a *"real street nigga that's in the field, we was thuggin' outside we ain't need cable"*, Bea sang the *Lil Boosie* song that blasted out of the stereo. Bea danced and swayed her way through the club until she took a pause in front of table 13. "Can I buy you a drink sexy?" Meme offered her friend. Bea pointed to herself with a look of surprise. "Buy me a drink? What's the occasion?" Bea asked.

Meme wasn't alone. Sitting at the table with her was a fat brown skinned man. He wasn't sloppy fat but definitely overweight. She noticed his dress game was up to par, most big people with money could dress. He wore a pair of *Dior* shoes, a dark pair of *Moncler* jeans, a *B.B. Simons* Belt, and a *Versace* shirt. Plus, his bust down chain danced harder than the strippers in the club did. But it was Meme that caught Bea's attention. She looked like a real bad bitch in her all-purple *Dolce & Gabbana* gown. It was open so her back and shoulders were out, her lips looked extra sexy and super glossy.

Just like her choke chain that read Meme wrapped around her neck, six-inch *Prada* shoes fitted her feet that complimented her French pedicure.

"The occasion is making new friends," Meme told her. "Ok so y'all want to be my friend?" Bea asked, looking at the duo. "You didn't even ask me my name," Bea said with a sad face. She fell right into the roll. "How rude of me," Meme stood to greet Bea, her ass poked out like a horse. She was a true stallion. "Allow me to introduce myself," my name is Jalisa, and this is my man Curtis, Meme said with raised eyebrows, telling Bea we got one. Bea shook both Meme's and Curtis' hands gently. "Nice to meet you both, my name is Chinks," Bea said. This time it was Curtis who spoke up. "What you drinking ma? Everything on me all night," the big man stated. "My choice of alcohol is Henny or Patron, but I don't drink while on duty so I'm gonna have to take a rain check. Sorry!" Bea explained. Meme took Bea by the hand, giving her sister the puppy dog eyes. 'Maybe we can have a drink or two after you get off," Meme asked softly. Bea looked from Curtis to Meme back to Curtis. "I don't know," Bea said, unsure. "It's an opportunity of a lifetime," Meme tells Bea with a smile.

Opportunity was the girls' code word for come up or money. They were up on funds; their net worth was a little over a quarter million altogether. *We have been doing a lot of spending,*

Bea thought to herself, and money could be gone at the drop of a dime. "How about this, give me your number and if I'm not too tired when I clock out, I might hit you up and see about them drinks. How's that sound?" Bea asked Meme. "How's that sound?" Meme asked Curtis. Curtis bounced his head to the music while looking Bea up and down. Her pussy print popped out something crazy. Just the thought of being inside her made his dick grow and throb. "Sounds good!," he yelled over the music. The girls acted as if they were exchanging numbers, Curtis lived in New York but had a couple houses in North Carolina. Meme sent a text of the location she knew.

Meme had met Curtis at a *North Carolina Panthers* game a year ago. She noticed that he traveled to NC every month and stuck to himself. She wasn't sure what he did, most likely drugs. All she did know was that when he came to town, he had large amounts of cash, and he spent that bread on her. She had had threesomes with him before, so her trying to bag Bea wasn't out of the ordinary. Curtis had quickly fallen for Meme and in return, she gained his trust. Bea made her way through the club, a bee line straight to the manager's office. She burst into the office unannounced, finding Diddy sitting behind a desk counting money. "Damn Bea, what I tell you about barging into my shit without knocking?" Diddy asked. She had a

look of shock with her hand over her mouth.
"Don't just stand there looking all crazy, close the
door," he demanded. She obeyed, closing the door,
and drowning the music into the background.
Diddy counted out a couple more stacks before
looking up at Bea with the mean mug.

She stood with her feet pigeon toed and her
hands behind her back. She held her head down,
looking at the floor. "I sorry," she spoke like a
three-year-old who had just gotten in trouble.
Damn this bitch fine, he thought to himself. She
smiled, knowing what he was thinking. She always
did. Men are so predictable, she thought. He
smiled back and wondered why he couldn't stay
angry with her. "Yes, how many I assist you?" he
asked with a sigh. "I need the rest of the night off,
she answered back." Diddy was in his late 30's,
6'3 light skin with a muscular build. 360 waves
spun around his head. He was a pretty boy. "You
just got here, it's only one o'clock, you probably
ain't made $100 yet", Diddy teased her. Bea took
her tip bag from around her wrist and pulled out a
bundle of cash. "Nah I'm good," she said
nonchalantly. "Let me guess, Ugly. If he wasn't
spending as much money as he be spending, I'd
ban his ass. He gone make you quit, all the bread
he be giving you," Diddy joked. They shared a
laugh. "Nah, but for real, I need the rest of the
night off, seriously. Opportunity has arrived," she
told her boss.

Diddy didn't know what she did outside of the club for money, but he knew it probably would get her killed or sent to prison. He'd heard rumors she would put that pistol on a nigga, but nothing was fact. He knew she only asked to leave out of respect, she didn't need permission from anybody. She was one of the realest street niggas he knew, even though she was a woman, she was more solid than half the guys in the club. "Aight get outta here before I change my mind," he said. "Aye aye Captain," she saluted Diddy and walked away without another word.

Meme and Curtis watched closely as Bea made her way through the club to their table and sat down to join them. Lust in both Meme's and Curtis' eyes, one lusting over Bea's flesh and the other lusting for the come up. Bea couldn't help rubbing her thighs against each other, all the lust in the air made her pussy moist. Bea snuggled in close to Curtis and squeezed his inner thigh. She put her lips so close to his ear he could feel heat as she whispered, "is it too late for those drinks?" She was all over him, damn near sitting in his lap. His dick was rock hard, he had to have her. "Not at all ma," he said in a heavy New York accent. Bea pulled Meme and they shared a long kiss. Curtis watched with excitement. Other men looked at Curtis with hating eyes, wondering who he was and why Chinks fucked with him. Little did they know, if Bea or Meme chose you, it was like

Halloween. You're getting tricked out of your treats. Curtis broke the two girls away from each other. "Why don't I grab a couple bottles and we get outta here and go to my place?" Curtis said to Meme but looked at Bea. Bea stopped a bottle girl named Quandra. "What's up Chinks?," she asked. "Get us a bottle of henny and patron to go!."

****

"Where is it? Hoe ass nigga," Meme yelled at Curtis. "Jalisa, please baby, why are you doing this?" Curtis asked in confusion. They had left the club around 2:30 after some heavy drinking. Now it was 5 o'clock in the morning. The three of them were at Curtis's house in Browns Summit, which was 45 minutes outside of Greensboro down Highway 29. This area of North Carolina was deep country.

Bea had followed behind Curtis and Meme in her '97 Honda. Bea sent Meme a text message saying *she was tired, then warned she wasn't about to play with this fat ass nigga when they arrived at his house*. They walked into the house. Once Bea checked to make sure they were alone, she began to get undressed. Meme helped her and did the same. They danced and strip-teased Curtis as they removed his clothes. The sisters were on

37

their knees, about to pull down his boxers, when
he stopped them. "What is it baby?" Meme asked
Curtis. "Nothing's wrong ma, a nigga just gotta
piss bad as a motherfucka," he told them. Curtis
walked out of the room, going to the bathroom.
Bea made her move. She ran outside to her Honda,
grabbed a *Fendi* handbag, then reached into the
back seat and snatched a baseball bat. She raced
back into the house and rushed into the room
where Meme was.

Her feet had dirt and grass all over, plus they
were wet. Her nipples were super hard from the
outside breeze. Bea tossed Meme the *Fendi* bag
and took deep, controlled breaths, preparing for
her attack, standing in a baseball players' stance
with the bat at the ready. Curtis walked out of the
bathroom and whoop! Bea cracked a home run
upside his head. He was already drunk as hell, so
sleep came easy. Meme reached into the designer
bag and pulled out a roll of duct tape. The girls
worked to tape his wrists and ankles together. The
girls then searched the house top to bottom but
came up empty handed. There was no sight of
money, except for the twelve bands he had in his
pocket and the bust down around his neck.

Bea became upset with her sister. *We put in
all this work for six punk ass bands a piece*! She
thought to herself. But then she couldn't even be
mad, at least they did get something. Bea had sent
them on a few dummy missions and Meme had

never complained. Bea suggested that they leave, they'd looked everywhere. She know for a fact that there was no cash in the house or in Curtis' car. But Meme wasn't trying to hear it. Nah sis, we gone wait right here until his fat ass wake up, I can feel it in my stomach this nigga got it. Finally, Curtis began to wake, and Meme was on his ass.

"I said where is the money!" Meme stomped his head downwards, then kicked him in the face. His right eye shut instantly. The girls had changed into sweatpants, t-shirts, and Tim boots. "I don't have any money; I swear to God!" Curtis cried out in pain, his hands and feet numb from lack of circulation. "Please Jalisa stop this", he pleaded, holding his duct taped hands up. "Shut yo fat sloppy ass up," Meme said. She was furious. "Give me the bat!," Meme screamed, spit shot from her mouth. Her eyes were open wide, making her look like a mad woman. Meme's chest heaved up and down, she held a hand out, waiting on the bat. As much as Bea didn't want to, she had to give her sister the bat. They had been best friends since teenagers, she didn't want to make it seem like she wasn't on her side. Bea handed the bat over to Meme and the beating began.

"Where is it?" She hit Curtis' body and he jerked in pain. "Where is it?" Whoop! "Where is it?" Whoop! She screamed with rage. She beat on

him until she had nothing left. She dropped to her
knees by his head and the floor made a thud sound.
Meme's eyes were red from tears of frustration.
Bea put a hand on her sisters' shoulder. Meme held
her hand up to Bea without looking. Bea gave
Meme the *Fendi* bag. She went into the bag and
pulled out a 0.40. The pistol was military green,
outlined with hot pink. She pressed the gun to the
back of Curtis' head and whispered into his ear. "I
hate yo fat ass." He mumbled something under his
breath, but she couldn't make it out. "What you
say?" Meme asked. She leaned down, damn near
laying her face on the floor next to his. "U-u-u-
under th-there, under what nigga? Spit it out!,"
Meme yelled in his face. "Under my doghouse,"
Curtis struggled with his speech. Meme looked up
at her bestie with newfound excitement.

The girls left Curtis on the floor bleeding.
They walked into the kitchen, which led them to
the backyard door. A growling Pitbull chained to a
tree beside the doghouse rushed the couple. Meme
upped the 0.40 and blew the side of the dogs' face
away. The pistol echoed in the night air, and the
dog made a yelp noise before dropping dead. The
sisters walked to the doghouse and examined it.
They pushed the doghouse over and discovered a
trap door. Bea bent down and opened the door.
Looking up at them was a black duffle bag. "I told
you bitch, and you didn't believe me," Meme
expressed her feelings. "I did to believe you!" Bea

lied. Meme was about to protest but Bea cut her off. "Girl if you don't shut up and open the bag," Bea said. Meme opened the bag and became upset. "What in the fuck we gone do with this?" she asked, looking at her bestie. "We'll figure something out, go finish off the fat bastard and I'll put this in the trunk."

****

"That shit stink girl, it smell like vinegar", Meme said with a scrunched up face. "I know right, I thought it was coke, but I've never seen white girl that smells like this," Bea gave her assumption. It took the sisters a little over two hours to wipe the house, covering their tracks over at Curtis' place. They were going on 24 hours of no sleep, 11:45am. They stared at 20 neatly stacked kilos of heroin. They were now at home in the kitchen. They had been in the streets their whole life without ever seeing these many drugs.

Once they robbed a weed man for 15 pounds of Zaza, but that was easy to get off and they smoked most of it. The rest they just sold to the dancers at the club. They didn't like people in their business, that's how you got fucked up. "It's got to be heroin, and I don't know nothing about this shit," Bea said. "Who can we sell it to without making us hot?" Meme asked her friend. Bea sat in her own thoughts, trying to think of someone. "What about Diddy?" Meme suggested. "Nah he's legit now, plus he'd have to be a middleman. We need somebody that's gone grab and go. I bet you your homebody Ugly can grab and go, he got paper," Meme said with raised eyebrows. "Yeah, you right, he do got bread. But we don't know if we can trust him". Bea put her down. "I thought you said he was one of the good ones," Meme rolled her eyes, teasing her friend. "What I meant was he not a trick ass bitch, he might see all this work and think we sweet and try and rob us." "Scared money don't make money", Meme blurted out of frustration. "Bitch don't come for me, you know I ain't scared of nothing. Remember dead bitches can't spend money".

They sat in silence, staring at the bricks. "What about my bae?," Meme said to Bea. "What bae?." "My bae bae," Meme replied with the girl-stop-playing face. "Who, your little jail bird? How a nigga in prison gone help us move this shit?", Bea asked with a you-gotta-be-kidding-me face. Meme frowned at her sister. "He might be locked up but he far from lame. He got connections, plus people won't be in our business because we not dealing with people we see regularly". Bea would never admit it, but she liked Meme's boyfriend, he was good to her sister. He'd come through more

42

than once to pay a bill or two for them when they were dead broke. He never argued with her unless she picked a fight trying to get a reaction out of him. He always tried to build her up and never tear her down.

He was in prison with a cell phone, so he probably did have connections, Bea thought. "Fuck it, call him. If you trust him, I trust him," she told Meme. Meme smiled then rushed out of the room to get her phone. Bea heard Meme speaking with someone as she walked back into the kitchen. She held the phone out in front of her, she had KB on speaker phone. "You said it smell like vinegar?" He asked. "Yes baby, and it's off white in color", she explained. He went silent for a second. "Okay baby sounds like you got your hands on some China White. If it's A1 shit, you could sell it for 40 to 50 g's a brick. I'ma send my young boy through. You can trust him, he's my extension to the streets. I'm telling y'all now, be patient and take your time with him. Because somebody is most definitely gone be looking for that much work."

"Ok my soulmate, I love you daddy. I love you more baby girl," KB told her. Meme hung the phone up and let out a sigh of relief. The girls stared at each other, Bea did math in her head. If KB was right, they were about to be millionaires. But his last statement had her thinking as well. Someone was definitely going to be looking for a

missing million. More money, more problems.
"Now we wait," Meme interrupted Bea's thoughts.
"Now we wait," Bea repeated Meme. "We rich
bitch."

Chapter 3

The hook landed square in the jaw, he let the man punch him in his shit. The lick stunned him, but he was the only one who noticed. *You gotta take some to give some* he thought to himself. Boolaid needed to know if the man he faced was weak. He wasn't he definitely had knock out strength, the blow was hard and stiff but also slow. The man moved in on Boolaid and delivered a two piece, Boolaid bobbed and weaved with his guard up. He tried a three piece, he missed because his moves were easily telegraphed. The man became enraged and swung a wild fury of combo's but only hit air. "Come on the man yelled out of frustration," he clapped his boxing gloves together, put his chin on his chest and walked towards Boolaid. He had gotten into the man's head, this fight is already won Boolaid though, "Fight back, scary ass nigga," somebody commented on the sideline. Boolaid watched the guy through his peripheral vision, he was a dark skin man with a high-top box that had a gold patch in the front. *If this nigga jump in I'm fye his ass up.*

Boolaid had found himself in the middle of a makeshift boxing ring, fighting in a backyard brawl with a grand prize of 10 stacks. Boolaid was the underdog, nobody knew who he was, and he didn't know a soul in the backyard. He'd only been out of prison a couple of months off a five-year sentence, he needed some quick cash. While in prison he met a man named KB, they had become close friends. Even though he was in prison he still had connections. KB sent Boolaid to a man named Keith, Keith owned an underground fight club. It took some convincing, but Keith finally agreed to give Boolaid a shot, since no one knew who he was, no one bet on him to win. Everybody was praying on his downfall, his opponents name was Cheeno and his record was 5 and 0, all five fights end with Cheeno

knocking a nigga the fuck out. He looked like he belonged in the NFL, 6'3 275 pounds with a beer belly. Boolaid on the other hand 5'11 205 pounds all muscle, his body was cut up more than two pairs of scissors. His skin tone was an almond color. He sported a low haircut with 360 spinning waves. His eyes had slants making him always look serious. People said he resembled the model Tyson but brown skin and gangsta. Boolaid watched Cheeno's footwork and knew when he would strike. Cheeno moved in and bounced while throwing a mean right hook. "Nah ah my nigga too slow," Boolaid told him, he ducked and delivered a right hook of his own to Cheeno's mid-section. This move wasn't his attack; he only did it to create momentum because the next blow was a left uppercut that rattled Cheeno's brain
and shattered his chin like broken glass. The whole backyard went "uuuuwww," Boolaid saw Cheeno's eyes rolled and knew he couldn't take much more melee. For the next several seconds Boolaid beat the shit out of the wanna be NFL player. Boolaid swung a two-piece, knuckle cracking against bone was all he heard, Cheeno dropped to the ground knocked out cold. The backyard watched their champ crumble in stunned silence, Boolaid walked to his corner to get his belongings, he had a shirt and pair of jeans folded neatly. He picked the clothes up carefully and watched the crowd because in between the clothes

hidden was a Glock 21, a 45-caliber pistol. *All my niggas see red all my niggas keep one in the head* he rapped *Pooh Shiesty* to himself as he approached Keith.

"Good fight, kid, good fuckin fight," the fight club owner told Boolaid, he gave Boolaid a stack of cash. "Everybody bet against you today, but KB wanted you in that ring too damn bad, so I knew better than to go against his judgment. You made me a lot of cash today young man," "I made me some cash today too OG," he replied with a smirk. "I like you already kid, so can I depend on you when I set up the next bout," Keith asked. "That's Boolaid" he told the owner then walked away without another word heading for his car. "Boolaid," Keith said watching the young man walk away. These children are weird as hell nowadays. Boolaid sat in his car and waited, he watched the people spill out the backyard to the front when he saw his target. He quickly jumped out of his car rushing over to the man with the box with the gold patch, the guy saw Boolaid approach and remember he called Boolaid scary. The man with the box reached a hand out as a peace offering, "good fight" were the only words he got out before Boolaid jawed his ass knocking him out cold. When he got back to the car his phone was ringing in the cup holder.

"What's good bigger bro" he, answered. "What's good nigga?." The voice he heard was a

man named Kevin Brooks, but everybody called
him KB for short. He was serving a life sentence
for organized crime. Boolaid had gotten sentenced
to five years but only served 3 and a half. He was
sent to federal prison after getting caught selling
guns he had stolen off of North Carolina's Fort
Bragg army base. Boolaid was 22 at the time of his
arrest, he had been in the military for a little over 4
years. His mother had died when he was a baby
and his father had abandoned him at an early age.
Raised by his mother's sister who was a recovering
drug addict, he grew up poor. By the time he was
12 he was a wild animal totally out of control, his
aunt tried to discipline him, but she failed. He
would just get up and leave home and be gone for
days at a time worrying his poor Auntie sick. He
never went to school and when he did, he got into
fist fights with classmates and teachers, he had no
respect for authority. *What the fuck do they know?
They don't understand.* the teenage Boolaid would
tell himself. Auntie couldn't put up with his
rebelliousness any longer so when he turned 18,
she enrolled him into the army, "yo stupid ass
going to prison" she would tell him. "The
army gone teach you how to be a man." He never
paid her no never mind, everything she said went
in one ear then right out the other. Boolaid decided
he would just go. On one hand his aunt wouldn't
be on his wig anymore. On the other hand, he'd get
out the hood and be on his own. As a child he

would run away because he felt like he was looking for something, but never found anything and always came up empty handed.

Six months after he finished basic training he got deployed, first he went to South Africa then finished in Afghanistan. He lived in the third world for 2 years 9 months before he returned back to the United States, he had witnessed death on both sides, He knew death firsthand, according to the United States government Boolaid had ten confirmed kills but off the record there were more, Auntie was right about one thing they taught him how to be a man that could turn a kill switch on or off. Only the strong survive and the weak die off Boolaid thought, he had been almost halfway around the world and back. Yet again somehow, he still came up empty handed. He still had so many unanswered questions until he came to prison and met KB. KB gave Boolaid the understanding of man's responsibility.

KB was good with the youth; he always knew what to say. He understood Boolaid's issues, he could relate to Boolaid. KB saw himself in Boolaid, so he put him under his wing spending a lot of his time with him dropping jewels. The boy got a lot of potential KB would tell his other comrades. During their time together KB taught Boolaid about religion, politics, investments, women and true black history, KB treated him like

a little brother but in Boolaid's eyes he saw much
more. He saw KB as a father he always wanted.
Before Boolaid was released from prison he made
an oath with KB, he would treat his aunt with the
utmost respect and would always take care of her.
When he touched down, he would live by the true
street code death before dishonor. Always staying
loyal to his principles as a man, he would respect
those who respected him. He pledged he would be
KB's extension to the street to continue his legacy.
KB made an oath to guide Boolaid righteously,
show him how not to be a fuck nigga. Holding
down the code until death and beyond. "What's
good nigga! Is that how your mother taught you to
greet people?" Boolaid asked his role model.
"Nigga shut up KB laughed," Boolaid's
government name was Bulak. KB gave him the
name Boolaid because of his hot temper. Niggas
would try him on in the yard, they would go into
the cell to fight. Boolaid would beat the shit out of
anybody that called him out. After the fight he
would still be hot, KB would tell him cool down in
response he would tell KB nigga "I'm Boolaid."
"The only time you call me bigger bro is when you
done did some ignorant shit," Boolaid couldn't
help smiling. Still sitting in his car counting the
money he'd just won, watching a small crowd of
people helping the nigga he just dropped off. "You
crazy" Boolaid said, "nah yo ass crazy nigga,
Keith just called me and told me you just came out

there and showed out. Knock'n shit out ain't you,"
KB joked, "yea I am!" Boolaid answered. "I bet
you are, you knock'n out fighters and spectators,"
both men burst out with laughter. "Check tho big
bro I won that 10-piece chicken nugget for us,
where you want me to send your
half?" Boolaid asked. He promised he would look
out for his friend no matter what. "I'm straight bro
whatever you was gonna send me give to your
mom dukes" KB told his little brother, "And ask
her I said when she gone write a nigga" he joked,
"aight I got you" Boolaid said with a face like
nigga please. "Aye bro do you remember shorty I
been fuckin with, the one that's in the streets."
"Yes, you talking about the bad dark skin chick
Meme, how could I forget she was the only thing
you ever talked about when we were on the yard
together with your tender dick ass" Boolaid joked
this time. "I'ma, pretend you didn't just try the
pimp, she done ran into a little bump in the road
and I need you to pull up and change her tires. Im
text you her number so yall can link up, she live in
Greensboro" KB said. "Oh, ok remember I told
you I used to live in the Boro until my Auntie
moved us to Burlington when I was 15" Boolaid
informed KB. "Ima drop this paper off to her and
chill for a while after I get myself together Im hit
your wifey up-n-see what she was talking about,"
Boolaid said. "Say less" KB disconnected the call,
Boolaid wondered what his mentor was up to.

"Why would you want me checking on your bitch for, I hope this nigga ain't got me on no stalking shit" Boolaid said out loud. KB had put Boolaid in nothing but good positions since he'd gotten out, so he had no reason to second guess him. I haven't been to the Boro in a while, Boolaid cranked up the car then pulled away from the curb. *Money Bagg Yo* blast out the radio, *I just looked at my wrist I got time today fuck it I'm crossing the line today.*

****

"Slow down baby it ain't going nowhere," Aunt Robin watched in amusement as her nephew punished the plate of food, she'd just sat in front of him. Boolaid hovered over his plate, steak with A1 sauce, baked potato loaded with sour cream butter and melted cheese, a salad mixed with ranch and Italian dressing. He kept his face in the plate and demolished it. That's how they made everybody eat in the army, then going to prison afterwards didn't help. By the time Auntie Robin finished making her plate. So, before she could join Boolaid at the table, his plate had been wiped clean, "Mamma," he called out to his Auntie as if he just became angry about something, he stood up from the table then began looking around the room searching. He rushed out the dining room, "Bulak!" Aunt Robin called after him. He came

53

back into the room with a look of concern in his
facial expression.

"What's wrong son." Aunt Robin began to
worry, "who been in the house mamma?." "Ain't
nobody been in my house but you and I, is there
something missing?" she asked. "Yes, ma'am
somebody broke into the house and stole my food
it was just right here a minute ago." He pointed at
the empty plate. Aunt Robin looked at Boolaid like
nigga you can't be serious, he stared back with a
goofy smirk on his face. "Oh boy stop playing so
much she laughed you almost gave me a heart
attack with yo bad self." "Aww, I'm sorry baby,"
he said as he came around the table to meet his
Auntie. He embraced her around the shoulders and
placed his face beside hers. "I'm just playing ma,"
Boolaid kissed her cheek. When he was younger,
he didn't realize how important she was to him.
Over the years she got older, and he knew one day
she would be gone, he felt a pain in his chest
because she was all he had in the world.
"Whatever boy" she joked as she cuddled in his
hug, "I was about to call the Army and tell them
they owe us a check because they messed my
baby's head up. I don't see how you even tasted
any of the food you ate it so fast" Aunt Robin said
looking at the empty plate, "believe me mamma, I
tasted every bite, and nobody can do it better than
you". She smiled at her son's praise, but then her
face became very serious as she watched Boolaid

54

drop a stack of money on the kitchen table. "What is that??" she nodded her head at the money. "It's money" he told her nonchalantly as he poured himself a cup of apple juice he'd just taken from the refrigerator. "Bulak Maquay Smith don't play with me boy." She only called him by his whole government name when she meant business. "Look ma! I'm grown now, you can't keep trying to baby me", he explained. "You've been taking care of me my whole life now it's my time to hold you down. You deserve it," Boolaid said.

Aunt Robin couldn't believe this was the same bad ass little boy she was trying to raise before he went to the army then prison. He had really grown, she sighed "I know you're a man now. I just been so worried when you out there in them streets, you get so much like your mother." Aunt Robin didn't talk too much about Boolaid's mom, but when she did, she would tell him she was the life of the party, very smart, had her own mind but the streets don't show favoritism she was just another victim. "You don't have to worry I'm not out there doing crazy stuff or hurting people, besides this money didn't even come from me. This is a gift somebody wanted me to give to you he said with a smile." "A gift?," she said curiously but becoming suspicious at the same moment. "Who is it from?," She wanted to know, "my big homie KB", he let her know. "KB? Yo lil friend in prison" she asked in a surprised tone with raised eyebrows, "yes momma my lil friend in prison" Boolaid mocked. "Well how much is it?," she asked looking at the stack of cash on the table, "$10,000 dollars". "TEN thousand" she shouted, "ain't no nigga in jail giving away that much money boy." Boolaid choked and spit apple juice out his mouth, caught off guard by his Auntie's reaction. He laughed out loud, "Mamma you silly, I think he got a crush on you. He told me to tell you to write him." "I don't got no time to be writing no jail bird", she said seriously. Boolaid gave her another kiss on the cheek, "Hey ma I'm about to go hit the shower. I got some things I need to handle. So, I'ma be gone a couple days. You need me to do anything for you before I leave," he asked her. Aunt Robin sat in her own thoughts for a second, she reached for the money on the table and pulled off a 100-dollar bill. "Yeah, son run to the store for ya mamma and buy me a hundred dollars worth of stamps and envelopes," Auntie Robin took one look at Boolaid and burst out in laughter. "I don't see nothing funny ma" he told her with a serious mean mug, "good cause I'm not joking now gone head and get up outta here I got a letter I need to write."

Boolaid laughed to himself, *my momma crazy talking about some damn stamps and envelopes*, Boolaid had been driving for the past hour.

KB told him Meme stayed in Greensboro, but his GPS told him something different. He and Meme hadn't spoken over the phone only by text, she sent him an address and he told her he was on the way. He had driven through the city of Greensboro and was now entering a town called Kernersville, "Drive West 3 miles and you will have arrived at your destination in 5 minutes", his GPS informed him. Boolaid sent Meme a text message saying, he was about to pull up.

"I hope this nigga not on no funny shit" Bea said to Meme what seemed like the thousandth time, "ugh bitch stop being so negative" Meme shot back. "We gone tell him what we want and he's going to deliver" Meme said, "I hope you're right sis" Bea said. They had given Boolaid the address to a double wide trailer in Kernersville, the girls had bought the trailer a few summers back it was their little duck off spot. They felt buying the place was a good investment for their line of work, just in case shit hit the fan they could get low. Plus, they didn't want some random nigga to know where they really stayed. Meme's phone chimed. It was a text from Boolaid that read I'm outside. "Here goes nothing," Meme said.

Boolaid sat his phone in the cup holder and checked his surroundings, the GPS he followed had brought him in front of a double wide trailer out in the country. You could see other trailers off in the distance, *a mile, and a half down the road* Boolaid thought to himself. The military taught him how to estimate distance, it had become second nature for him to look for multiple entrance and exit points. You never knew when your life would be endangered, there was an I8 BMW in the driveway smoked gray he thought. He didn't pull in the driveway but parked at the curb, He drove a white Chevy Impala '09. "Damn this bitch got that bread," he said out loud. The front door to the trailer shot open and a woman appeared in the doorway, Boolaid got out of the car.

Bea stood in the doorway and watched the stranger approach, the first thing she noticed about him was his mannerism in each stride he made. It was a hot summer day; he wore a fitted white fruit of the loom tank top. He walked with his back straight making his chest poke out. His arms and shoulders looked strong and well developed, all in all he was chiseled. On his feet were a pair of cocaine white *Jordan* ones, which went well with the red and white Nike basketball shorts. The young man's legs weren't skinny like most men, they were athletic and matched his upper body. He climbed the steps to the front porch then stopped in front of Bea, she took a closer look, his hair was cut low that had deep waves wrapping around his groomed Crown. Almond colored tanned skin

from the summer sun, with slants in his eyes
making him look so serious. Bea couldn't help
noticing the bulging dick print in his short, *aite he
cute* she thought to herself. "Hey, is Meme here?"
Boolaid broke the ice, "and you are," was all Bea
shot back with an attitude. Normally he would
have been a straight ass hole about things, but he
was the newcomer, so he stayed calm and played it
smooth. "My name is Boolaid," he introduced
himself, "is Meme here?" he asked once
again. "How you know I'm not the person you
looking for?", Bea questioned him.
Boolaid stared Bea in her eyes. She had chinky
eyes like his but hers were deeper. She was
amazing in the face, he had to admit. Her hair was
braided corn roll style, the braids were long
flowing down stopping at her hips and her baby
hair laid smoothly around the edges. She looked
like a life size China doll. Boolaid knew she
wasn't Meme, he'd seen pictures of her before,
matter of fact KB would show him Meme's flicks
every time she pushed the free prints. The woman
was testing, checking his temperament he couldn't
even be mad she was protecting her friend; he'd do
the same thing. "I did time with KB," Meme's
nigga. "He had pictures of her posted all over his
cell. So, I know for big facts you're not her. You
must be her sister or either a bodyguard". He
smiled, letting her know he was only joking, trying
to be friendly. Bea was caught by surprise by his

comment, *9 times out of ten she would have had a nigga at a loss for words or pissed off, so he's not easily controlled* she thought as she returned a smile. Boolaid reached out and took her hand. "It's nice to meet you, Meme's sister guard." He made her blush, which was rare. Bea accepted his hand, and they shook, "my name is Bea it's nice to meet you as well." They shared a moment where Boolaid felt he'd met this woman before but couldn't put a finger on it. "Do we know each other? I'm sorry you just look so familiar I had to ask" Boolaid said. "No, we don't know each other, maybe we did in our past lives," she told him. "Yeah, maybe" he replied then just brushed off the subject. "Well come on in, it's hot as hell out here Booo-laid" she joked, opening the door, and letting him inside. She turned to lead the way and he followed, she had on a pair of red
Marine Serre leggings that gripped her booty like a fist, he watched her ass jiggle with every step. They came into a large living room. An 80-inch LG plasma flat screen was mounted along one of the walls. The girls had bought an expensive royal color living room set; the couch was a wrap-around with matching lazy boys on each end. Meme sat in one of the lazy boys with the chair reclined back, her feet in the air as she played GTA 5. These bitches got it made he thought, Bea flopped down on the sofa, Boolaid noticed she was barefoot. Bea's feet were small and well

pedicured, Meme paused the game then stood to greet Boolaid. "Hey Booo-laid!" she joked with a warm smile letting the two know she'd heard their conversation outside. "Hey! How you doing Meme, nice to finally meet you", Boolaid said. Meme wore a white t-shirt and some SpongeBob boy shorts; they were snug around the crotch. Boolaid had a hard time looking Meme in the face because her pussy print was also trying to say hello without using words.

"Nice to finally meet you, my nigga talks very highly about you. Me and my sister were hoping that you could assist us on something" she said, getting straight to the point. "Oh yeah, what might that something be?." Bea hopped up and quickly moved to the closet in the corner of the room, grabbed a black duffle bag, brought it to Boolaid then dropped it at his feet. Bea flopped back down on the lazy boy. Boolaid looked down at the dirty duffle bag then back to these two ladies. They had gone from friendly to straight to business plus he noticed both girls with a pillow by their side. He'd seen plenty of ambushes before he was positive those were guns, they kept nearby. *I knew I should have brought my Blick in this bitch I hope I ain't gotta drop these crazy ass chicks*, Boolaid thought. "I see you ladies are cautious about what's in this bag, so I'm going to have a seat to calm everyone's nerves," Boolaid said as he sat down. "Why would you say we're nervous?,"

Meme asked while holding onto her pillow. "Go ahead and open the bag," Bea urged him. "The fact that both of yall are clutching pillows tells me you're nervous," he said as he unzipped the bag to look inside. Instantly, he knew he was looking at heroin at least 10 to 15 chickens, he'd never sold it, but he'd seen plenty of it while on tour in Afghanistan, which is the capital of heroin for the whole world. Boolaid spoke calmly but seriously, "take your guns out, KB sent me, so you know I'm not your enemy." The sisters were speechless. *How could he have known they had guns hidden?* Bea was sure they had played everything cool. Meme and Bea obeyed moving their pillows, revealing their weapons. Meme held on a 40-caliber pistol military green outlined in hot pink, Bea brandished a Glock 30 which is a 45-caliber pistol but small and compact. "Okay, now that we're being honest and the cat's out of the bag," Boolaid pointed to the drugs. "I want to take an educated guess; all this work just so happens to fall in your lap. Y'all don't want to move because you can't or don't want to risk the chance of becoming hot. So, it's obvious you ladies want me to free your face and take all the heat from either the nigga who is looking for their shit or the feds". "Exactly!" Bea blurted out, Meme smacked her sister on the thigh and told her to stop it in a whispered and a face saying stop being mean because we need him. "No not exactly but you took a good guess, we were hoping you would just buy all of it, or maybe knew somebody that would grab them from you" Meme told him. There wasn't much that shocked Boolaid, but he'd never met real live Gangsta Boo's. These bitches were trap queens for sure. *What in the fuck you done got me in to bigger bro* he thought to himself. "Listen ladies, I'm not gonna lie, I've only been out of prison a couple months, and I don't have that kind of money," he said referring to the bricks. "I don't know how many blocks are in that bag but," "it's 20 keys" Bea interrupted. "Okay 20 keys" repeated. "I do have a few people in mind that got bread they'll snatch a couple here and there the rest would take me a little networking," Boolaid stated as a matter of fact. He'd never sold drugs, but he remembered what KB taught him about drugs, work will sell itself. Bea wanted to say something but kept her mouth closed, she wanted to talk shit at first but then thought about Meme's boyfriend, niggas were definitely going to be looking for that much work this way might be for the best she thought. The three of them sat quietly just staring at each other trying to read each other's minds. Meme broke the silence; she sighed letting out a deep breath. "Okay Boolaid my nigga, wouldn't have sent you if he thought you couldn't help us. Since you say you know people that will buy our China White" Meme spoke like a plug. "My sister and I propose 50 thousand each key, there are twenty of them if you get rid of them for us, taking the risk from beef and possible heat will give you 10% of the profits. That would be 200,000 dollars". Boolaid laughed out loud, what's so funny the women asked in unison. My bad, ain't nothing funny, he wasn't going to tell them why he laughed but the truth was these two females in front of him acted like some real street niggas. They were fly popped guns and got paid. They did it all.

Boolaid felt his adrenaline begin to rush, the thought of moving that much work, knowing somebody would be looking for their bricks. If Boolaid made the wrong move it could all mean sudden death or a prison sentence. It was like being back in the battlefield of a place where he performed best. Plus, 200 bands was more money than he had ever seen. "I'm sorry he apologized again, ladies, there's nothing funny it's just," he paused in thought. "Just what nigga? Spit it out" Bea ice grilled him. He smiled on the inside. He loved to play his own mind games. "It's just I've never met one let alone two bad ass boss bitches before, y'all are amazing and I'm honored to have met you both." His statement caught the sisters off guard; they were used to men praising their bodies, not their minds as businesswomen. They both seemed to melt under his gaze, "thank you" they told him with a blush. *Damn, this nigga is smooth as hell, but he got a bitch fucked up if he think I won't beat his ass up.* "Are you in or out" Bea asked, "I'm in," he answered, "but I need something from you both." He had their undivided attention, "I need a key to this spot," he said. "A key, what the hell you need a key for?" Bea jumped down his throat. "Calm down no need for attitude, this place is a good location to keep the work, the area is out of the way not many people so if I get a tail I'll know if I'm being followed. Since technically now I work for you, I need an office to work out of. I can come here to grab and bag the product as needed, then we can also meet for cash drops. Now that I've had a decent conversation with the both of you, I know this is not where y'all actually live, this is more of a duck off spot" he said as he admired their living room. *This nigga think he James Bond and shit*, "Okay a key done anything else", Meme questioned. Boolaid grabbed a kilo out of the duffle, "see this stamp?" He showed them. "What is that? A chess piece?" Bea asked. "Not just any chess piece it's the Queen, the most powerful piece on the chess board. When I was in the Army, I had been stationed in the heroin capital of the world. The queen means this brick is all the best," Boolaid tossed the kilo into the air and caught it. "We should be able to double the price, so I want $400,000 and I'll give you 1.5 M's give or take". Bea and Meme watched and studied Boolaid's face looking for signs of deceit but saw none. Nobody in the room was a drug dealer, they had come this far, and somebody had to take the first step of trust. Bea looked to Meme for assurance. It was her boyfriend that had set this meeting up so she would only approve of it if her sister did. Meme took a moment to think before she nodded her head in agreement. "Agreed, but if you play us there will be hell to pay," Bea warned. Bea and Meme looked at Boolaid with dead seriousness and right then at that moment Boolaid knew that both women had killed before. "I'm sure there will be hell to pay for I have no doubt in my mind," *I'm right at home with these two* he thought. "I'm going to take this with me" he said, showing off the brick, "text me when you've made a key for me." "If I make 50 before you hit me I'ma just text you", Boolaid said to Meme. "It was nice meeting both of you, but I think it's time for me to make my exit. I don't want to wear out my welcome", he said. "I'll walk you to the door" Bea said getting up off the couch, Boolaid followed her to the door. "Here," Bea grabbed a set of keys off the wall and un-looped a single key from the key ring then handed it to him. Their hands touched and lingered a little longer than they should have. "Me and my sister don't let people into our circle," she told him. Looking directly into her eyes, letting her know he meant what he was about to say. "Maybe it's time for a change." "Yea, maybe you're" right she sighed. Boolaid gave her another smile before walking off without another word. Bea watched him get into his car then pull away from the curb. She went back into the house to join her best friend.

"So!" Meme had a big Kool Aid smile on her face, "what do you think biitchh?," Meme asked as soon as Bea entered the room. Bea sat down then shrugged her shoulders like she wasn't interested. I'm not sure, I can't say right now she answered. Meme threw a pillow at Bea "stop lying, bitch you like him" she laughed. Bea flung a pillow back, "I do not," she blushed. "Mhm, I saw how you were looking at him," Meme pressed her. "Well, he is cute," Bea admitted with a smile. "And he is not a trick type. We had all this ass and titties in his face and he didn't' lust", Meme said, giving herself a smack on the ass. "I thought this nigga was gone run when I had this cat in his face," Meme patted her pussy, and the girls shared a laugh. That's how they found victims by wearing clothes that mad men drool showing their true colors, they just knew he was going to try and holla and see if he could get some pussy but he passed the test by being all business. "It's something about that boy," Bea said out loud. "It's like he looked at us like soldiers instead of normal women." "I'ma tell you something I do know" Meme said, "what girl?," Bea listened. "That nigga got a big dick, girlll did you see that dick print in his shorts?," Meme asked with her arms spread wide. "I know right" Bea said, "I thought the nigga went and stole the turkey pepper log out of the refrigerator." Both girls cried out with laughter. "Nah but for real I get good vibes; I see hunger in his eyes. We had that same hunger at one time in our lives. He don't got shit but he want it. And when he gets it, he gone keep it. All he need is opportunity and we're the ones that gone give it to him", Meme said. "I hope you're right," Bea told her sister. Bea didn't want to admit it because she didn't trust anybody but Meme. "For some odd reason she felt the same vibe Meme felt." "What's the coincidence we meet a nigga that's like us," Meme asked. "I don't believe in coincidences," she answered. "Well, it must be fate."

Chapter 4

Boolaid walked into the house and embraced his friend with a handshake. Boolaid, "what's good my brother from another mother," Justin said, happy to see his childhood friend. "Another day, another dollar," Boolaid said. "Now that's triple facts" Justin said as he closed the front door. "Come on me and lil bra in the kitchen," Boolaid followed Justin through the living room into a small kitchen, the kitchen had a table set with six chairs. One of the chairs was occupied by a man with long dreads that hung low, concealing his face. His head turned in the direction of the two men entering the room. "Boolaid, my nigga!" He stood and greeted him with a hug tap. "Max" was the only word Boolaid said. He could barely see the man's facial expression because of Max's dreads but he knew the gangsta was smiling. Justin and Max took seats at the table, but Boolaid stayed standing. He wore a small sports bag, removed it, and tossed it on the table in front of Justin then joined his boys at the table.

"So, how's life treating you? Or should I say how's fight club treating you Kimbo Bruce Leeroy Jr " Justin joked making a waaataaaa sound swinging a karate chop. You could hear snickers coming from behind Max's dreads.
"It's actually not that bad" Boolaid said "Oh yea! Well, whenever you ready to get money with us just let me know, I told you when you touchdown I got you I look at you like a lil brother" Justo told Boolaid. "That's why I'm here" said Boolaid. Leaning forward patting the sports bag on the table. Justin and Max shared a quick look at each other before Justin unzipped the bag taking out a kilo of heroin. "Where you get a whole chicken of doggy from?" Justin asked in a

surprised tone. "Just fell in my lap." Boolaid
nonchalantly shrugged his shoulders like it was
nothing "just fell in your lap!" Justin said with the
screw face. "Ain't no coincidence you show the
fuck up at my doorstep and magically pull this
doggy of ron out a hat ", Justin said now becoming
suspicious. "I don't believe in coincidences,"
Boolaid told his friend. "So, it must be fate" the lil
brother joined into the conversation. Max's real
name was Jason, he was Justin's little brother, and
they were Boolaid's childhood friends.

****

They were misfits as kids, the three bandits would
get into all types of shit. Children would laugh at
them because of their hand me down shoes and
clothes. Being poor wasn't funny. The three got
into multiple fights. At first, they started to commit
B&E, breaking, and entering. One day they kicked
in somebody's door and the person was home, they
jumped the guy and took all his money.
Afterwards the three decided to get a gun and just
rob people because it was easier to just make a
nigga give it up. Putting in work together splitting
the money buying clothes and shoes felt good to
the boys. They were thick as thieves back then.
Boolaid turned 18 when his Aunt Robin sent him

to the army. And the Bryant brothers continued to
live the street life. Justin and Jason both went into
the drug dealing business. Mid-level dealers: they
could buy two bricks at a time. They were in tune
with the streets and could move work. They were
the only people Boolaid felt he could trust, so he
chose to reveal his hand to them. "Now fate, I do
believe in because one day we all gotta die"
Boolaid stated as a matter of fact. "Nigga I'm not
trying to hear all that philosophical bullshit,
where'd you get all this work from? This isn't like
you" Justin said. Justin was 6'4, 225 pounds dark
skin with a Boosie fade. His voice was raspy when
he spoke, tattoo all over his face markings of his
gang. When he smiled, he showed off a small gap
that the ladies loved for some reason. People said
he resembled Jamie Foxx, the hood called him
Justo Mr. No Nonsense because of his quick
temper. From the west side of Greensboro his
hood's name was called the Heights. A long street
that consisted of many different apartments. So
treacherous the neighborhood was you might find
a dead body just laying out in the field. Justin's
hands looked permanently swollen from niggas
he'd punched and beat on. Knuckles that had
gashes that needed stitches from hitting people in
their mouths knocking out teeth. Never going to
the hospital for treatment so his hands healed ugly.
He was your gangsta's gangsta. Justin was very
intelligent; he was the brains of the brothers'

operation. Now Jason on the other hand was something totally different. He was a hustler at heart and knew how to get money. If you didn't get money you didn't eat. Having money was a necessity like food and clothing and he knew that. But for real Jason was the muscle. The bodyguard's bodyguard. If your shooters had a shooter, he would be it. The streets gave him the name Mad Max because he had an unnatural thirst for blood like the Jamaican shotta. When he was 14, he was arrested for murder one. Police couldn't prove he did the crime, so they let him go. Rumor had it that Mad Max had over one hundred bodies under his belt that wasn't fact, nobody really knew. What niggas did know was that anybody who tried him, or his big brother paid with there life or was given a shit bag as a gift and that was fact. Mad Max stood at 5" 7, 165 pounds he was very dark skin with thick bushy rude boy type dreads that fell chest length. For some reason, his dreads covered his face at all times. It was like his hair instinctively knew to hide his face because he might slide and catch a body at any moment.

Mad Max was on demon time twenty-four hours a day, the type of nigga who'd rather catch a head shot before catching a nut. "I thought we were done hitting licks?", Justin said to his friend sincerely. "I didn't rob anyone", Boolaid answered. "Oh, ok you found a plug on the work then?" Mad Max acted like everything was a joke, his face revealing an evil grin the entire time. Boolaid knew this wasn't just any normal joke but a serious joke. "Yeah, something like that", Boolaid said. "My nigga I love you an all but you gotta stop with all this James Bond double 0 seven shit. Boolaid, you don't sell drugs", Justo explained. "You just just got outta the feds and all of a sudden you the brick man? That shit doesn't sit well with me my nigga. So, either your gonna put us on game and let me know what type time you on or your gonna get the fuck up out my trap and take that bag with you". Justo said, meaning every word.

The trap being a location people used to sell drugs or stash money. The brothers had two. This one was a two-bedroom apartment in the suburbs, Justo only counted money and bagged narcotics here. The apartment belonged to an older white man named Freeman. At the sudden outburst of Justo's demands towards Boolaid. Mad Max jumped into action, standing from the table upping his firearm. Boolaid stared down the barrel of an F&N hand pistol which shot assault rifle ammunition. Mad Max knew Boolaid was no slouch. He definitely was about that action, so he moved first to ensure he had the upper hand. Boolaid stayed calm all the while gripping on to his Glock 30 under the table. Boolaid knew his life depended on his next move, because Mad Max was too close for him to try an attack. There would be zero chance of survival if Mad Max hit him with the f&n point blank range. The two childhood friends studied each other. Boolaid liked to play on people's emotions. He would have been surprised if they didn't carry it the way they were at this moment, because if it were vice versa, he would have done the same thing. Three best friends that shared mad love for each other, but this was a dirty game they played. Friends turned on one another everyday. As far as Justo and Mad Max knew, Boolaid could have been cooperating with the Feds. Boolaid held the glizzy so tight he thought he might crush the handle. He decided to tell the brothers everything.

They deserved to know, because if they chose to fuck with him, they might get into beef behind some bitches they didn't even know. "OK but before I tell y'all anything! Max, you need to get that gun up out my face and you already no we gotta shoot the fade for you even coming at a real nigga like that", Boolaid said in a cool calm and collective tone.

Boolaid stared directly at Mad Max and still couldn't make out his whole face, Mad Max gave Boolaid a sinister smile. He loved that Boolaid didn't fear death. Ever since children Boolaid never folded under pressure, he never moved out of emotions but thought mathematically. If it didn't add up it wasn't Boolaid. Mad Max tucked his pistol into the waistband of his G star jeans then sat down at the table and acted as if an altercation

75

never happened. For the next 45 minutes Boolaid
gave the brothers the run down on his last 72
hours, he explained how his mentor KB sent him
to the sisters. How many kilos they had shown
him. "So, you telling me your man sent you to see
some random bitches and when you got there, they
pulled out 20 joints and asked you to move them
on consignment? Where'd they get them from?
They robbed sum sucka nigga?" Justo asked.
"They didn't give me details but I'm positive that's
what probably happened ". Justo fumbled the kilo
from hand to hand giving it a close inspection, "it
has a Queen chess piece stamp on it!" Justo said,
looking at Boolaid. "Never seen that", Mad Max
interrupted. "I have when I was in Afghanistan. I
was stationed in a village called Shirac. The city
was under control by the Taliban. Our team was
sent there on a mission to find and extract a man
named Yusuf Iman, a leader of their cartel. He got
away but the building was filled with bricks that
had that same exact stamp."

Boolaid pointed at the small block. "I think
we got pure Afghan heroin", Boolaid told them.
"It's only one way to find out, aye yooo Freeman!"
Justo called out. Movement could be heard in the
back of the apartment which surprised Boolaid
because he thought the three of them were alone.
He told himself to *tighten up and pay more
attention to his surroundings.*

A few moments went by before an older white man appeared. He had long shaggy hair and wore a tie dye shirt with a marijuana pot plant in the middle. His glasses hung on the edge of his pointy nose, a real hippy. "What can I do for you groovy fellas?" Freeman asked, already knowing Justo was going to give him a fix. Freeman was the tester; Justo wouldn't buy anything without Freeman's approval. "Freeman, I need you to let me know if this is good dope" Justo passed the kilo to freeman so he could do what he did best. "I haven't seen the Queen stamp in over 40 years, that's far out man" Freeman said putting the kilo down on the table then swiftly moved to the sink to fix a cup of water. "Got damn weirdo" Mad Max said in a low mumble. Freeman grabbed a leather case from the cabinet then joined the boys at the table. Freeman opened the case revealing a junkie's kit. A spoon, needle, lighter, cotton balls and an elastic band. He carefully placed each item on the table like he was preparing a dinner. Everyone watched it in silence. Freeman drew water from the cup with the needle then pushed the water into the spoon. "Food, please!" He asked. Justo took a knife, cutting through the plastic wrap of the kilo. Taking a small amount of heroin out with the tip of the knife Justo tapped the off-white powder into the spoon. "Far out man!" Freeman said big eyed watching the liquid in the spoon. "What is it?" Justo asked curiously. Freeman held the spoon outward for everyone to see. "The cotton balls are used to catch the cut when you pull the dope up through the needle, but this has no cut at all it just dissolved completely. "I don't even have to put heat to this" Freeman said, licking his lips hungrily. Justo helped Freeman tie the elastic band around his arm just above the elbow. It only took minutes before a strong healthy vein bulged. Freeman pulled the poison from the spoon up into the needle and quickly but carefully plunged the syringe down into his arm. He pushed down on the needle then pulled up drawing blood to mix the substance. Finally, he gave the needle one last push injecting himself with pure uncut Afghan China White. Freeman's eyelids immediately began to flutter. Then rolled to the back of his head. He let out a low moan, the kind of sound you only heard when a man released himself during sex. "Ahhhh" Freeman said with his mouth wide open. His arms fell freely to his sides. His head rolled around for a few seconds then stiffened up before leaning forwards then backwards. His body did a long hard shiver. The room watched him closely. Freeman's head fell limp, his chin crashing into chest. Then Freeman stopped moving all together.

The three friends all looked at each other then back to Freeman's motionless body. "Yooooo" Boolaid said with a hand covering his mouth. "That nigga look dead" "nah he always do

that when its fire work. Yo Freeman! Freeman!"
Justo called out but got no response. Justo
smacked the shit outta Freeman but still nothing.
"Freeman" Justo shook him by the shoulders he
leaned over then fell out the chair into the floor.
"Yeah, that nigga is defiantly dead" Boolaid said.
Mad Max laughed at the comment. "Yo, that shit
not funny Jason. He my best fien," Justo told his
little brother. Justo's face was priceless, it looked
like he was about to cry at any moment. Boolaid
tried his best to keep from smiling but Mad Max
wouldn't let'm "y'all niggas lame as hell. I don't
know what type time y'all on but I'm not feeling it"
Justo was pissed the fuck off. "My bad big bro"
Mad Max patted Justo on the shoulder. "Freeman
always said he wanted that far out shit! You can't
even be mad, it's all groovy baby", Mad Max
joked. "Fuck you bruh! You still play'n," Justo
said. "Bro really look at him." Mad Max pointed.
Freeman's eyes were wide open with a blank stare.
His lips turned upwards with a strange smile, "now
what?" Mad Max asked. "Clean the whole house.
Move the work and money. Afterwards call
Freeman's sister and tell her to come over because
you haven't heard from him all day." Mad Max
nodded his head in agreement.

"OK guys now that y'all got everything
under control I need to know if you in or out!"
Boolaid said acting as if there wasn't a dead man
lying in the kitchen floor. "Nigga the shit you got

just knocked Freeman off. I've seen him hit the best of the best. I'm in, just name your price." Justo said. Boolaid explained his loyalty towards KB and that he was getting the bricks from KB's girlfriend for fifty bands a kilo. Boolaid knew he could cut the heroin to make more profits. So, his proposal was for Justo to stretch the work as much as possible without killing the potency so people that were buying could cut it as well and the heroin would still be an 8% or 10% on the quality scale. Then Boolaid, Justo, and Mad Max would split the profits 50/50 with Meme and Bea. If everything went according to plan, they all would be rich. Once the heroin was gone the girls could then lead them in the right direction to find more. "I don't like the idea of bust'n down fifty fifty with some hoes I don't know. The only plus I see is I won't have to buy shit just sale and make free bandz fuck it! let's get money ". Justo spoke arrogantly. "So, to be clear we all agree? Because if shit get ugly for any reason down the line, I'm not trying to hear nothing" Boolaid said. "I'm cool. You cool Max?" Justo asked his little brother. "Hell, naw I'm not cool wit it". Mad Max told the room "O' lord what's the problem?", Boolaid questioned. "No problem, I'm just not cool wit it. I'm bool with it tho." Mad Max said with a mischievous smile. "I'm out y'all. I gotta hit this gym up, gotta fight lined up for next week. Call me when y'all get the trap situated," he was referring to the dead man. "Max

Ima get with you later, I still gotta get my one on one" Boolaid told his friend. Fighting didn't mean anything to them, it wouldn't affect the relationship more or less. Mad Max pulled his pistol out then sat it on the table. "You ain't gotta see me later. We can get this shit out the way right now!" Mad Max said. Boolaid drew his weapon and placed it beside Mad Max's F&N they both squared off right there in the kitchen. Justo watched with excitement he loved to see niggas wreck. "I don't see nobody but me, who I'ma lose too?" Boolaid rapped Lil Baby lyrics to himself before throwing a jab. He and Mad Max squabbled it out fighting fist to fist settling their differences as men. Boolaid had told Mad Max he wanted his fade over the gun being pulled out on him, but little did Justo know this fight was long overdue. The two had an issue from their past that they needed to get off their chest. Once they finished, they embraced each other with a handshake and a hug and most importantly their respect. They looked into one another's eyes still catching their breath then nodded to each other. Now that they had fought, the three of them shared an unspoken law. If you fight the issue is dead simple as that. "Love you bra" Boolaid said, "love you more my nigga" Mad Max said back. "Niggas get punched in they shit then get soft". Justo shook his head. "Boolaid, we got business to attend to, we gon get wit'cha" Justo said telling Boolaid it was time to bounce. "I'm gone" he grabbed the now empty sports bag off the table then headed for the door.

7 months later

When he walked into the house he almost threw up. He never got used to the smell of death. He covered his mouth and nose with the handkerchief he'd taken from the breast pocket of his cheap suit. The house was full of forensics, people taking pictures and bagging evidence. He walked through the living room which led him to a hallway. A decomposing body lay stretched out, most of the body lay in the hallway but his feet were positioned just pass the threshold of the bathroom "what do we got partner?" homicide detective James Ford questioned. "We've got a deceased African American male age 33 looks like lots of blunt force trauma to the body." Detective Tim Mcdon. Ford took a closer look and saw the body had bruise marks from top to bottom, "yeah someone beat this guy to a pulp." The legs, abdominal section, and head. "But what killed him was a single gunshot to the back of his head." Ford's partner Tim Mcdon said, pointing to the back of the dead man's head with a click pen. Flies buzzed and swarmed in the air for a few seconds before landing back atop the carcass. " How long has this guy been maggot food?", asked Ford. "The estimated time of death is at least 90 days; the coroner needs to get him to the morgue to know for sure" replied Mcdon. " God damn Tim! What took so long to find the poor bastard", "no neighbors for miles mailman reported it. He said it took him a while to notice the difference between animal and human decay. Out here in the country you smell rotten animals all the time but after a while the smell goes away due to the animal decomposing back into the earth.

The mail man said the stench became stronger and stronger. So strong you could tell the odor came from inside the house" Mcdon explained. "Have we got a positive ID" Ford asked looking down at the body, "sure Curtis Lewis" Mcdon read off his notepad. "He is a native of Queens, New York. I had his name run through the FBI's database and got a hit." "Why am I not surprised a dead New Yorker found in the sticks. What did the database tell you?", he did ten years fed upstate New York for trafficking, got out did 6 months at a halfway house in Harlem. He'd been quiet ever since just disappeared off the radar" Mcdon said, flipping through the pages of his notepad. "Now he's loud as ever without saying one word", Ford pinched his nose shut. "Who's next of kin?." "His mother lives in Queens, we've sent a squad car to transport her so she can make a positive ID." "Huh, so we got a dead ex-trafficker for NY in NC" said Ford "and we've got a dead pit bull in the back yard with a flipped over doghouse that had a trap door under it. An empty trapped door I might add" detective Ford continued. " The motive was robbery. Most likely inside job". "Excuse me, detectives!" a rookie officer said as he approached. "The coroner is ready to transport the victim to the morgue." "10-4 rookie tell em the place is all his". Mcdon answered. "Yes sir!" The rookie said then left. "It's gonna be a long day Tim, let's start it off with black coffee and a ton of sugar, plus more donuts," Ford said to his partner. "Now that's a big 10-4" Mcdon replied.

****

"Girl look!" Bea passed meme her iPhone meme watched the video that Bea had just watched. "Damn!" Was all she had to say about what she'd just seen. She nonchalantly gave her friend the phone back to Bea "really bitch! That's all you got to say about that" Meme rolled her eyes showing off her aggravation. "What you want me to do Bea, cry?" Meme said with a light sigh. They had just watched a video on the news on your side app. Bea would check the app daily. She liked to be informed on things like the weather and current events. Covid-19, some unknown virus that came from out of nowhere had spread worldwide. The

84

whole planet was in a crisis plus on top of that you never knew when a black person was gonna get killed by a white person or cop for no reason at all. Black lives did matter even though some black people deserved to die Bea thought to herself. What caught her attention was an article that was titled man found dead in house discovered by mail man. It took five months to find him. "It took way longer than I expected" Bea expressed her thoughts out loud. "I know right", Meme said with a mouth full of the huge bite she took from her cajun filet chicken biscuit. They were parked at the *Bojangles* on Bessemer Ave having lunch. Meme saw a worried look on Bea's face. "What's wrong Bestie? We cleaned up the house, good they can't trace nothing back to us" she let her sister know. "It's not that!" Bea answered, "it just took them so long to find him now the news people making more of a scene about it. It's like more of a mystery than anybody else getting found murdered in a house. First, police like to solve big mysteries and second thing is now that his fat ass has been found who ever he owed them keys to, gonna know for sure that he got robbed then killed. The idea that he ran off is out the window. You remember what KB said! Somebody was defiantly about to be looking for a million dollars worth of drugs." Bea said, putting her mouth around a straw, taking a couple long gulps. Meme looked at Bea with a face full of disbelief. "Bitch since when you started listening to what my man got to say?" Meme asked with her head cocked to the side waiting for an answer. "Ever since KB sent Boolaid to us and made us rich, might I add" Bea said back. Meme still held her head to the side. Her mouth dropped open in shock from what she'd just heard. Bea never admitted to anything. "KB said trust him and he would do right by us, and he has. Then Boolaid has brought us almost two mill a piece in only five months girl!." " You ain't lied about that" Meme said, doing a ratchet moment. With a big smile she and Bea gave each other a high five. "Did he not convince us to invest in a business and help start-up our hair and nail shop?" Boolaid had told the sisters they should consider becoming business owners so they could generate generational wealth. Money for the long run. He even went as far as helping write the business plan.

"Yesss, bitch he did all that" Meme said. "Even tho he helped us a lil bit" Meme measured with her thumb and pointer finger, " doesn't take away the face that yo ass is star struck over this nigga". "What!" Bea shouted, jumping in her seat almost hitting her head on the ceiling. Meme laughed at Bea's reaction. "Yeah, girl I'm no fool he's the first man we've met that ain't trying to fuck on us and that shit got you all hot in the ass." "Meme you trippin". "Bea stop the lies KB told me that the last time you met Boolaid to get a payment you tried to throw that pussy and he told yo lil thot ass no because it would be bad for business or a possible long term future friendship. Ummm hmmm thought I didn't know didn't you". Bea put her face into her hands, she was so embarrassed. "Bitch don't come for me" was all Bea Could think to say. "You thought the nigga might be low key gay because what man wouldn't want the bad bitch Bea huh? But after looking at his Facebook and IG we know that's not the case he definitely slanging that big dick and the bitches he fuckin is bad". "Ok Meme you can stop now!" Bea said to Meme with a *stop picking on me* tone. "He's not pointing that dick in your direction or mine for that matter," Meme said, biting into her biscuit then chuckling at the thought of giving Boolaid some pussy because she never would have.

She loved KB too much to ever disrespect him like that. "Meme I'm being for real I got a funny feeling about all this. I think we should tell him", Bea said. Meme was about to take another bite of her biscuit but stopped in mid air. "tell'm what?" Bea stared and said nothing. "Tell him that the police found the body of one of the few motherfuckas we murdered?" Bea still said nothing.
"Bitch you really trippin we don't tell people about the shit we've done in our past all me and you gotta do is stay black and die." The sisters stared at each other not saying anything for a long moment. "I'm not playing Bea don't tell that boy our business. I

know you like em and all, but we can't trust him on something like that". A red F 150 swung into the parking lot then backed in beside the girl's money green 97 Honda. Meme made eye contact with the driver; her pussy became moist. He was a young male mid 20's and very handsome. He noticed Meme watching so he smiled. "Damn he fine" she said out loud. Bea leaned over Meme's seat to see who she was admiring. She saw the man and smiled just as hard. He opened his door then stepped out of the truck onto the pavement. Bea hit the unlock button Boolaid opened the back door to their Honda then climbed in. The women turned in their seats to look at their guest. "Hey ladies" Boolaid said.

“Hey!" They said in unison. *These some silly bitche*s Boolaid smiled to himself. He tossed a small Gucci handbag up front, and Meme caught it. Then peeped inside. Stacks of money wrapped with rubber bands. Bea saw the money she looked at Meme with raised eyebrows. Meme stutters. "Boolaid there's something we need to tell you" Bea said. Meme made a bitch Ima kill you face. Boolaid saw the stand off the girls were having so he decided to instigate. "Oh yeah what up is everything okay?" he asked, watching both women very closely. "No well um, well I mean yeah everything's fine. Actually, more than fine. The shop is doing numbers shit's great we couldn't be more happy" Bea said "It's just our deal was 1.6

M's and you've already paid your debt. You don't owe us anymore money" Meme thought Bea was about to put the Curtis murder on blast but relaxed when she heard her statement. "Oh! That's all you had to say, nothing else to tell me?" "Nope! Nothing Else!" Bea lied. "I'm glad we all can be so honest with each other that's why I fucks wit you two so much" Boolaid said to the couple. Bea felt bad. She felt she was hiding something he should know. "All I wanted to do is make sure we all eat that's what y'all hire me for. There's 400 bandz in the bag I just gave you. So, I've just made you two wonderful ladies a mill a piece. I can't thank you enough for such an opportunity. You two are angels. Heaven sent, even though I've paid you I can't ever really repay you if that makes any sense. I love the both of you very much, if you ever need anything just let me know I'm there", Boolaid said dead serious. Bea and Meme showed confusion on their faces.

"What're you tryna say?" Meme asked. "What I'm saying is goodbye." His statement melted their hearts. He was actually trying to leave them, and it came to them as a real shocker. They had never met a nigga like this. In reality they all were so much alike he was doing the very thing they did to their trick ass niggas. Get the money and be gone. "We love you too," the girls said back. "Since you're saying your goodbyes and shit, at least let us take you out to eat" Meme suggested, Bea put a chicken tender to her lips ready to take a bite. Boolaid leaned up between the seats and took it from her "hey! that's mine" she said with a smirk. He licked the honey mustard sauce off before eating the whole tender in one bite. The sisters watched in silence. Chicken supreme, seasoned fries, honey mustard, large sweet tea with extra ice is my favorite " Boolaid told the girls, "for real? That's exactly what I get every time I eat here" Bea told him. "Now that's weird y'all are just alike, even down to the food. I think you two are meant to be together" Meme tried to throw any ally for her friend. Boolaid caught on to the invitation but didn't bite. Instead, he grabbed another chicken tender. "Thanks for the meal but I gotta run!." He ate the chicken tender as he opened the door to get out the back seat. "No wait!" Bea stopped him. Boolaid sat with one foot in the car and one outside. "What up!" He turned to see what she wanted. Bea had to think fast. For some odd reason she wanted this man to stay in her life. There was more to figure out about him. She'd been dealing with him for the past 6 months and still he was a mystery. If she let him get out the car this could be her last time, she might ever see him.

"Well, uhmm! Will you at least go out with me" Bea said. Boolaid raised his eyebrows curiously. "I mean go out with us" she corrected herself looking at Meme for help. "Yeah, well you go out with us this weekend it'll be fun" Meme teased. "You always talking bout business before pleasure and since our business is over it's time for pleasure. Let's go out and celebrate our success and newfound love! I mean friendship "Meme winked at Boolaid giving hints that Bea secretly like him, "pleeassse!" both girls said at the same time. Boolaid thought about it, "nigga it ain't nothing to think about!" Meme said, reading his mind.

"Now say yes" Meme added with an attitude and a smile,"what do you have in mind?". " Well since you're not trying let my sister throw that ass in a circle," she joked, "let's go to a strip club and make it rain a little". Boolaid hadn't gone out to enjoy himself since he'd come home from prison. Maybe the girls were right, it was time to kick back a little. "OK this weekend! I'm in hit my phone." He said climbing out of the vehicle without another word. "I don't care what he say we gonna make him give you some of that dick and if he get to actin funny we gonna date rape his ass and then you gonna take the D!" Meme joked. There car filled with laughter as they watch Boolaid pull off.

.... "*A love letter came in the mail it said I miss you*" Boolaid rapped *Lil Baby*. He turned the radio down he needed a moment to think about a few things. *Like why Bea and Meme were keeping something from him?* Meme looked like she was about to shoot to Bea's ass when Bea mentioned she needed to tell him something. Boolaid also thought about the heroin he had left because it would run out soon. He had told the girls he wanted to go his own separate way, but really never had that intention. He was only fishing hoping they would stop him from leaving because they still had more bricks they needed him to move. Maybe that's what Bea really wanted to tell him. That she had more kilos. Whatever the case may be Boolaid would find out this weekend. He decided to just ask them did they have more and if not where'd they come from. Hopefully, he'd get the answers he wanted. Boolaid's phone beeped it was a message from his fb message app. He could tell by the sound his phone made. He grabbed the phone from the cupholder and opened the message. It read. *When Ima see you, (eyes emoji) with smiley face with hearts eyes a heart emoji and eggplant emoji a 100% emoji and ended with the thumbs up.*

He replied. *Ima be through there in a couple hours, cook somthin for a nigga. I'm text you when I'm omw!.* Bubbles began moving across the bottom of the screen letting you know the message was being read. The phone beeped. A simple text came through that said *K!*. Boolaid went to his contacts and called Justo. The phone rang a few times then went to voicemail. Boolaid dropped the phone into the cupholder and turned the radio up.

Lil Durk blasted through the speaker *my celly was 23 but got 96 and he aint get caught for a murder he was moving bricks.*

Chapter 5

"Yea! Ride that dick girl" Toya held both hands on Justo's chest while her hips moved back and forth, "faster! faster!" Justo said as he massaged her nipples. She rode all 10 inches like a dirt bike. "Oh my god baby.... You in my stomach "Toya cried out. He wrapped one arm around her back then pulled her body closer to his. She kissed

his neck licking up to the ear. Then bit gently.
With Justo's free hand he palmed her ass cheek
open and pounded her out. Toya's skin was soft
and super smooth to the touch. Her booty was fat
and plump. Just the feel of her skin on Justo's
made his dick swell deep inside her. Toya's pussy
was hot and wet. He rammed up into her harder
and harder. She began to cream around his pole. "
I'm cumin, baby" she moaned. Every time he
pumped into her wetness he nailed her g-spot with
the long stroke. At first slow but then picked up
speed going crazy. "Ah ah ah ah " was all she
could yelp out. Justo roughly grabbed Toya,
rolling over on top of her in one swift motion. He
delivered a few deep strokes before backing out of
kitty cat. He sat up on his knees to take a breath.
Their California king size bed was so comfortable.
"Turn over" Justo demanded. Her eyes were
closed, breathing heavily. Her body twitched from
the sexual climax she just had. Toya loved Justo's
dick; she was a fiend that needed a dick fix. She
slowly turned over positioning, one leg stretched
straight out, and the leg was bent in a 90-degree
angle. She laid flat on her stomach. Her juicy wet
swollen pussy poked out in between her ass
cheeks. Justo watched at how her ass jiggled as he
climbed on top of her from behind. "blop! blop!
blop!" Was the sound of his nuts smacking down
on Toya's pussy the headboard knocked against
the wall. They were making sex music, "ooh baby!

Yes yessss!" she whined, "fuck me fuck me yes fuck momma's pussy", she screamed. Toya stuffed a mouth full of cover to muffle a loud yell. Justo's phone buzzed on the nightstand; the vibration was loud against the oak wood. He grabbed the phone to see who it was. The number belonged to his friend Boolaid "noooo baby don't stop I'm... Im about to cum" Toya said. Justo was about to answer but Toya's threw her ass back like a wild horse. Her pussy ate Justo's penis in the same motion. He dropped the phone then grabbed her ponytail yanking her head back and began pounding out her bottom half. "You gonna nut for me?". Justo's asked in a deep voice "yeessss... Im cu-cumin for you daddy I'm... Cum-min" Toya cried. Her orgasm made Justo's dick rock hard, swollen with nut. "Ooh shit girl I'M about to bust" his strokes went from hard fast and powerful to soft and weak. They came together. She creamed all over his penis and he shot a load on semen inside of her. Justo's phone rang again. He rolled over not wanting to miss his brother's call again. "What's good!" He answered while looking at the screen. "What up doggy" the person on the other end spoke. Justo looked at the caller ID. The voice he'd heard wasn't Boolaid's. "What's the word O" Justo said. "You already know! Tryna stay out the way", Omar replied.

Omar was an associate of Justo's; they'd known each other for the past three years. Justo had started asking for more drugs than his dealer at the time could handle, so his dealer introduced him to Omar who had been supplying Justo until just recently. "I'm calling to see if you still got me on what we talked about, what's understood don't need to be explained!," "I told you I got you, I'm a man of my word." Justo said. He smacked Toya on the ass they shared a smile and silent laugh as she made it wobble. "Aite bet then!" Omar said. "Ima shoot you a text once I put everything together" Justo said then hung up without another word. He saw he had a text message from Boolaid. He opened it. "*OTW*" it read. "Shit!" Justo said, checking the time he had to meet up with his friend but know he was going to be late. "What's wrong baby?" Justo's baby mother asked, blowing out a cloud of funnel cake. Which was a type of exotic weed. Justo would purchase a couple pounds at a time just to smoke. She put the blunt to his lips. He took a long pull, the cherry on the blunt turned bright red. He inhaled then choked before speaking. "Nothin bae, I forgot I had to handle some business with Boolaid today", Justo said, letting smoke escape from his nostrils. "But baeee! I thought we was going shopping", Toya whined like a six-year-old. "Girl don't start that crybaby shit. Ima take ya spoiled ass shopping. If you wanna continue to be taken on shopping sprees, you'll go get the shower ready for us". Toya's face lightened up with a smile, she kissed Justo on the cheek. She happily jumped out of bed, her perky breast bounced, and ass wobbled as she quickly made her way to the bathroom. "*OTW*", Justo sent Boolaid a reply. Then finished his blunt.

2 hours later......

****

Justo walked into the house; it was one of his many traps. He was accompanied by a bald-headed man with bug eyes. "What's good big homie?" Bigs said when Justo walked through the door. Bigz was Justo's little homie, they were part of the GBG Greensboro Blood Gang. Bigz was also Justo's employee. He ran the trap house on the east side of town, Florida St, and Willow Rd. He was 17 years old. He had no family; they were all dead. So, he was loyal to Justo and eager to learn how to make money and prove himself. Bigz paused the latest version of *2K Basketball* for *PS5*. He sat the controller down on the table then picked up another set of sticks. A micro ak47 which had a "honey bunn" attached. Honey bunn was slang the youth use when referring to a clip that held 100 rounds. He did this because he'd never seen the man Justo was with. "Yo lil nigga this my man Omar everything one hunnit!" Justo said, talking to the assault rifle Bigz held and not Bigz. Bigz just held his position with the weapon like a soldier, and said nothing, "what up lil nigga? "Omar said to Bigz. "The only lil nigga I see in this room is my stick and he don't even know you!" Bigz said with the screw face. "Do you know this nigga Omar lil nigga?" Bigz asked his baby AK. He moved the rifle side to side as if the gun shook its head *no*. "Would you like to get to know Omar?" The rifle slowly went up and down in agreement. "Aite lil bruh! That's enough" Justo spoke up. He laughed to himself because everyone that knew Bigz knew he named his gun little nigga. So even though at this moment Bigz wasn't playing around it was still like a serious joke. "Where Boolaid?" Justo changed the subject, "aw yea he told me to tell you not to leave nowhere and that he'll be back in an hour. That was about 45 minutes ago" Bigz said.

Justo was running late. He and Toya couldn't get enough of each other; they had to have another round while in the shower. So, he couldn't even be mad Boolaid had left, "aite call'm and let bruh know I'm here". Bigz watched the two men head towards the kitchen. Bigz thought he'd seen Omar somewhere before but wasn't sure. What he was sure about was he didn't like Omar's vibes; *he just seemed toxic in every way* Bigz thought. "If I catch that nigga down low Ima slide on his ass off gp," Bigz mumbled getting back to his video game. Omar followed Justo into the kitchen. Justo opened the refrigerator and grabbed a kilo then

98

tossed it on the table. Omar noticed two more keys on the bottom shelf before Justo closed the door. "Damn my nigga you really done came up in the world just a few months ago you was grabbin from me, now you my plug", Omar laughed. Omar's plug Curtis had gone mia- missing in action. Omar thought he might have gotten locked up, but when he hadn't heard from him after a few months he turned to Justo and started to buy from him. "Yeah, it be like that sometime," Justo said ignoring Omar's last comment. "I'm only doing this favor one time. And I'm only putting you on game because you came through for a nigga when my momma died. My partner wouldn't approve me doing this, but I fucks wit you O!"

"That's what friends are for" Omar said, embracing Justo with a strong handshake then brotherly hug. Omar wore a *Gucci* bag with shoulder straps. He passed the bag to Justo, "that's 80 bandz right there! Now bro is you sure the doggy is jumping out the gym?" Omar asked. "Look my nigga this shit is so fire you can turn one chicken into ten but I'm only doing one to five. Leaves room for the next man to eat a little bit" Justo explained turning the bag upside down the money fell from the bag. Four 20 band stacks of cash landed on top of the table. Justo replaced the money with the kilo. "This should have you straight until you find out what's up with Curtis." Omar nodded his head in agreement. Justo had no

idea who Curtis was until a few months ago when
Omar told him about his disappearance, "good
look my nigga but duty calls, Ima holla at you after
awhile to let you know what my people think"
Omar said, then gave Justo dap. He left the kitchen
and went into the living room. Bigz still watched
Omar with choppa in hand.

Omar was far from a bitch nigga but knew
better temping a young gangsta with an AK 47. So,
he walked through the room to the front door only
giving Bigz a slight head nod. "Say bye lil nigga"
Bigz whispered to his weapon. Omar walked
outside oblivious to the green dot beam Bigz
aimed at the back of Omar's head. "Bye, bye pow!"
Bigz pretending his rifle could talk. Omar got into
his car and then sped away from the curb. As he
drove off Boolaid pulled into the driveway.
Boolaid walked into the house, Bigz didn't budge
he just continued to play the game. "Big homie in
the kitchen" Bigz said keeping his eyes glued to
the tv screen. "Who was that that just left" that
question made Bigz give Boolaid his full attention.
"I don't know big homie, some nigga name Omar
straight weirdo if you ask me. I was bout to put lil
nigga on his ass" Bigz said with an evil grin. "Justo
would have been super-hot tho so I left it alone"
Bigz explained.

Although Bigz was under Justo in the blood
gang, Boolaid had been the one who brought him
around. Boolaid and Bigz older brother Eric were

tight back in the day Boolaid stopped fucking with him because he had too many flawed ways.

Soon after Boolaid had gotten out of prison Eric had gotten himself killed. Eight months ago, Boolaid saw Bigz posted up at the local Marathon hood store, off Randleman Road. He was selling dime rocks of crack, Boolaid recognized him from his past and felt like it was his duty not to let Bigz become anything like his brother. So, he put him under his wing. Boolaid introduced the teenager to Justo and Mad Max. They took a liking to him as well. Bigz was already blood. Mad Max knew Bigz big homie was a bitch and wasn't respected by him. So, Justo put Bigz under him. The young boy was now in real life street boot camp. They put him to work in each and every way. Justo showed him how to get money, and Mad Max taught him how to slide. For starters Bigz former big homie Cooper needed to be dealt with so they killed him. The four of them created their own brotherhood. They were called the Urban Millionaire Gangsters; their goal was to make everyone a millionaire. Bigz was a good little brother. Boolaid still had connections on guns through an old army Buddy, so on Bigz 17th birthday he got him the micro-AK 47 also known as "lil nigga".

"Lil nigga won't gone do shit!" "Yeah, I know that's right", Bigz said picking up his controller going back to playing the game. Boolaid walked into the kitchen Justo had his back turned smoking a blunt of Zaza as he plugged up a money counter. He felt someone present in the room. He turned around then smiled. "What's good dog?" "What's good!" Boolaid said, looking at the money on the table. "What's this the monthly net?" "Nah, I just made a play to Omar" Boolaid knew very little about Omar. He didn't come into the picture until he had gone to prison. He'd met him once and didn't care for him. Boolaid didn't dislike him, but he didn't like him either. One thing was for sure. Bigz was right. The guy was definitely a weirdo. There was just something off about him.

"How much is it? Hunnit thou?" Boolaid asked picking up one of the four large stacks of cash. "Nah that's an 80 piece. But check it bro I sold Omar one of the raw uncut bricks" Justo truthfully told his business partner. Hearing this Boolaid became furious but kept his temper in check. "Bruh, I can't tell you what to do with your operation but selling people uncut not only keeps us away from reaching our goal we're working so hard to accomplish, it's dangerous. Justo! We don't know who those keys belong to. We could start an invisible war and we can't beat a motherfucka we can't see coming" Boolaid's voice raised a couple octaves. "I thought about all that already! I'll take the loss on that brick and as far as a war we don't gotta worry about Omar bruh. He good. I promise

you that. And if an issue comes up, I'll handle it."
Justo said.

Boolaid didn't like it but nodded his head "ok my
nigga, I trust your word. But we can't serve any
more uncut", "agreed" when Boolaid brought the
first kilo to Justo they needed to see how far they
could stretch it. Justo turned one into ten, even
with adding that much cut his buyers still said the
drugs were a 7 on a scale of 1-10. A seven wasn't
that bad so Boolaid devised a way for everyone to
get rich. They had 20 uncut kilos at their access.
Boolaid suggested they should turn one into five
which would give them one hundred keys. If sold
at fifty thousand a piece like Meme and Bea asked
everybody would come off with a cool million.
Justo had spots where he met people to make plays
but what he didn't have was trap houses that stayed
open 12 to 24 hours shifts. The three brothers all
invested their money into opening a trap on each
side of town. Boolaid would look after one and the
brothers would operate the other three locations.

Their objective was to sell whole bricks in
all breakdown so that way they could double or
even triple their profits. Justo could hire the people
he fucked with. People who deserved to be put on.
Boolaid estimated they would make at least six
million dollars. Boolaid ran the trap house on the
east side of Greensboro, an area they called duty
heights. Florida Street and Willow Road. The
neighborhood was middle class, right down the

street from the trap was James B. Dudley, a historically black high school known for its football, basketball, and amazing drumline. Boolaid chose Bigz to be the manager over the movement of heroin on the east side. He didn't know anybody else he could trust with that much money and drugs coming in and out. This wasn't his operation he only made up the business proposal. Boolaid's only job was to make sure everybody took full advantage of making as much money as possible because after they made all those millions his plan was to become a legit businessman in the urban community. After doing a short tour in Africa while in the Army, then going to prison, Boolaid wanted to learn about his own black history, so he read. Throughout all of time civilizations got their hands dirty to get ahead including the United States through the Atlantic slave trade. *They owe me and mine* Boolaid thought to himself.

Meme and Bea had given him the opportunity of a lifetime. Justo ran the show; he had all the manpower with providing the hustlers to hold the traps down. Boolaid thought of himself basically as their financial advisor. It took two months to get the traps off the ground. Within a whole five month span each location was moving at least two keys a month in all break down. Justo and Mad Max had wholesale buyers as well. "I paid the girls the last portion of money we owed them so it's smooth sailing from here. Everything's all profit from here on out. How many we got left?" "So far we've moved fifty chickens. I just sold Omar an uncut so that's like five. Each trap has two uncut so that's eight" Justo explained, "aite so we got 40 birds technically speaking!" "And them bitches moving fast." Justo placed money into the slot of the money counter then pressed the button. "Beeep!" The bills began to flutter in the machine. "Did you ask the girls if they had more keys?" "Nah I didn't, but Ima find out this weekend" Boolaid said. The counter stopped, the digital reading said 20,000. Justo put two more piles of money on the table. There were four piles altogether 20 thousand in each pile. Boolaid grabbed 40 bands stuffing the money into his G star jeans. Justo said nothing. "When I got here Bigz had a hunnit thou bagged and tagged, I put 60 of that in the back room for you and Max. I paid Bigz 10 bands then gave him an extra five".

"I've been noticing some funny activity around the spots over here and the one on the north side where Drama works. Cars I've never seen driving through. White people walking dogs and cable vans posted. These are telltale signs for police. I suggest you shut down all traps. Relocate and reopen in about 60 days, everybody that's on the clock should have enough bread to hold out until then. If not they in the way and Mad Max and Bigz should get them outta the way. I'm not trying to get locked up before I can get a chance to spend my money plus that should give me enough time to see what's up with more of that Afghan shit" Boolaid said. "Say less" Justo answered. "Yo, I'm going with Meme and Bea to the strip club this weekend. You should come". "Oh, hell yeah nigga I remember when I went with you to meet them, to drop off some money. Both them bitches bad. I can't see how you sit around them sexy women and not try to fuck". "I'm not gone lie its hard." Boolaid laughed off his friend's comment. "Nah, on the real they my home girls". "Ok well when we go to the club, I'ma bag one of they asses if not both and Ima tell you what it's hittin for" Justo told Boolaid as they followed each other to the living room. "Yo, Bigz! Shit hot right now so we shutting shit down until further notice." Justo informed his protégé. "Bet big homie!" "What y'all about to do?" Bigz asked his two elders putting his controller down on the coffee table. "I gotta holla at Mad Max then Ima take the bm shopping." "Damn she got a nigga spending all his money straight goofy" Bigz joked. Justo shot a quick jab at Bigz 'chest making him flinch, laughing "where you going Boolaid?" Bigz asked "shit lil bo I'm about to go to this shorty spot, she posta cook for a nigga". "Well, I could eat so I guess I'm riding with you" Bigz said standing up to stretch. Boolaid loved his nigga he didn't care if bro rode with him.

Bigz was just gonna be stuck with him so if he complained he had only himself to blame.

The crazy thing about it was Bigz had his own car, a brand-new Lincoln Continental but on the low Bigz had abandonment issues. He'd seen so much death as a child with his own family he'd felt if he was away from his newfound brothers for too long, he might not ever see them again. Boolaid was the only person that knew this secret fear Bigz carried. People tended to think like that when they lost important people in their lives. Boolaid saw a lot of that in the Army he wanted Bigz to know his new family would never abandon him. They were locked in from until death and beyond. "Come on lil bruh pack the ps5 and bring lil nigga. Justo we out".

Chapter 6

Assalaamualaykumwarahmatulah the man said, looking to his right. He slowly turned his head in the opposite direction then repeated the ancient language. He was in prostration praying to his God Allah. Omar watched in silence. Omar had been blind folded then driven to an unknown location, once he confirmed he'd found the kilos marked with the queen stamp. The praying man opened his eyes then stood to his feet. His skin tone was dark brown. His nose was big and long like a shark fin. Black and shiny hair pulled into a tight ponytail. His beard was thick, full, and very healthy. The Middle Eastern man wore all white silk top and bottoms. He was bare footed.

He was a general of a cartel. Not the cartel most people thought about like the Mexicans or Cubans. He was part of an elite one-of-a-kind cartel. Rafiq was part of the Afghan cartel. And the name of the group he worked for was called Shirac. Shirac was a city in Afghanistan that was fully under control by the Taliban. Afghanistan was the capital of heroin. The Taliban sold 93% of all the heroin in the world.
"Assalaamualaykum! I am Rafiq welcome to my home" Rafiq held his arms stretched out. "Thank you for inviting me" Omar said looking around the room. They were in a room that looked more like a palace. The ceiling was at least 30 feet high with Arabic writing trimmed in gold all over the place. Twenty-four karat chandeliers hung low. Omar had never seen anything like this in his life. This one room had to be worth a

cool mill Omar thought. There were nine armed guards in the room as well. Two in each corner and one last guard stood beside a desk table that sat in the middle of the room. Everyone in the room was barefooted. The carpet seemed extra comfortable to the touch. Rafiq walked around the desk then took a seat on his throne. "Have a seat" he spoke with a deep Middle Eastern accent. "Thank you but I'll stand" " I wasn't asking" Rafiq smiled polity he spoke in a cheerful voice.

The guard standing next to the desk put a firm hand on Omar's shoulder. The other eight guards moved in with fully automatic weapons aimed to kill. Seeing this Omar made a wise decision to sit. "You are here and may I add still alive for only one reason." Rafiq spoke to Omar while staring him in the eyes. Omar felt like he was about to shit a brick. "You are not responsible for Curtis's death. At first, I assumed you betrayed your own friend. I knew you and Curtis were very close, so I had you followed for a little over two months. You were unaware of this." Rafiq said loving every moment of putting fear into Omar. Omar felt a cold chill run down his spin at the thought of being spied on by a group of people responsible for killing hundreds of people. "So! I shut down shop as you call it. I knew the streets would soon dry up. After you realized you couldn't contact Curtis you went searching for more product elsewhere like I knew you would. At this point in time there should have been only one other source still able to supply wholesale. Your friend Justo was very smart to cut the product and break it down. I would have missed his activities if it were not for you." Rafiq smiled for a moment, "Curtis worked for me for many many years. Not only was he a great employee he was my friend but now he is dead!" He clapped his hands leaving them in a prayer-like position.

Omar was shocked when he heard the news about Curtis body being found. But Rafiq had not. He knew Curtis had a house out in Browns Summit. He sent men out there to check because Curtis had not been in touch which was unlike him. Once Rafiq's men reported they'd found Curtis in the house dead. He ordered them to leave but to make sure they cleaned their own tracks. "Would you like to replace your friend's position and I supply you with Afghan heroin the best of the best! Hmmmm!" Omar didn't know if this was a trick question, so he chose to say nothing. "You may answer now" "hell yeah"! I want

you to put a nigga on" Omar said, "very well
I put you on!," "After you go get my heroin
back" he told Omar nonchalantly. "Huh!
Rafiq I don't think my nigga Justo had
anything to do with taking your bricks he
doesn't even know Curtis. Somebody had to
put him on plus I only saw two more keys in
the frig" Omar told the Muslim.

"Can you prove what you say?" Rafiq
asked with raised eyebrows. "No! I can't
but..." "no buts! Buts I can not do! But!
Since you say this Justo had nothing to do
with taking my kilos you go and tell him he
owes me one million dollars." Rafiq spoke
as if he were talking about one dollar. "So,
you're telling me you want me to just walk
into a real street niggas house and tell' m he
gotta come up off a mill? I'm telling you
now that's not going to end well" Omar said.
"Very well my friend you leave me no
choice! How you gangsta say! I'm with all
the smoke" Rafiq said with a quick flash of
anger showing. "You want my heroin
connections; you go kill this so-called real
street nigga and anybody that means
something to him. I'll send a solider with
you to make sure it happens, and if you do
not kill this man. I kill your family" "Wait!
Hold up bruh, I did everything you asked. I
helped you find your work" Omar said in a

panic. "Yes, you did. Now you help me kill! Taliban! "Rafiq called his guard standing beside the desk. Taliban was very light skinned and fat. Two hundred ninety pounds with beard that hung down to his round belly. They spoke to each other in Pashto. Everyone in the room understood Rafiq's orders except Omar. Taliban said one last thing to his commander then spoke out loud to the rest of the soldiers. One of them moved in putting a blind fold over Omar's eyes. "Come now we leave" Taliban roughly stood Omar to his feet.

Omar wanted to plead his case but knew better. They slowly led him out of the room. "Assalaamualaykum. "Don't let me down Omar" Rafiq yelled after him.

****

Amber's back was pressed against the wall. Her legs wrapped around Boolaid's waist, her arms around his neck and hung over his shoulder. Water fell raining from the shower into his face then drizzled down in between both bodies. Hot steam made the couple feel on fire even if they were wet. Boolaid palmed Amber's ass cheeks wide open so he could guide his manhood into her gushy pussy. His chest smushed against her breast making her nipples become super hard. Their bodies were soapy and slippery from the mango body wash. "Ooh baby" she moaned long loud and hard. Her body raised up then her back slid down the shower wall. Boolaid dug deeper and deeper with each stroke.

"Oouh ummm. Hmm... O shit! Bae, o.. Ba..by I'm cummin on your dick I'm cu..min ahhh my pussy" she yelled. Boolaid had her pent to the wall and was grinding her hard. She orgasmed against the wall. He slowly let her down to her feet, they embraced. She laid her head on his chest having to catch her breath. She knew she was still in for a hell of a ride. Boolaid's dick was still brick hard pressed up against her stomach. He turned her around taking her by the waist. She leaned forward, putting her hands on the wall bracing herself for the beatdown she knew she was about to get. Amber was petite with a very nice shape. Her ass wasn't fat though. Her pussy made up for that because it was super fat stayed wet and was on fire at the same time. She had a face like *Chloe* the singer. Boolaid fell into the pussy at first with long slow deep strokes he watched his dick go in and out of her. Just the sight made him bulge. "Oh yes baby", she moaned. He held on to her hips with a tight grip then went faster ramming her bottom out " pop! pop! pop!" Was the sound that echoed in the shower from his thighs smacking against her ass along with the water in between.

Boolaid reached around taking hold of Amber's titties. He gave them a hard squeeze. She leaned backward into his chest. The more she leaned back the more he punished her from behind. "O god you killing this pussy!" She whined. Boolaid seemed to pick up speed drilling deep. "Uh. Uh I'm about to nut girl..." Boolaid told Amber he was ready to bust. He repeatedly rammed inside her, each stroke getting closer to   his release. Amber pulled away from him falling to her knees she grabbed his penis with both hands then began jacking him while sucking the tip. She looked into his eyes and moaned. "Ahhhh!" Boolaid said trying to keep eye contact but couldn't. His eyes rolled backwards like he'd just popped a triple stack ecstasy pill. He palmed the back of her head she deep swallowed then sucked on it like a straw. Boolaid shot a load, she caught it letting it run down her throat. She pulled his dick out of her mouth and let the next three cum shots spray her in the face. Boolaid aimed shooting cum up her nose, into her eyes then all over the lips. Amber used his dick like a washrag. Wiping cum all over her face like it was facial cream. "Ummmm you taste sweet. You like that baby" she asked still jerking his now soft penis. Boolaid's body jerked each time. hell...yeah uh damn." *This bitch is a whole porn star he thought to himself.* "I think I love her" Boolaid laughed looking down at her. "Boolaid, you don't love, Boolaid you don't love me."

She sang into his dick like it was a microphone, he jolted every time she touched his private part. He helped her to her feet. "Come on let's get washed up. I'm hungry as hell and my lil brother don't know how to cook. Ima be mad if you let that BBQ chicken burn over some dick." "Boy you crazy hand me the body wash". Amber rolled her eyes jokingly.

****

Mad Max placed two more bricks into the duffle bag. There were 8 total, Justo had come to see Mad Max a few hours earlier to give him a portion of the sixty bands that Boolaid had collected from Bigz. Justo also informed Mad Max that they were closing shop until further notice, Justo asked his little brother to go move the kilos that were stashed at each trap location. Mad Max was at his last stop for the night. He was at the trap on the east side. The location Boolaid and Bigz watched over. Mad Max threw the duffle bag strap over his shoulder preparing to leave when his cell phone rang. "Yoooo what up?" "A my nigga! I called Justo because I saw his car in the driveway, but he said yall switched whips" 2 times aka 2x said. 2x was the neighborhoods tattoo man he lived directly across the street from the trap. He didn't sell drugs but had a Cali plug on the pounds that's how he got tight with the urban millionaires they would smoke and get tatted.

"O damn bro I forgot we had a tatt appointment yesterday let's reschedule for this weekend plus we gotta try some of that new gas that just landed this morning." Mad Max said as he turned out the lights, heading for the door. "Nah Bruh fuck that tattoo and smoke." 2x quickly changed subjects. "I'm calling you because it's two cars full of niggas sitting outside." "Is it the police?" Mad Max asked he clutched his f&n then peeped out the window. "Don't know, I can't tell if it's the hop out boys" 2x said, meaning under cover law enforcement. "All

I know is they been out there for about 20 minutes, and it don't look right". Mad Max put his back against the wall to think for a second. Two cars 7 heads he counted. This was more like a robbery or a hit, Mad Max thought to himself. Mad Max switched the hallway lights back on. If niggas were going to slide, he wanted to see his death coming. Mad Max had been having dreams of untimely murders for years "is this the one" he spoke to a dark corner in the living room. For a moment he thought he saw a moving silhouette. "What they doing now?" Mad Max asked 2x, "hold on bruh I stepped into another room right quick. 2x walked back into his living room then looked out of the blinds. "Shitt! bro they getting out the car", 2x said in a slight panic. "Good look my nigga" was all Mad Max said before disconnecting the phone.

****

Omar had been trying to call Justo for the past three hours but got nothing but a voice mail. He needed Justo's whereabouts so he could kill him in order to get the plug and get things back to regular business. "Fuck that nigga Justo! He'd do the same thing to me" Omar mumbled trying to boost

himself up. He didn't know where Justo
lived so he took Taliban to the spot he'd met
Justo at earlier today. It was 8:30 at night
and the street was quiet. Omar was in the
back seat he'd rode with Taliban and another
Middle Eastern man named Muhammad.
Omar's little cousin Drew and some of
Drew's home boys followed them to the east
side. Two cars deep, seven shooters
altogether. Omar told Drew that when they
hit the house, he and his home boys were to
search for cash and that there were at least
two bricks in the bottom rack of the
refrigerator. He would be the one to kill
Justo. "Are you sure this is the place?"
Taliban asked checking out his
surroundings. "Yeah, I'm sure the BMW in
the driveway belongs to him. That's the car I
saw him in when we met earlier" Taliban
said something to Muhammad in Pashto.
Muhammad nodded his head in agreement.
They watched the lights go out in the front
of the house. "He is about to come out!
Prepare yourselves" Taliban said drawing
his Glock.

Omar sent a text message to Drew, it
read Lights, Camera, Action, telling the
team to get active. The lights in the house
flicked on. "We've been made, load up and
move out", Taliban said as he got quickly

got out of the front seat with gun in hand. Everybody else followed suit. "You four through the front door" Taliban pointed to Drew and his friends. "We'll kick in the back door" he told Omar and Muhammad. Mad Max watched four men rush the front yard three others moved towards the back. They were blitzing the house trying to flush him out back. Mad Max wasn't worried about the back door. You needed more than a kick to knock down its reinforced steel. It was dark walking around to the back. Mad Max was hoping they missed the side door. If they didn't, he most likely would die tonight. Especially if these men were official steppers. One of the four men carried an AR-15 assault rifle, the other three held pistols. Mad Max had to think fast. He went into his pocket hitting the push start button on his key remote. The s class 6 series BMW roared to life.

The bright high beams lit the entire front yard. The lights also allowed Mad Max to see three silhouettes moving through the blinds. The front door to the living room made a loud cracking noise before giving away crashing inwards. Mad Max upped his f&n then fired at the man entering the house. Two bullets rocked the man's chest and he fell in the way dead. Mad Max swung the pistol at the moving shadows "ka! ka! ka! ka! ka! ka!" 7.5 rounds flipped and twisted out the gun shattering the house's front windows. A stray bullet hit the man totaling the AR-15, he dropped to the ground with a hard thud. He wasn't dead but the blow he took to the face was life threatening death was most certain. The two men felt in the front yard fled for cover as they sent bullets of their own trying to catch a stain. Bullets rained down into the living room. Sparks flew off the flat screen mounted on the wall. Bullets whizzed and sailed all around Mad Max as he low crawled to the side door in the kitchen. He jumped to his feet, took a few deep breaths preparing for death. He pushed the door open then stepped outside into the night air. He looked to his left and saw his getaway car sitting ideally in the driveway. A sudden noise caused him to look to his right. There was a heavy-set man with a large beard gun in hand and aimed at Mad Max. The breaded man fired two shots, Mad Max shot back. The man with the beard ducked back into the shadows. The shots Mad Max let off hit nothing but air. The shots Taliban delivered were more precise. One bullet zoomed an inch away from Mad Max's head. The heat from the bullet burned his scalp and knocked off a couple of dreads. The second shot was a direct hit to the gut. If it weren't for the duffle bag full of narcotics catching the bullet Mad Max would have been done for. He turned and raced for his brother's BMW. He made it to the front seat without more injury. He jumped in. put the car in reverse and smashed down on the gas. The car flew backwards, bullets began smacking and rocking the vehicle. Mad Max ducked down trying his best not to get hit by a stray. The front windshield shattered, so did the back along with anything else made of glass. Mad max felt heat from the slugs that entered his body. The car jumped the curb then rolled to a stop directly across the street in the neighbor's front yard. Mad Max sat still slumped over the starring wheel. His body burned all over. He knew if he made any sudden moves, they would lite his ass up. He looked down at the floorboard and saw his F&N next to the brake pedal. He couldn't feel his right arm, so he slowly tried to reach with his left as five armed men approached. Mad Max had gunned down two of the seven men one of them were Omar's little cousin Drew. They all crept up on the BMW not wanting to be caught by surprise again. Smoke escaped from up under the hood.

One of the headlights had been shot out. Dust from heroin filled the air.

The men now could clearly see who they thought was Justo wasn't. Muhammad stepped into the yard with his Glock 40 aimed ready to give a kill shot. Muhammad took one step closer when he was knocked off balance by a hail of bullets that tic tac toed his body from the face down. 2x came from around the side of his house firing a fully automatic mp5 sub machine gun trying to spank something. Everybody tried to retreat at the sound of the gun's fire. One of Drew's friends tried to up his pistol but fumbled. 2x did him bad pumping bullets into the man. 2x jumped into the passenger seat. "Yo Max!" He called his friend. Mad Max sat up at the sound of a familiar voice. "Can you drive? "2x said in a panic. Mad Max looked terrible. But still threw the car into drive, he pressed down on the gas the BMW fishtailed. 2x hung out the window spraying bullets at all targets he saw. The car sped out into the street going from zero to sixty. The duo flew down the road then bent the corner and were gone.

Chapter 7

"Damn! Amber you can cook yo azz off. This shit is a missile" Bigz said as he smashed his plate filled with BBQ chicken, mac & cheese, mashed potatoes and sweet Jiffy cornbread. Bigz was a big young boy. Seventeen but looked 21 standing at 6'3 225 pounds. He had long thick dreads that fell waist length and a full bread like a viking.

Everybody said he looked a lot like *J Cole*.
"Thank you Bigz. I'm glad you're enjoying
the meal there's plenty more if you like", she
said with a happy smile. "Yeah, Amber this
mac & cheese is all the way like that!"
Boolaid added his own two cents, stuffing
his face. Amber blushed at his comment.
"Like your mac & cheese" she told him in a
seductive voice. "Girl, like more than some
damn macaroni. I couldn't tell if y'all was
fucken or fighting the way my brother had
you back there yellin". Bigz said licking
BBQ sauce from his fingers like he was
Pops off *Friday*.

     Amber covered her wide-open mouth
with both hands looking at Boolaid filled
with embarrassment. Boolaid laughed Bigz
joke off. He knew his little brother was
ignorant and had no filter. "Nah don't look at
him like that! All that hammering and loud
banging against the wall y'all was doing I
thought you niggas worked for a
construction company". Everybody at the
table broke out with laughter.

     Amber's phone rang, it was in her
bedroom, "let me get that." She excused
herself from the table leaving the two men
alone. "Shit, lil bruh I guess we on vacation
until we get the trap back jumping. Whatcha
gonna do with the bread I gave you cuz last

round you gave all your money to your lil girlfriend Keke" Boolaid joked all though Bigz knew he wasn't playing. "I didn't give her all my money; I spent all my money on her" he corrected Boolaid with a goofy grin. "Nah! but for real you remember my home boy Stupid Dude, he can rap his ass off I was thinking about getting into the music business, promoting, and managing." "That can be a real lucrative investment if you got the right connections. I met some good people involved in the rap game when I was in the Feds. I was thinking about shooting down to the A next weekend you tryna roll with me? We can do some networking while we down there". "Hell yeah, big bro you already know I'm wit it" Bigz said excited. Amber came back into the kitchen she sat down at the table with her eyes glued to the screen, "there you go on that phone fb is your life" Boolaid told Amber. "I have a real job thank you" she said rolling her eyes. "Facebook is my past time Keyosha just posted four people shot three killed one life support. I think I know one of the people killed because she commented under the post rip *Drew you will be missed*. That is so sad" Amber said with the sad face. "You said somebody named Drew died?" Bigz questioned. "Yeah look!" She passed him her phone. "What's good lil bruh with that nigga, you over there locked in on the screen". Boolaid became serious. "Nah I don't know him, he's a nobody". Bigz tossed the phone to Boolaid. Boolaid saw worry in Bigz facial expression but kept it to his self. He looked at the post and began to read. There weren't any pictures of the people but there was an image of their trap house on the east side. You could clearly see the house was shot to hell. Windows blown out and there was yellow tape everywhere. Boolaid quickly reached for his phone. "Justo's phone is going straight to voicemail." Bigz said with his phone to his ear. Boolaid called Mad Max but got the same result. "What is it? Do you know them people bae?" Amber asked. Boolaid and Bigz talked around her like she wasn't in the room, she smacked her lips pouting like a six-year-old child. "What we need to do?" Bigz asked. "First thing is calm down at this point all we can do is wait. None of their names are posted as dead and since we know its not our niggas stretched out theres only three options hospital, in jail, or on the run. Either way we'll get a call once there situated".

****

The room was quiet except for the sudden outburst of sobs from a woman being consoled by her companion, she'd probably gotten bad news of a mother or father no longer amongst the living. Justo sat with his face in his hands. Toya gently rubbed his back trying her best to comfort him. They were in the Moses Cone Hospital emergency waiting area. "I can't lose my baby brother" he spoke into his hands, tears streaming down his face. "You're not gonna Jason! Everything's gonna be fine baby." Toya said while hugging and kissing her man. But the truth was she didn't really know she was just afraid as he was. The engine of the BMW had stalled causing the vehicle to shut down. That car was a total loss from bullet damage. Steam shot from the radiator and the car beeped. Mad Max passed out with the key chain dangling in his hand. 2x had called Justo to tell him what had happened. Where they were and for him to come fast.

2x let Justo know they were parked in the middle of a street off Summit Ave. Which one! Justo demanded "Don't know! The street behind the Texaco and McDonald's." When Justo arrived, he couldn't believe the condition his little brother was in, blood was everywhere Mad

Max looked dead. Toya followed Justo in her own car so 2x could get rid of their guns and stash away the kilos. Justo and 2x hurriedly carried Mad Max from the BMW to the back seat of Justo's Ford Expedition. Toya called 911 so paramedics would be waiting when they arrived at the emergency room. "Mr Bryant!" Justo looked up at the sound of his last name being called.

His eyes glossy and blood shot red. Smeared blood on his face, t shirt soaked with blood from touching his brother's body. He stood to face the doctor. "Hello, my name is Doctor Allen. "Is he gonna live?" Justo cut the doctor off. Doctor Allen was an older black male, somewhere in his mid fifty's. Bald headed with a five o' clock shadow. His eyes were alert but looked tired from working nonstop for the past 72 hours trying to save lives including Mad Max's. "Your brother has sustained multiple gun shots and has lost a lot of blood" Justo grabbed the doctor by the collar of his lab coat and got into the man's face. "Answer! my got damn question" Justo said in a deadly whisper. A nurse standing nearby rushed over to help but the doctor held out a hand stopping her. The two men had a staring contest. Doctor Allen saw an angry, confused, and afraid person. "Baby no he's here to help," Toya cried to her baby, while still rubbing his back. "Listen young man" he said in a calm tone. "I know you're scared but, being scared doesn't make you weak it only means your human." Justo loosened his grip then let the doctor go all together. The doctor continued to speak as if there never was a conflict between the two. "Your brother is out of surgery and is stable he's lost a lot of blood and has fallen into a coma. A coma what does that mean?" Justo asked frantically. "Calm down son it doesn't mean anything his body has been through a lot, sometimes that's how the human body behaves. Your brother has just been through 13 hours of surgery we lost him twice and he's still kicking so believe me when I say he's a fighter" the doctor told Justo with a reassuring face. Then his voice became really low. "I'm not supposed to say anything but..." Doctor Allen looked around making sure no one was listening. "There is a detective here. He has a detainer on your little brother until he finds out what his involvements are. I was told not to allow any visitors but tonight I'll make an exception. Now come on before the officer returns." Doctor Allen walked away without another word. Justo and Toya trailed closely behind. They passed by a nurse's station then turned down a hall. Justo took notice that some room doors hung open. He saw sick people lying in bed with supportive family members at their bedside. What he saw made him become dizzy. The realization that he probably would be doing the same thing for his brother had him sick to the stomach. "You'll have about 20 minutes" the doctor said when they stopped at a closed door. "When the detective comes back, I'll stall'm for as long as I can." "Thanks doc. Justo gave him a firm handshake and also gained a newfound respect for the man." Justo looked at Toya with sad eyes. "I'll stay out here if you need time alone" Justo gave her a long kiss then one in the middle of her forehead. She hugged him tightly. "I love you baby." "I love you more" he said before opening the room door then closing it shut. The lighting in the room was dim. One look at Mad Max broke Justo down. His little brother had IVs sticking into his arms, tubes were in his mouth and his nose had a tube in it tied down with medical tape. There was a breathing machine that hummed other monitors hooked to Mad Max's body beeped and vibrated. Mad Max always kept his face hidden but tonight his hair was pulled back. Justo almost forgot how much his little brother looked like their mother. At that moment he missed her desperately. She had died three years ago. She lost her battle with cancer. Leaving the boys to fend for themselves.

"Momma I wish you were here. Look at what they did to our baby boy." He looked to the sky. Mad Max had been shot six times. Neck, shoulder, arms, stomach, and thighs. "Max! Who did this to you?" Justo asked, as if his sibling would speak back. He laid his head on Mad Max's chest listening to his heartbeat. They became one person for a second. IMA find out who did this and I'm gonna kill them all. Justo sat up at the at the sound of someone entering the room. "Mr. Bryant, my name is detective Ford." "I don't have anything to say Justo cut him off." "I'm sorry all this happened to your brother. I'm just trying to figure out what happened". "Look! My brother called me and said he'd been shot and needed my help so I came running like any big brother would". "Ok!" "So, who was your brother with?" Ford asked with his pen and pad out writing. "He wasn't with anyone" Ford stopped writing just to look at Justo. "Ummm hmmm according to paramedics your brother was moved from a BMW to a Ford Expedition." "Yeah, that's right!" "So, you're telling me you moved this grown ass man all by yourself?" Detective Ford studied Justo closely, "yes, I moved that grown ass man all alone". "So, your brother wasn't alone" Ford tried to trick Justo up. "Nah he was alone" Justo answered already knowing the police tactics. "That's funny because the evidence I've gathered tells me that your brother was possibly attacked." Ford stepped a little closer to Justo, "and my evidence says some one helped him, probably saved his life," "sounds like a classic case of self-defense." "You just told me you came running when he called. You sure you didn't run over to that neighborhood to bust your gun. If so, come clean now while I can still help." Ford warned.

"I don't know what you talking bout, my alibi is solid. I was at the house with my o' lady when my brother called. I picked him up then brought him here to the hospital. Now unless you plan on putting cuffs on me like you came to do to my lil bruh I suggest you get the fuck outta my way!" Justo said purposely standing in the detective's way. They had a stare down Ford knew Justo was telling the truth for the most part and didn't have enough to make an arrest or even hold him. Detective Ford stood to the side; Justo

walked past they bumped shoulders. When
Justo stepped into the hallway, he saw Toya
being grilled by another detective. "I don't
want to speak without my lawyer present",
"good girl." Justo said proudly to himself.
"Come on baby" he said reaching for Toya's
hand. She quickly accepted. "I'm tired, let's
go home," Justo told her. "Why talk with a
lawyer if you don't have anything to hide",
detective Mcdon called out to the fleeing
couple. They kept their stride never looking
back. "Let me guess you didn't get squat",
Ford asked his partner. "Not a damn thing!"
Mcdon said in a funny voice. "What movie
is that from," Ford looked at his partner
strangely. "Friday, man! Chris Tucker, come
on man everybody know that. Your black
people card has just officially been
revoked". "All this serious shit going on and
you wanna act like Smokey," Ford shook his
head. "Come on let's get some coffee, it
looks like another sleepless night".

****

Justo passed the blunt to Boolaid. He
didn't smoke, but tonight he made an
exception. It had been two days before Justo
reached out to anybody. When he did the
first person, he called was Boolaid. Boolaid

put the blunt to his lips and inhaled the potent London pound cake. He chokcd as he exhaled. He instantly became lightheaded. Then felt his eye lids become heavy. He passed the blunt to Bigz. They were at Toya's house in a back-room Justo called the bat cave. The three of them sat in silence and smoked. Boolaid and Bigz both knew Justo was stressed out. He had a lot on his mind. So, they waited for him to speak first. "It was meant for me!" Justo finally spoke, his eyes low and glossy. "What was meant for you bro?" Boolaid said. "The shit that happened to my brother the other night. It was a hit and the niggas that tried to kill Max thought he was me". "Who tried to kill Max? And how do you know for sure that drill was for you and not him. Let's be real you know like I know Mad Max got hella enemies". Justo stood to his feet and put his hands on top of his head. "That's just the thing, I don't know who it could have been let alone who would want me dead. All I do know is we swapped out cars. So, whoever it was thought it was me in the house." Bigz or Boolaid said nothing they were just as confused. "Omar!" Bigz broke the silence. "Nah hell no! Not O that's my nigga. Plus, he has no reason to come for me like that" Justo said to his little bro but Bigz shook his head in disagreement. "I'm telling you big homie that bitch as nigga is a snake, I can feel it". "Bigz does have a point. You know what you did for him. And he knew you wouldn't sell him anymore uncut so he probably planned to rob you but knew if he did, that he would have to kill you so decided why waste time just kill you take the work and whatever else he could find".

"Didn't you tell me he used to be your plug and now you serving him. Justo that nigga probably jealous that type of shit happens all the time. We been getting money damn near half a year with no issues. You sell this nigga one block of A1 and then all of sudden niggas tryna do drills?" Boolaid looked at his childhood friend seriously. "I'm just saying big homie think about it " Justo sat back down blunt in hand he hit the blunt long and hard.
Nobody had called to check on him or the well being of Mad Max, except for the two people in front of him and the six others Justo had running the three trap locations. Omar hadn't even sent a text. Everybody had heard about the shooting by now. *Omar not reaching out was a little suspect, maybe even a sign of guilt* Justo thought. "Fuck it we going to war!" Justo said blowing out a long cloud of smoke. "Call up the team and

tell'm it's on-site wit Omar and anybody with him" hc told Bigz. "Say less big homie" Bigz said with a satisfied smile. He left the room with his cell phone plastered to his ear. "2x got the food stashed. He's out of town just to make an alibi solid in case he needs one. If you need to get the work call'm", "nah I'm good it's probably best he keep it put up until the smoke we about to cause clears up" "Yeah your right!"Justo agreed. "I'm still going out this weekend with the girls you coming?" "Are you serious? Bulak Max is in the hospital fighting for his life and you thinking about some bitches" Justo said pissed, "nah my nigga I'm on your side and nobody else's. Don't you forget that. You also need not forget we still trying to see if we can get more blocks of doggy. And them bitches!", Boolaid pointed out, "are our only way; besides Mad Max would blank if he saw you all cooped up in this room."

"Max is mental health right" Justo laughed at the thought of his brother. "Damn right he is. We gonna get the niggas soon enough" Boolaid patted Justo on the shoulder. Boolaid was right, they needed more keys to continue getting money. Besides, he needed to link up with his team so they could find all of Omar's locations. Then they would get shit poppin. "When you going out?" "Tomorrow night", Boolaid said rubbing his stomach. "When Toya gone be finished cooking them tacos? I got the munchies," Justo laughed seeing how high his best friend looked. His eyes were already slanted now they were extra chinky. "Nah bruh for real my nigga I can't rest until Omar laying in blood. *The one who killed my blood is laying in blood I can rest!*" The friends rapped *Lil Durk's* song together.

****

"How could you let this happen?" Rafiq yelled ferociously at Taliban in broken English. "How could you let Muhammad die!", Rafiq had lost soldiers before but only in Afghanistan where you were in constant danger everyday of your life. He felt people in America were soft, weak, and spoiled. Americans had it made over here and shouldn't be able to defeat a real warrior like Muhammad. But Mad Max and 2x had proven Rafiq wrong. "Sir the target was clever and unafraid of death. He stayed calm and performed like a solider through out the whole assault." Taliban spoke with respect towards his new opponent's.

We had him cornered Muhammad moved in to deliver a kill shot but was killed by a neighbor who joined the battle on his own free will. The sudden ambush is how he got away. "So, this Mad Max person is in the hospital?" "Yessir and he is the younger brother of the man you were supposed to kill? Hmmmm?" Rafiq asked. They were back at his mansion but in a different part. He spoke to everyone while relaxing in a hot tub with a beautiful naked Middle Eastern woman who sat behind him massing his shoulders. Omar was now part of their team, so they didn't blind fold him. "Yeah, Max is the younger brother. I thought he was Justo because of the car in the driveway. The two must of switched cars, when I left", Omar explained himself. "So, these so-called street niggas are not so called after all" Rafiq took a sip of some very expensive champagne. The foreign woman held the cup to his lips. "Taliban tells me you also lost some one in the battlefield when we lost Muhammad." "Yeah, I did my cousin. I never should have gotten him involved he wasn't built for nothing like that!" Omar said feeling guilty about Drew's death. "In my country, my cousin die in car bomb boom!" Rafiq said smacking down at the water around him, the splash made the woman yelp and giggle.

"Very very sad, so I understand. You and I now have a common enemy. In my country we crush enemies," he said balling his hand into a tight fist. You could see the fire and pain in Rafiq's eyes due to his tragic past. "I will make you my new local distributor, I will send people to you to buy, and you may sell to people as you see fit. I will give you all access to my drugs. Twenty kilos of pure Afghan opium, twenty kilos of uncut cocaine and 200 pounds of the best premium marijuana once a month how's that sound?" Rafiq asked Omar at that moment. Omar knew he had sold his soul to the devil and that his life had just changed for ever. "Sounds like mothafucking music to my ears" Omar said rubbing his hand together, "good" Rafiq smiled. "You now have Curtis's responsibilities and with that responsibility you must avenge his death and your cousin's." Omar nodded his head with understanding. "I'll be sending you soldiers to help you sell drugs and to kill. How you say? The ops!" Taliban put the team together.

"Hit the streets sell my drugs and get revenge" Rafiq said dismissing everybody. "I want weekly reports on this Justo" he called out as they left.

****

"You have reached a voice mail box that has not yet been set up" the automated service said. Bea gently sat the phone down on its phone stand. The girls were at their nail shop getting fresh manicures. "He still hasn't answered any calls, neither one of my phones," Bea said to Meme "and he's not active on the book, do you think what happened to his friend had anything to do with the drugs we took from Curtis?" Bea spoke in a whisper so their nail stylist Kisha and Toy Toy wouldn't hear their conversation. Meme watched Kisha and Toy Toy work on their hands as she told Bea what she felt. "Girl, I seriously doubt it! Them niggas Boolaid deals with are deep in the streets. It could have been a million other reasons why it went down like that over there on the east side." Meme said even though she didn't believe her own words. She didn't want to admit it but deep down she knew Boolaid's friend laid up in the hospital fighting for his life because of their actions. Bea saw the shooting on her news app. At first glance she didn't think nothing of it just another senseless shooting.

But then she saw the picture of the man hospitalized, she recognized him. She'd met him before twice to be exact. Boolaid brought mad Max with him to drop cash off to the girls at their nail shop. "Has KB said anything to you about Boolaid?" "Damn, girl I forgot to tell you KB azz done got caught with his cell phone. He wrote me a letter and said they gonna keep him in restrictive housing for at least six months." "For real when all this happen?" Bea asked her best friend with a face full of concern, "last week but I wouldn't be surprised if he called me tomorrow talking bout, he back on line. You know he a straight bae bae kid." They shared a laugh while keeping their hands flat down on the table watching their nail tech's paint away. Bea looked at her sister with puppy dog eyes. "What bitch?" Meme asked wide eyed, "can you call him for me pleaseee!" she said with a shy smile. "I'm not about to be on this niggas nutz!" Meme's voice rose a few octaves. Near by customers looked in their direction, "excuse you" Meme said looking crazy as hell head cocked to the side. The two women Meme bucked on said nothing but did make stank faces and rolled their eyes before going back to minding their own business. "Thought so," Meme talked a lil more shit then returned her attention to Bea. Her face was still scrunched up making her look hard core. She smiled at Bea. But Bea didn't feel like playing.

Meme smacked her lips with an attitude. Meme's conscious was eating at her. *She didn't know what she would do if someone did something to Bea and she not know why it happened.* Meme's phone rang taking her away from her thoughts. Her phone sat up on the table by a phone stand. The caller was trying to connect with facetime. Hold up one second Kisha, Meme said to the young girl doing her nails. She gently swiped her finger across the screen making sure not to mess up her nails. "Heey!" Meme said, with a nigga grin when

she saw who appeared. "Hey sis what you doing?"
Boolaid asked with a smile of his own. "Nothing!
Bea and I at the shop getting dolled up," she said
in a sweet tone. Bea's head appeared on the screen
she was shoulder to shoulder with Meme but kept
her hands flat on the table. "Hey Boolaid," Bea
blushed she couldn't help it. There was just
something about him, she just couldn't put a finger
on it. "Why have you been ignoring my calls?,"
Bea said with an instant attitude. "Yeah, about that
I've been really busy a good friend of mine is in
the hospital and it's not looking good," Boolaid
watched the girls' reactions, but they made no
indications they knew what he was talking about.
He continued, "my nigga Justo lil brother Mad
Max is in the hospital and he's taking this shit
really hard. So that's why I've been out of reach",
he said becoming serious. "Well, I guess that's a
good enough excuse, so IMA let you slide" Meme
said with a sad face. "And if you have any other
family emergencies, will you let us know?! We do
care about you if you haven't noticed. And I
remember meeting both your friend's Justo and
Mad Max I'm so sorry to hear about them". The
girls saw anger flash across Boolaids face. "Yeah,
shit got my nigga stressed out. That's why I was
hitting you up to see if were still on for tomorrow
night, because I wanted to bring my bro along so
he can clear his head". "Hell yeah we still on for
tomorrow night turn up! turn up!" Bea sang,

"period!" Meme added her two cents. Boolaid laughed at their ratchetness, *he loved how they gave it up because they weren't faking, these women were the real thing.* "Baby! I'm ready", a female voice called out in Boolaids background. "Aite, give me one second" he said back to the mysterious female voice. "Who is that?" Meme said being nosy trying to see more of Boolaid's back drop. "Noneya," "noneya who?" Bea jumped in, "noneya business," he laughed because the girls fell right into his joke. "Nah nigga don't do that," Bea became defensive. "Aite y'all got it my bad my bad," he said with his hand up in surrender. "Ima call y'all when I'm on my way out the door tomorrow," "ok!" they told Boolaid in unison. The call ended; Meme's home screen popped up. "Bitch did you hear that?," Meme asked in a shocked tone. "Yeah, I hear that thot in the background. I'm ready baby" Meme mimicked the unknown voice she'd just heard. "Girl, it sounded like she was tryna to get hit from the back" Meme teased her friend. Bea knew Meme was only joking but she still felt some type of way. *Bea get your shit together, he's like any other man*, Bea told herself. "Come on sis my nails dry. We gotta hit the mall and find something to wear for our Boo," she nudged Bea on the shoulder. Bea rolled her eyes then laughed, "bitch you childish."

Chapter 8

"Damn girl its cold as hell", Meme said to Bea. She hugged herself as they walked towards the entrance to the strip club. A chilly November night, fall was coming to an end and winter was right around the corner. "Well, you should have put on some clothes, ain't nobody tell you to come out here naked" she joked. Meme's hair was braided on the sides pulling the rest of her hair into an all-natural Mohawk. She batted her long beautiful full length eye lashes at a passing man making him bump into a parked car. Her dark brownish and gold eyes seemed to glow in the night. She wore a very short very tight *Prada* dress, its pink color complimented her dark chocolate complexion to the max. Every few strides she would have to pull the dress down to keep her ass from showing. Around her neck was a twenty thousand dollar bust down choker with a charm that read "Meme." The v.v.s diamonds lit up like the night sky. The couple wore a matching pair of six-inch *Gucci* heels that showed off their fresh pedicures. There hills clicked and clacked in unison as they stepped into the long club line. "How you doing?" A man already in line said to Bea. Hunger and lust were in his eyes as he admired her beauty. Bea's jet-black hair flowed down shoulder length then cut into a Bob with streaks of blonde. Her slanted eyes made her features look so much more exotic. But at the same time, she looked vulnerable which is why men always fell victim to her game.

Bea's *Versace* dressed wrapped tight around her thick frame, her back was exposed, the dress's shoulder loops laid across the front barely keeping her perky breast covered. Men and even some women eye's wondered, all wishing they could see just a little more. Four tennis chains fell in between her cleavage with dancing diamonds. Four matching tennis bracelets, two on each wrist also did their own two step. "I'm fine," Bea bit her bottom lips as she flirted. The guy didn't stand a chance in hell, but she didn't mind stroking his ego. "Have you been in this club yet?" The man asked. "No this is my first time" she said looking up at the building. They were at a strip club called Platinum. It had only been open two months and had already grown a name for it's self. The building was an old warehouse that had been gutted out. The place was huge. It had five stages, three bars and its own photo section. Exotic dancers came from across the country just to dance here. Rappers and different other famous people in the urban community came here every weekend. This weekend was no different, *Da Baby* and *Stunna 4 Vegas* were here making a guest appearance. Bea chose to come here tonight because she didn't want an interrogation from Diddy or anybody else

who knew her at the Cabaret. She and Meme
intended to have a good time with Boolaid
uninterrupted.

"Since this is your first time here, I'm
hoping you'll let me be the first to buy you a
drink!" The man asked cooly. "Cut line VIP
cut line! Thousand-dollar entry!" yelled a
man waring a bust down Chain that read
"double L's hunnit gang." He stood at a side
door a few feet down from where the club
line was. "Uh com'on bitch its cold" Meme
took hold of Bea's arm pulling her towards
the cheat line."Sorry! You better hurry if
you want to be my first", Bea smiled at the
man who offered the drink. He smiled back
as she turned to walk away. They entered
the club and stopped at a counter where the
man with the double L's chain stood. Music
blasted through a door to the left of them
people could be seen moving about dancing
or just partying hard. "2 bandz" Mr. Bust
down said. Meme reached into her *Birkin*
bag "is your manager around" she asked
pulling out a stack of money. It had a white
and blue band wrapped around it with a
label that read 10,000 "my name is Tank and
I own the place how can I assist you" Tank
said becoming thirsty at the sight of their
money. "Are there any booths available?"
Meme asked handing Tank two grand.

Normally he would have told the average group of women no or told them they could join him at his booth, a sure way to get some pussy. He watched Meme closely, her and Bea danced all over each other while they flashed cash. These two are far from average. Tank thought to himself. "Yes baby we do have a booth available. Its actually our last one. Booth ten! When you go through the door it's going to be the last booth on the right. Right over there by stage four you can't miss it", Tank pointed in the direction they needed to go. "How much?" "Twenty-five hunnit" Meme gave Tank the whole stack of cash she held. "Give me the rest in one's," "yes ma'am." "I'm about to head to the bar and get us something to drink while you waiting on the ones. I'm ready to turn the fuck up!" Bea said. "Period!" Meme answered. "Meet me at the booth when you're finished," Meme told her. A bouncer standing at the door moved out of Bea's way. She walked through the door and stepped into the club. *It looked amazing*, she thought. The music echoed through the building perfectly. Everyone seemed to be having the greatest time of their lives.

Really handsome men dressed to impress, posted up hollering at some of the most beautiful women Bea had ever seen, strippers and club hoppers. Lights of all types of colors flashed. Dancers where high in the air from climbing 20 feet stage poles Bea watched with a face of approval as the dancers slid down with there legs wide open.

The tables were big and nice. Chairs with cushions gave people maximum comfort while they spent cash. Men and women threw money up into the sky. Strippers gave lap dances, niggas smacked ass and slid bills of all denominations into thongs. Club Platinum even had its own photo area with several different back drops. Local rappers, dope boys and get money niggas took flicks flexing with stacks of cash and bad bitches on there sides. Bea made her way through the crowd to the bar she had to squeeze in between a group of people in order for the bar tender to notice her waving. "What can I get you?," the bartender shouted over the music. She was really pretty. She was a high yellow bone with tattoos that covered her whole body. Ear gages and nose piercings with red and pink dreads, which gave her a real rock star look. Two double shots of Henny, good choice that'll be 40 dollars, she told Bea as she bounced her shoulder to the newest *Megan the stallion* song. Bea reached into her *Birkin* to pay for her drinks but was stopped by a warm touch from a hand. She was actually caught by surprise when she saw who it was. "Is it too late or can I still be your first?" Bea smiled. "I shouldn't have wasted my money on cut line if the line we were in moved that fast," she said pulling a fifty-dollar bill out of her pocketbook. The man laughed, "nah I paid to cut too." "I didn't follow you because I was waiting on a couple friends," he said stopping her from paying for her drinks. He went into his *Balmain* jeans pulling out a fat knot of cash. He peeled off a blue face hundred then gave it to the bartender. She took the money and left to fulfill the orders. "My name is Omar by the way," he extended his hand. "Kendra," Bea lied excepting his hand with a gentle shake. She never gave men her real government. Tonight, she was Kendra. Omar kissed the back side of her hand before letting it go. "Why don't you and your friend I saw you with come hang out with me and my gang? I promise it'll be worth your while" Omar said looking Bea up and down with his bug eyes. Damn I gotta have that pussy he thought to himself. "As much fun as it sounds, I'm going to have to decline your invitation, I'm here with my own lil gang and I don't think he'll approve." Bea politely let Omar down. "OK respect, respect" Omar said with his hands in the air. "How about this? We exchange numbers and sometime in the near future we can have a lunch date?" She didn't find Omar attractive at all, but she had to admit he was defiantly fly plus persistent which gave him sex appeal in his own way.

The girls agreed their robbery days were over after they killed Curtis. But for some reason she felt he might have something she wanted. Something she needed. "Okay Omar let's do it!" She decided to swap numbers. The bartender returned with the drinks. "It was really nice meeting you Omar and thanks for being the first", she held up the two cups of brown liquid. "No problem." She left the bar throwing her ass as she walked away. Omar watched Bea's every move. Even though her dress was black he could still make out the outline of her pumpkin shaped ass. It clapped with every step. She disappeared into the crowd and out of Omar's sight. Bea balanced the cups of Henny as she made her way through the club. She had to climb a few steps to enter the VIP and booth ten. A bouncer tried to block her. But Meme stopped him. "Where you been?" Meme shouted happily. She wasn't alone, Boolaid was at her side. He helped Bea up the steps by taking her drinks and sitting them down on the table. The two shared a moment of eye contact before embracing each other with a hug. Bea felt his hard muscles through his fitted shirt. Boolaid's grip was strong and firm. Bea felt strangely secure in his arms. The only time she'd ever gotten a feeling like that was with her father and he'd been dead for over 14 years. "You look beautiful", Boolaid said holding her arms length apart so he could have a better look.

"Thank you," she blushed. "But look at you. I didn't think you wore anything other than sweatpants and balling shorts" Bea joked. Boolaid wasn't the dress up type but that didn't mean he didn't know how to get fresh. He had gotten a hair cut only hours ago. His 360 waves were thick and smooth. A diamond pendent necklace hung around his neck with a picture of his deceased mother in a bust down charm in the shape of a heart.

His outfit was *Armani* from top to bottom, finished off with a thousand-dollar pair of *Dior* shoes. Tonight, he held the image of a famous rap star.

"Bea this is my brother Justo!," I believe I introduced the two of you before,

Boolaid spoke loudly over the music. "Hey Justo!" she said in a cheerful tone. "Yeah, we've met but it's nice to meet you officially." They gave each other a friendly hug. "Nice to meet you back, Boolaid talks a lot about you." Justo gave Bea a secret wink. "Oh really? I hope only good things," she gave Boolaid a seductive grin. "No question he thinks very highly of you and your sister. Which is something rare" Justo said giving Bea a look up and down, *this bitch is really fine as hell* he thought.

Bea was only 5'2 Justo looked like a giant standing next to her. "Speaking of Meme, I'm sure you've met her by now." "Who her?" He pointed at Meme. She had three exotic dancers all over her, it was a real freak show going on. One sat in Meme's lap while the other two did splits on the floor then bounced their fat ass up and down to the beat of *Juicy J's* song *Bandz a Make Her Dance*. Meme threw ones in the air and slid dollars into g strings. Meme kissed one of the dances on the cheek then whispered something into her ear. She seductively slid out of Meme's lap then made her way over to Justo, her booty wobbled with every step she took. "Happy birthday daddy" she said, to Justo running a hand down his *Versace* shirt. "Who? Me?"

He pointed to himself with a giant smirk. "Your friend is crazy knowing damn well it's not my birthday" Justo said to Bea, Bea laughed and shrugged her shoulders. She took him to the wrap around sofa pushed him down then straddled him, her breast caressed his cheek; her nipple became hard. The other two dances followed suit. It looked like Justo was in a soft porn movie and he was loving every moment. Meme and Bea threw back their double shots and began to entertain Boolaid with their own little strip tease. Boolaid watched as the besties kissed and caressed one another. Excitement shot straight to his penis at the thought of fucking the both of them at the same time.

But the girls would never know this because he contained his facial expressions. The slants in his eyes always made him look so serious. He grabbed both women by their wrist pulling them down beside him on the sofa. Two beautiful women snuggled in closely beside Boolaid with silly giggles turning him into a human sandwich. "Aite that's enough you too!" Boolaid called out over the loud music. He knew what they were trying to do and to be honest it was starting to work. A brown skinned woman wearing a short black skirt and white blouse stepped into the booth stopping in front of the three musketeers. She was very pretty, thick as a Snicker, getting tips would be easy for a woman with this type of body. "My name is Kandis and I'll be your bottle girl tonight. So, what can I get for you" she asked with a big smile giving Boolaid some extra I contact. "Yes, sweetie bring us a bottle of Henny and a bottle of Patron", Meme requested. "Coming right up" Kandis left to fulfill the orders. The girls brought their full attention back to Boolaid, throwing their legs over his knees, pushing their bodies up against his to the max. The mixture of their body fragrances crept up his nostrils. They smelt like something sweet and tasty. "Why you gotta be such a party pooper?" Meme said with her bottom lip poked out. She looked like the moment right before an infant baby began to cry.

"Yes, us girls just wanna have a little fun", Bea said running a finger down his chest. She would have grabbed his dick if Boolaid wouldn't have stopped her before she could get any further. "I understand what you're trying to say, I do! Really, but I'm having fun just by being in your presence. The kind of fun you're talking about having can ruin a lifelong relationship. Listen, Bea! For some odd reason you remind me of someone I don't even know"

Bool- aid said, looking unsure of himself.
Bea raised her eyebrows puzzled by his
statement. "What do you mean by that?" "I
don't know my mother!" Boolaid stopped
speaking and shrugged his shoulders, "I
can't explain it when I look at you, I feel this
connection, but I can't elaborate." He stared
Bea directly in the eyes. Bea felt the same
emotion but didn't understand why as well.
"And Meme you're like the crazy ass female
cousin I never had. I never had really had a
family growing up but with you two and my
niggas I finally have one." Boolaid
expressed his inner thoughts. He made the
sister's hearts melt. "awww.." Meme said
putting a hand on his knee. "That was so
sweet let me just suck the head" she joked,
the three of them all shared a hard laugh.
"See! my point made crazy ass cousin."

"No nigga! You crazy if you think
you gone play me Boolaid", Bea and Meme
all looked up at once. The bottle girl Kandis
had returned, and she wasn't alone. "See girl
I told you your man was over here all
hugged up with some thot as hoes," Kandis
said to Amber with a mean mug. Amber's
looked heart broken at the site of Boolaid
sitting in between two bad bitches. Although
she really didn't have any room to talk
because she was just in a booth with another

nigga just a few moments ago. "Amber chill out! it's not what it looks like" Boolaid tried to explain. "Ummm hmmm whateva nigga. Which' cha lyin ass", Amber clapped her hands in Boolaid's face with every word she used. "You said to me that you was going to go handle some business this weekend but instead you at the club in these ho's face". Amber yelled over the music. "I told you he was a dog", Kandis added her two cents. Boolaid couldn't believe how bold some women could be, like Kandis wasn't just in his DM the other day sending nasty photos, trying to give him the pussy behind Amber's back. He was about to speak but Bea beat him to it. "What makes you think he's not handling business right now" Bea cupped her breast giving them a light bounce. Then she stood to address Amber face to face.

"And believe her bitch! Because when she say he handles business she means he handles business real well". Meme said as she spread her legs wide open showing off her pretty little shave pussy. She gave it a double tap trying her best to piss Amber off and it was working. She stood beside her sister. Normally Boolaid would have tried to stop such a confrontation, but Amber had overstepped her boundaries. They hadn't even made things official. She was definitely tripping. He decided to just let the entire situation play itself out. "Boolaid you just gonna sit there and not say nothing," Amber folded her arms. "He's not talking is he bitch" Meme said disrespecting Amber. "Who you call"n bitch, bitch!" Amber rolled her neck becoming more aggressive. It was Bea who answered that question with a punch straight to the middle of Amber's face. The hit instantly drew blood busting Amber's nose. Bea swung again but Amber ducked the next blow. Meme jumped into action catching Amber with her own punches one connected hard to Amber's jaw. Meme then grabbed a hand full of Amber's hair flinging her to the floor. Kandis dove head first into the mayhem at the site of her friend being jumped. She punched and swung the Henny bottle she brought to serve. The bottle cracked Bea in the side of the head. She fell to the club floor seeing stars. Justo witnessed what was taking place. He tossed the dancer sitting in his lap off him onto the couch then rushed over to assist the situation if need be.

Meme punched Amber nonstop then banged her head on the floor. Kandis held the liquor bottle high to the sky ready to deliver a finishing blow to Bea's head. Boolaid had no choice, he couldn't allow

Kandis to harm her any longer. He had been invited out by Bea and Meme they were his company. He could have just yoked Kandis up then overpowering her by taking the bottle. But he didn't like how she instigated the whole situation. Tonight, was all her fault. He side stepped to get a better view of Kandis' face then delivered a right upper cut that connected with the bottom of her chin sending Kandis two feet off the ground. The blow knocked the poor girl out cold.

Security rushed over to stop the mêlée. The first bouncer stepped into the booth then dropped to his knees from a three-piece combo Justo sent to his head. Every punch connected with perfect precision. Boolaid finished the deal with a knee to the bouncer's face. The man fell to the floor bloody and down for the count. Another bouncer tried to sneak Justo, but Boolaid crushed his jaw with a powerful punch, sending the man to the floor with his coworker. Justo bobbed, weaved, and swung knocking out three people. Two bouncers and one stripper, that had gotten in his way. A bouncer quickly moved in yoking Boolaid up into a full Nelson head lock.

Bea jumped onto the security's back. Justo tried to help his friend, but a giant guard overpowered him which lead to a body slam that knocked the wind out of Justo's body. Within a matter of seconds, the security team had overpowered all four. Boolaid, Bea, Justo, and Meme all struggled to free themselves from the team of ex cops, ex convicts and body builders but failed. Boolaid and Bea had been separated from Justo and Meme in the mix of their battle royale. Both couples carried to opposite exits of the club.

****

East parking lot 1:15 am

Justo licked his lip tasting his own blood. His bottom lip split open from a cheap shot from a bouncer while he'd been held down. It stung but at the same time numb because of the cold night air. "chill out lady" a guard said when Meme tried to run past the security for the third time attempting to get back into the club. "No! I told you I want my *Birkin* bag and I'm not going anywhere until I get my shit!" She said. The man at the door shook his head at Meme's ratchetness. One of her titties bounced loosely where her dress had been ripped. The bottom of her dress ridden so high up her ass was out for all to see; she was bare foot from kicking off her hills during the fight. She stood with her hands on her hips like she was about to pose for an Instagram photo. The security guard said something to a nearby coworker. He disappeared into the club. Moments later returning with two identical *Birkin* bags. "Here! I assume the other bag is your friend's. Now that you have your belongings will you please leave the premises?" the security begged. Meme pulled her dress down rubbed her hands through her Mohawk getting herself together. "Thank you" she smiled. "Come on Justo, me and Bea parked over there" she pointed. "You can ride with me, and we can meet them somewhere. Let's get outta here". "I'm calling them now" Justo said with his phone to his ear.

****

West parking lot 1:15am

"I'm not going anywhere until I get my bag!" demanded Bea. The bouncer blocked the entrance of the club. Boolaid watched Bea with amusement. Not even minutes ago she'd just been smacked upside the head with a liquor bottle. *You still ain't had enough? that ass soft* he thought. He felt his phone vibrant in his pocket. "Yo! Bruh yall good? "Haha, yeah I saw you sock that nigga down to the floor" Boolaid laughed giving Justo his props. "Oh yeah! aile bet that!" Boolaid hung the phone up. "Bea, Meme said she got your bag. Come on, Justo's gonna hop in the whip with Meme and we gonna meet them down the street at the *Waffle House*. My truck parked over there." He pointed. Bea still eye grilled the bouncer, on the real she was still pissed off about the fight and wanted somebody to blame. Boolaid wrapped an arm around her waist pulling her away. She gave in and began to walk with him. She looped both arms around his waist then looked up to him with a sweet smile. "I see you looking at me", he smiled back, "why you hit that girl in her face? Wit yo bad self." Bea burst out laughing, "you sound like somebody's grandmama" Bea said. "But to answer your question I had to go! Before my father died, he always taught me that disrespect is not to be tolerated." "You be acting all tough, but I know on the real you just a big softy" Boolaid teased even though he agreed with her one hundred percent.

They reached the F150 pickup. Boolaid unlocked the doors then helped Bea into the vehicle. He jogged to the other side then jumped into the driver's seat. He shut his door and the outside world became quiet. He started to put the key in its ignition but noticed Bea had her head leaned over touching around the area shed been hit in. "Aww, that baby got a boo boo you want me to kiss it?" She said nothing but answered him by nodding her head yes with her bottom lip pocked out. He leaned over the middle console softly kissing her on top of the head. "Does that feel better?" Boolaid asked looking into Bea's eyes, "yes" she moved in to kiss his sexy lips but instead kissed him on the cheek. He turned his head. She became pissed once again when he'd hit her with the spin moved. She started to open her mouth to speak her mind, but he silenced her by throwing a hand up in the air. "Ssssshhhh! You hear that?" he said with wide eyes and alert ears. Bea did hear it, gunshots, and a lot of them.

****

East parking lot 1:27am

"Damn! Meme, you riding clean in this i8 BMW" Justo said when they arrived in front of the luxury vehicle. "Real boss bitch," he gave her a salute. "Well, I try", she said then added a curtsey of her own

164

knowing that if it wasn't for Boolaid and this man she didn't even no standing in front of her shed still probably be somewhere hitting licks. "I can't tell which bag is which. Here help me find the key remote," Meme passed one of the designer bags across the hood of the car to Justo. "And you better not steal nothing!" she joked, "girl bye!" Justo opened the bag and began his search. He immediately noticed a small black gun. He took hold of the weapon to get a closer look. He thought it was a nine-millimeter at first because it belonged to a female, Glock 30, Justo read the across the top of the firearm. That was a surprise to him this gun was a compact 45 caliber pistol. The kind of guns he used. "Y'all some gangsta bitches too!" Justo said out loud flashing Meme the gun. He was defiantly impressed and finally started to realize why Boolaid liked them so much. It wasn't every day you met a real genuine trap queen and gangsta boo all rolled in one and Boolaid had found two of them. "So, you in the field," he joked, "ladies gotta protect herself" Meme said as she continued to dig into her bag. She pushed around a couple more items before she spotted the remote key.

She also kept in her bag a military green XD 40 caliber pistol outlined with hot pink. She clutched the gun instead of the keys. Meme upped the pistol in Justo's direction then squeezed off two shots. The bullets zoomed passed Justo's face. One bullet knocked out someone's windshield nearby, the second bullet hit its target. A light skinned man with a short bushy beard pointed a gun at the back of Justo's head. The bullet he took to the chest made him do a spin move. Meme fired again and again. Two direct hits right to the middle of the man's face sent him to the concrete where he would stay until paramedics transported his body to the morgue. Justo grabbed Bea's Glock 30 pointed it and fired at his attackers. They all sent shots back. Meme aimed and pulled the trigger. Gunfire erupted turning the parking lot into a war zone. There were five men moving in between parked cars. They moved in unison. Two of the five men sent bullets at Meme making her duck down and take cover. She felt heat from whizzing fire balls. The other three moved in military formation gunning only for Justo. Bullets beat, wrecked, and crashed into nearby cars. Meme only could let off one or two shots at a time before having to take refuge behind the i8. Fire and brim stone rained down on the couple like it was the end of the world. The gun battle suddenly stopped. "Meme you good?" "I'm good," she called. Justo took a quick glance and saw three men slowly approaching. "These niggas are not practicing" Justo said as he sat with his back against the car next to Meme. He popped the clip out to see how much ammunition he had left. "Five bullets! I gotta make this shit count he slid the clip back into place. "Meme stay low! Ima count to three and I want you to get outta here. One... Two.... Three!" Justo rose to his feet and took aim over the hood of someone's car at that moment all three men were out in the open. Boom! Boom! Boom! Boom! Boom! Boom! Justo opened fire letting off all five shots the gun cocked on the empty clip. Justo shot one of the men, he made a whine sound before falling out of sight. Justo saw the flash from the gun when his ops shot back. An unseen force smacked into Justo's chest. Once, then twice. He didn't want to fall to the ground, but he had no choice. The bullets that rocked him made him lose total control of his body movements. Meme held one hand on the driver's side door squatted low with gun in hand. Justo had told her to run but she didn't.

"Justo!", she called out but got no answer. She laid flat on her stomach trying

to see any movement, what she saw made
her heart skip a beat. Justo was on his back,
blood drooling from the side of his mouth.
"Meme if you gone die tonight then you
gonna die fighting bitch!," she told herself
prepared for what ever waited for her on the
other side of the car.
She took one last deep breath then stood and
then swung around the car with pistol aimed
ready to kill or be killed. She swung the gun
left, then right but there was nobody to face.
The group of men were nowhere to be
found. Gone just as quickly as they had
come, with the exception of the man Meme
killed. Justo had gunned another man he laid
off to the side slumped over on a Jeep
Cherokee. Meme rushed to Justo's aid,
"hold on baby we gonna get you some help",
she said in a panicked cry.

Boolaid's F-150 bent the corner then
skidded to a stop. He jumped out the whip
with a Glock 21 in hand. He raced to his
brother's side. "No! No! No!," he said,
lifting up Justo's shirt seeing the damage
done. Three gaping holes were in his chest.
He'd seen these types of injuries plenty of
times while on tour in the Army. Boolaid
knew his friend would not live to see
tomorrow. He sat down on the pavement and
pulled his best friend into his chest holding

him tight. "It's OK bro. Don't fight it. Just relax my G." Justo looked up to Boolaid tears fell down his face. "Te..tell my lil brother I love him" Justo said through grunts. "I will bro ima make sure he good and your son not gonna want for nothing, I swear to God!" Justo nodded his head that he understood. "Who did this?" Justo tried to speak but coughed up blood. "Easy, easy calm down bruh! You don't have to answer", "y'all got-ta go!" Justo mustered the strength to say. "I'm not going nowhere, fuck wrong with you nigga" Boolaid told him. Justo smiled showing off his blood-stained teeth. Although Justo was right, they definitely didn't need to be there when the police arrived.

Sirens could be heard in the distance. But Boolaid believed in no man left behind. You stayed as long as your comrade had air to breathe. Justo tried to sit up, he needed to tell Boolaid something. Boolaid leaned in closely. Justo whispered into his childhood friend's ear. "OK my nigga I believe you" Boolaid said looking his brother in the eyes. But Justo stared off looking pass Boolaid. Boolaid looked up but saw nothing, "what do you see my nigga?" he asked Justo knowing the end was near. "Momma!" was all he said then his head slumped sideways into Boolaid's chest. No longer breathing in Boolaid's arms. Boolaid slowly laid his friend to the ground then shut his open eyes. "R.I.P. Dog" he said barely above a whisper. He stood to face the girls. They looked sick. Instinct told Boolaid they had information he needed, but right now all that could wait because none of that matters if they were in jail. People were now spilling out of the club. "Com' on y'all we gotta go!"

Chapter 9

Boolaid blinked his eyes up at the bright sun, it was the middle of the day. The sun was at its highest peak. 93-degree heat beamed down on his face. Humidity at its all-time high so the temperature index read one hundred- and three-degrees Fahrenheit. "Move out men! Stay alert because if you get killed, you're stupid", Commanding

Officer Captain Mcraven said to his group
of soldiers. Boolaid had been in the military
for two and a half years. He'd earned stripes
early, taking up the position of a fallen
soldier. He was the youngest Sergeant on the
team. When they arrived in Afghanistan
eight months ago, he was with a team of 21
elite men handpicked by the United States
Government. But now they were down to
fifteen. Boolaid was a natural in the field he
could think in the middle of action and his
marksmanship was one of a kind. So, he was
chosen by Captain Mcraven to be part of a
Black Ops team called Ranger Battalion
Red. Ranger Battalion Red was a Special
Operations Unit. Right now, they were
traveling the desert foothills and valleys
headed towards the city of Jalalabad. The
team's mission was to find and destroy all
marijuana and poppy fields they
encountered Ranger Battalion Red split up
into two groups to cover more ground. Eight
went west while the other seven went east.
Boolaid accompanied the team moving East.
Members of Al Qaeda and Taliban all hated
Ranger Battalion Red. Any time they
crossed paths there was instant gunfire.

One of their number one resources to
fund their rebel movement was major drug
distribution. So, they would kill anyone who

bore the Red Battalion tag. "Joe Papi, ju think we run into O-sa-ma while we out here?" Colon spoke out loud as they traveled the unknown landscape. Boolaid was too hot to speak so he stayed quiet to save his energy. "Osama's been dead for like five years dumb ass!" Wilson said, as he wiped sweat from his forehead. Colon aka Porta Rock was from Puerto Rico, he had gotten into some trouble back in New York. The courts gave him a choice: join the army and be all you can be or join the D.O.C. he chose the army which Boolaid thought was both the same thing. Either way you were doing time. Porta Rock was light skin but had a dark brown tan from being in the sun all summer. Standing at 5'7 165 pounds he sported an army style high top buzz cut. And when he spoke his Spanish accent was strong.

Wilson on the other hand was the total opposite. A real redneck white boy from Texas 6" 3, 225 pounds all muscle. Wilson liked to push his weight around and never held back his tongue. Everybody called him Rooster because his neck turned dark red when he became embarrassed or angry. He also was biased as hell, and everybody knew. He had his own beliefs and at the same time so did everybody else. One thing

was for sure when it came time to put in
work you wanted Rooster on your side, he
was no slouch when it came to putting in
pain.

Porta Rock and Rooster fought all day
every day. Even had a few fist fights. But
the whole platoon knew they really fucked
with each other like brothers. Neither one
would ever admit it though. "Who ju callin
dumb ass, dumb ass!" Sweat dripped off his
chin with every word he used. "I don't hear
nobody else talking but you amigo. I'm
surprised the Taliban haven't tried to recruit
you as one of their premos" Rooster said
with a deep southern accent. "What I tell ju
about that racist shit puta! I'm not a cracker"
Porta Rock said, becoming angry. Boolaid
and the rest of Ranger Team Red knew Porta
Rock hated being compared to any other
race other than his own. The look on his face
was priceless. Boolaid couldn't help himself.
He had to laugh. "I'm poor leeeeqwa!" He
said nice and slow so that everybody
listening could hear. "Ju ma ma! She no
about dis long dick so, ju might be my ohja,
let me speak a engless so ju understand. Ju
might be my son" he told Rooster patting
him on the shoulder. All the soldiers
laughed. Rooster's neck turned a deep red.
"Now you looka here fe-lipa don't you go

and talk about my mama" Rooster said ready
to throw hands.

"Hey! You two, shut the fuck up
before I throw a grenade over there and kill
both you s.o.b's we got boogies at 12 o
clock. Take up positions and prepare to
engage" Captain Mcraven ordered. The
soldiers spread out in a tactical formation.
Each man taking cover in the nearest brush
they could find. Captain Mcraven was a 37-
year-old man, bald headed with a thick salt
and pepper beard from several months of not
shaving. Even though the captain was
pushing forty, he looked to be in his mid-
twenties. His body was sculpted like a
statue. He did hand signals telling everyone
what to do. Boolaid and a soldier named
Clarke had taken a position nearest to where
the unknown people were approaching.
Ranger Battalion Red sat waiting with M-4's
aimed at them ready to shoot to kill. Two
Middle Eastern men with long beards
wearing turbans walked around the bend in
the valley. They were also traveling with a
woman wearing a burqa.

Muslim women wore these outfits to
conceal their bodies so no man other than
her husband would know her shape. It
covered them from head to toe. It looked

like someone put a giant black sheet over her whole body then cut out the eyes. The soldiers wore tan and light brown camouflage so that they could blend in with the scenery. The passers-by didn't notice Boolaid and Clarke. Boolaid moved in with lighting fast speed punching one man in the face then snatched him off his feet. He slammed the man into the dirt. He screamed in pain from Boolaid's sneak attack. Boolaid dug his knee into the man's back, he wrenched with more pain. The Middle Eastern man tried to resist more but quickly stopped when Boolaid pulled his M1911 .45 from its holster then pointed it at the back of the man's head. Clarke followed suit and subdued the other man just as fast. The Muslim woman threw her hands into the air, surrendering. Captain Mcraven and the rest of the team moved in. "Taliban! Are you freak'n Taliban?," Clarke aggressively asked the man in Pashto.

Clarke was the team's translator and he spoke five different languages. They called him Mouse because he was quiet as a mouse only speaking when he had too. "No! No Taliban" the man fearfully shook his head. "Farmer, I farmer." "Don't fuck'n lie! Your fuck'n al-Qaida" Mouse screamed jamming his pistol into the man's right eye.

176

But the man still pleaded for his life
swearing to his God Allah that they were
only farmers and nothing else. "Sir! They're
claiming to be goat farmers from the next
village over", Mouse told the commanding
officer. He looked unconvinced. Ranger
Battalion Red held their desert storm tagged
M-4's at the ready. In this country
everything and everyone was dangerous.
They were in a land they knew nothing
about. You never knew if you'd just walked
into a trap or if your'e dealing with normal
people just living out their normal lives.
Boolaid and Mouse waited on orders from
their superior. Captain Mcraven gave them
the OK. "At ease soldiers," Boolaid and
Mouse put their weapons away and allowed
the two men to stand on their feet. "Wilson!"
"Yes commander," "search the women"
Captain Mcraven ordered pointing with his
rifle. "Yes sir!" He attempted to search the
Muslim lady but was stopped by one of the
farmers. The farmer spoke to Rooster in
Pashto. He talked very fast and seemed to be
angry by the tone of his voice. Rooster didn't
speak Pashto and couldn't tell what was
going on and he didn't care. "I don't
understand all that salami turkey bacon
gibberish you're saying because we
Americans speak English" Rooster

challenged the man. Mouse quickly jumped in between the two.

"He is saying it's a sin for another man to touch his wife. That's the law of the land around here" Mouse announced to Rooster and the rest of his squadron. "I don't give a fly'n fuck what law it is. It's not Americans law", Rooster's neck turned bloody red. "Stand down Rooster", Captain Mcraven said with a sigh. "Mouse tell'm to search his wife while we watch and tell'm do it slowly and carefully." Mouse spoke to the farmer, and he agreed. Ranger Battalion Red aimed their rifles at the farmer as he began the search. Boolaid took a quick glance up into the hills that surrounded them. He thought he saw some movement but saw nothing when he looked. He turned his attention back to the task at hand. A shot rang out into the air, breaking the silence. A round crashed dived into Boolaid's chest making him do a spin move before hitting the ground. He rolled out of the way of the next burst of shots that kicked dirt and rocks into the sky. He pressed his back against the mountain taking cover as a gun battle took place. The rest of the red squadron took cover wherever they could, sending gunfire back at their opps. "Booba you hit?", a nearby soldier named Johnson called out.

Booba was the name Boolaid's squad used for him. A year ago, they were in Johanneshurg, South Africa where Boolaid had met a young beautiful African woman named Niyoka. For some odd reason she wouldn't address him by his name. She preferred the name Booba. Boolaid's comrades would pick on him daily about his new name, calling him Niyoka's little boyfriend. After a while the jokes stopped and the name stuck. Boolaid pulled away the left shoulder strap of his level 4 military issued bullet proof vest then looked inside to see the damage. The round had penetrated two layers of the vest. The third layer was a ceramic plate, and that's where the bullet stopped. The area where the bullet should have entered his body was already turning purple and black. The pain was excruciating, but there was no time for pain. If anything, pain was a good feeling in a place like this because if you didn't feel any pain then most likely you were already dead. "Smith! you hit?" Johnson called out once again. "Nah I'm good". Boolaid yelled over the gun battle as he strapped his vest back into place. He grabbed his rifle, preparing himself for whatever. "Air support we got bogies all over our six. Do you have a visual? Over" Captain Mcraven spoke into his radio. He listened to it static for a few moments then a voice clearly came through. "That's a negative big red we have no visual repeat, no visual you're on your own, over!" Air support reported.

"Copy" Captain Mcraven looked to the sky. Everywhere Ranger Battalion Red traveled they were followed by nearby drones so if they needed assistance help could be deployed. But the route they traveled was inside a large mountain valley and some areas were blind spots for drones. In certain parts of the valley, trees, and hill walls could be as high as one hundred feet. Many places an enemy could hide. Captain Mcraven stepped from his cover but quickly ducked back in when bullets were sent his way. He'd gotten all he needed. Pinpoint of the shooter's locations. "Three shooters!" he yelled for all to hear. "Smith on your 2, Colon on your 12, Johnson on your 6". Captain Mcraven called out the shooter's positions and the people nearest. They needed to fight their way out fast before more Taliban showed up. Boolaid popped out trying to aim his rifle in the direction given to him by the Captain but was pushed back into the brush by gunfire. Dust and sand cracked off the wall. "Clarke! Give me cover" Boolaid instructed. Mouse

immediately stood, aimed his M-4 then fired
magazines at their enemy. The opp ducked
down behind a medium size sand mound.
Boolaid stepped out into the open for all to
see. He was unafraid of death.

He had to swipe sweat from the brow
before aiming his M-4 looking through the
scope. Gunfire echoed all around him and
yet he stayed calm keeping his breathing
smooth and even. He trusted his teammates
wouldn't allow anyone to sneak him. "Come
on out nigga!" Boolaid said to himself
holding his rifle firm. At that moment, the
man's head appeared into view from behind
the sand mound. The Middle Eastern man
saw Boolaid standing in the open, so he
swung his weapon down at him. Boolaid hit
the switch on his weapon changing fully
automatic to a semi-automatic. He fired. The
first round rocked the man's chest making a
hole the size of a golf ball, the second round
ripped through his neck obliterating the spin.
The Taliban fell to his knees, his head rolled
sideways. Boolaid watched the third round
sink into the man's head. The air exploded
with a mist of blood. The shot was fifty
yards away. Easy money for the poor black
boy from North Carolina.

"Two o'clock eliminated" Boolaid shouted, as he moved back into cover. *Only two threats left* he thought. Johnson and another soldier named Nelson ran down on their target when they saw him duck back into his cover. They took a gamble hoping he was reloading, they had to if they wanted to live. Johnson and Nelson bent the corner of the sand mound just as the Taliban man was popping in his banana clip. "Allah Akbar" he screamed before they mowed him down with a hail of bullets. "Six o'clock eliminated", Johnson announced. Other soldiers repeated to ensure the rest of the squadron heard. Now only one shooter is left. He was positioned about 20 feet above Boolaid and his squad. Almost impossible to get a clean shot. At the attacker's angle he could kill every last one of the Ranger Battalion Red members if he had the skill and time. The Middle Eastern man aimed his weapon then pulled the trigger. Johnson screamed in pain. He fell to the ground; Nelson quickly dragged him to cover. The Middle Eastern man shot again. Nelson hit the dirt dead, shot to the heart. "Nelson!", Johnson cried out, taking cover the best he could. Blood soaked the ground turning into mud where they hid. Johnson grunted in pain trying to stop his bleeding. The bullet entered the top of the thigh and exited out the side of the leg. Johnson gritted his teeth, tying an American flag around the wound.

"Johnson, you good?" Boolaid called after seeing his friend drop. "Hell, I fuck'n just got shot with a k". "Nelson?" Boolaid called. "Ne..Nelson didn't make it" Johnson mustered. "Damn Nelson" Boolaid hung his head low. You never know your final days out here. The band of brothers were sitting ducks, if anybody tried to come out of their hiding spots, they were sure to get smoked by the Taliban rebel. Someone would have to sacrifice their life to save the rest of the team. The Taliban soldier swung his ak-47 down in their direction and pulled the trigger again. His rifle came to life sounding like a mini helicopter sending mayhem where he aimed.

The man from the Middle East watched one of the Americans drop dead from his assault. Smiled evilly then aimed his ak-47 waiting to kill anybody dumb enough to step out. He had them all right where he wanted. "Joe Papi y ju try and kill my maneto's?" Porta Rock said, sneaking up on the enemy. The Middle Eastern man jumped from being caught by surprise. He tried to aim his weapon but there was no point. Porta Rock shot the man in his face knocking off the right side of the chin, then the ammunition exited the top left side of the head. He shot again. The already dead man's cheek blew open. "For Nelson!" Porta Rock unloaded the whole magazine, caving the man's entire head in. The body fell to the ground, twitched a few times then stopped moving altogether. "Twelve o'clock eliminated, All clear!" Porta Rock called down off the cliff. He waved the American flag a sign for safety. The troops stepped out from hiding. "Good work private!" Captain Mcraven held the thumbs up. "Doc get over here", Boolaid called, running to Johnson's side. Doctor Jones was the Medical Sergeant for the team. Everyone called him Doc for short. "Fuck!" Johnson said as Doc examined and cleaned the wound best, he could. "Commander, we got a flesh wound in and out, Johnson's very lucky." "I wish we would say the same for Nelson" Captain Mcraven looked down at Nelson's dead body. Everyone had a moment of silence. "Can he walk?" "I can stop the bleeding only so much we should be able to make it to the next village. But I need to get him out in the open to treat the wound."

"Good work Doc! The next village is ten miles that way", he pointed east. "Let's move out." The team began to follow the commander's orders, but Rooster still had unfinished business. "Now hold on one second lady you haven't been searched for any illegal contraband." Rooster blocked the woman's path. "Bomb!" Porta Rock yelled from the top of the cliff. He pointed in the direction of the danger. The Muslim woman held her arms in the air so Rooster could search. When her long sleeves fell down it revealed the detonator in her hand. Rooter's eyes became wide with fear, he tried to deliver a kill shot but it was useless. She pressed the button. The 50 pounds of explosives strapped to her chest exploded, death came instantly. The blast was loud and ferocious. The heat was so intense anybody nearby was sure to have second degree burns. The attack was over before it started. "Nooo!" Porta Rock cried from the cliff. Chunks of charred meat scattered the area. The remains looked like pieces of highway roadkill. "Damn Rooster" Boolaid shook his head looking at the carnage left behind from the bomb. "I know right that nigga cooking like bacon" Johnson said. "Huh?" Boolaid gave Johnson a confused look, not sure if he'd heard correctly. "What did you just say?" "I said I'm cooking bacon; do you want some?" Johnson repeated.

Boolaid blinked his eyes open, Bea came into view. He had been asleep, another memory of his past coming back to haunt him. "Hmm" he said sitting up. "I'm cooking breakfast, you want some bacon?" Bea asked with a sad smile. She knew the man in front of her was grieving. "Yeah, but I don't eat pork!" "Good because we don't either. Its beef bacon" the smell of food in the air made his stomach growl. "Yeah, I'll have some thanks sis." Bea blushed before walking outta the room. He was on a couch. He massaged his forehead, his body felt sluggish, and his mind was a little fuzzy. After Justo had gotten killed the three made a run for it in the F-150. While driving Boolaid lost his cool. He couldn't believe his brother was actually dead. Gunned down by someone unknown. Gunned down in the same parking lot and Boolaid still couldn't save his friend. He broke down right there at the wheel. The girls helped him pull the truck over. Meme jumped into the driver's seat then hit the gas. The realization of Justo not waking up tomorrow fucked with him bad. "Here baby take this!" Meme said, giving him a pill. He didn't do drugs, but he needed to ease the pain. He bit down on the pill chewing without water. The zanny bar kicked in within minutes, it knocked him out cold within an hour.

The sisters decided to hide out at the trailer in Kernersville. Meme tried to start the i8, but it wouldn't start, too much damage was done to the engine from bullets. Boolaid asked Meme to stay on the scene, but she refused. He thought that was a little fishy but figured she must have had warrants for her arrest, so he just left the issue alone. But today he would get all the answers he was looking for. He stood to his feet and stretched the Xanax was still on his ass. "I won't be taking any more of that shit" he told himself. His nose followed the smell of food. He slowly walked through the double wide mobile home then came to pause when he stumbled into the kitchen. He watched two beautiful women preparing breakfast. Bea over the stove cooking while Meme grabbed plates, silverware, and cups. They both had changed outfits to something more comfortable. Tight fitting t-shirts and boy shorts. Bea's were red and they hugged her perfectly. She had one of those bodies where you would have sworn, she worked out daily. Meme's shorts were pink, every time she moved that ass wobbled. Her booty was just so damn jiggly. Meme saw him quietly watching. She also noticed the drowsiness in

his face. He needed more sleep. She grabbed
a cup pouring some tropical fruit juice
Minute Maid. The juice was ice cold. "Hey"
she politely handed him the cup. "Thanks."

"You look like you about to fall out,
come over here and have a seat baby!" She
led him to the kitchen table. He sat down
then put the cup to his lips. The juice
seemed to taste better and better with each
gulp he took. Boolaid didn't realize how
thirsty he was. He put the cup down and
Meme refilled it. "Oh, I'm at the waffle
house" Boolaid asked, putting the cup back
to his mouth drinking. "We can be wherever
you want us to be", she shyly smiled. Meme
went back to helping Bea finish the meal.
Although Boolaid's thoughts were still
cloudy his eyesight was 20,20 because he
clearly saw how Meme's ass clapped as she
walked away. A few minutes later Bea
bought Boolaid two plates full of food. He
thought about his aunt Robin for a second,
he needed to check on her. He took hold of
his fork then scooped a mouth full of eggs
and with the other hand he grabbed a couple
strips of bacon. Bea smacked his hand
playfully, "boy slow down! It ain't going
nowhere. Plus, you gotta wait for everybody
to join the table." But he'd already jammed
his mouth full, yes ma'am he swallowed

what was in his mouth. Leaving his lips greasy in the corners.

Bea watched him closely making sure he wouldn't eat anymore. That's more like it, she went back into the kitchen satisfied. Yeah, she definitely reminds me of my aunt. From the way she told him to slow down. He pulled his phone out then sent an *I love you momma* text to his aunt Robin; life was just too short.

"Justo was dead, I'm about to be on straight bullshit! With whoever." He talked to himself. Boolaid brought his attention back to his plate of food. His stomach started to talk to him. He had to admire the black women's cooking skills because these two really threw down. Scramble eggs with cheese, bacon, Turkey sausage links, cheesy grits, waffles with whip cream and strawberry syrup, and lastly a pan of big soft buttery biscuits. The kind that you can peel off in layers. A meal fit for a king. Bea and Meme came back to the table, both carrying plates of their own, only their portions were much smaller. The kitchen table sat four, Bea and Boolaid across from each other, Meme to his right. "OK we gotta say grace now bow your head and close your eyes" Meme spoke to the table. Boolaid bowed his head but didn't close his eyes. Meme cocked her head sideways making a crazy face, "is you serious?" She said nothing. "Is she serious?" he asked Bea. She smiled but said nothing. He decided to play their little game only because he was hungry as a bitch. He sighed then closed his eyes.

"God is grace, God is good, Lord, we thank you for this food" Meme prayed. He couldn't help it, he had to open his eyes. Not to his surprise four eyes stared back at him. He smirked *these some childish females*. Meme finished. "Bow our heads we must be fed give thanks to our Lord for daily bread, amen" "Amen!" Bea and Boolaid said in unison. All three began to eat.

Boolaid inhaled his food like a human dirt devil. The girls couldn't believe how fast he ate. "Damn Major Payne" Bea laughed. He came up for air, his plate almost finished. The sisters had barely touched their food. Boolaid put his back to his chair, rubbing his stomach full. He burped "my bad you gotta eat fast in prison and eat even faster in the Army." "Well, you're not in prison anymore Damon!" Bea joked eating some eggs. "Those are two places I don't ever want to go" Meme said, peeling a fluffy layer off her biscuit. The table fell quiet. Boolaid watched them eat.

Now was the best time to confront the girls. He wanted to know what they were hiding. Something told him they knew something about Mad Max getting wet up. And if that was true depending on what they said depended on whether he would murder them both. Last night Justo whispered in Boolaid's ear. He told him to *fuck with the sisters* and that *they were solid. Why would he tell him that with his dying breath?* Boolaid trusted nobody but Mad Max and Bigz.

"The last time we met each other Bea you wanted to tell me something, but you didn't and I wanna know why?." Bea and Meme stopped eating. They didn't say anything, just paid Boolaid close attention. Bea knew where this conversion was going. She also knew Boolaid had a gun on him. She saw him tuck it into his jeans before they came into the house last night. Bea was from the streets; she'd lost somebody important to her at an early age. She knew Boolaid was in pain and confused about the things going on in his life. He wanted to take his anger out on anybody responsible for his confusion. Point blank he wanted answers.

Boolaid waited but neither sister spoke, which was fine with him, because he would ask only one more time. If he got no answers after that he was just going to kill them at the table and figure out shit on his own. "What was it you didn't tell me that day I brought y'all that money" he slammed his fist down on the table. The girls jumped in their chairs at the sudden outburst. The silverware clanked against the plates and everybody's cup rattled on the wooded table. Boolaid's eyes were low and extremely chinky from the zanny still traveling in his blood stream. Unseen he gripped his glizzy under the table, if they lied, they died. If they told the truth and it sounded like bullshit, he would still smoke their boots.

Bea wanted to tell him about Curtis that day at the *Bojangles* and she wanted to tell him now. But she was more loyal to her sister. Meme had never betrayed her trust so why would she. Bea didn't want to die but she believed wholeheartedly in death before dishonor. She was willing to take their secrets to the grave. Bea looked at Meme with pleading eyes. "We can trust him". Bea broke the silence. Meme knew Boolaid was hurting. He only wanted answers, she couldn't blame him. Meme sighed, "what the hell tell'm!" "OK Boolaid the day we met there was a news report about a man named Curtis Roger's. He'd been found dead in his house by his mail man". "The name does not ring a bell. Why are you telling me this?" "Curtis is the man we robbed for the 20 bricks". "Soo…so I killed Curtis" Meme said with her hand raised in the air like she was in school waiting to answer a question for the teacher. "So, when we heard something happen to Mad Max, we thought it might have been connected somehow, we just wasn't sure. Now, comes to why I didn't want to stay at the club last night and wait on the police. Because the gun I used to kill Curtis was the same gun I used last night and you don't have to say anything, I know I'm stupid I should have been gotten rid of the gun" Meme said, feeling much better now that she'd gotten something so heavy off her chest.

"So, there you have it" Meme smacked her thighs. "Now the cats out of the bag we've told you everything" "Well, so if your gonna shoot then just shoot nigga" Bea said seriously. "Just know we're not the enemy. The enemy is them fuck niggas that killed Justo and got Mad Max up in the hospital." "And luckily for you I know who them fuck niggas are!" Meme finished with revenge in her eyes. "Who killed my brother, well I don't know him know him, but I would recognize him if I saw him again." Meme turned to Bea. "You remember the nigga that tried to holla at you in the club line?"

"I do!" "Well, he's one of the niggas that ran down on me and Justo. I remember the big bug eyes from anywhere." "I dissed that nigga and everything. He followed me to the bar and I let'm buy my drinks with his lame ass." Bea became flaming hot on the inside. She felt used. "Wait!" Bea yelled, catching Meme and Boolaid off guard. "We exchanged numbers." "So, you got the nigga's phone number?" Boolaid made sure he heard correctly. "Yesss boy I got his number." She grabbed her cell off the counter. You could hear a roach fart. It was so quiet in the room while they waited for Bea to go through her phone contacts. "Omar!" She said, happy to be of some help. Hearing Omar's name made Boolaids armpits sweat, all his drowsiness gone. He felt alive with a new purpose in life. *Murder! Bigz was right all along. That's why Justo said Meme was solid. She'd seen his killer and so did he. Omar was a snake and needed his head cut off.*

Boolaid's mind began to race. His blood pressure rose. He needed to slow down his thought process. He needed to act and not react. A reaction was an action without thought. Reaction could get him killed or land him in prison, behind a wall for the rest of his life. He digested everything he'd just heard. *They were telling the truth and he believed them.* If Curtis and Omar were connected there's no way the girls could have known. But still they had to choose sides. No straddling the fence. "I'm about to go to war with this nigga Omar. People are going to die. Y'all are loyal to each other, and I respect it because I know it's real. But I'm now asking for your loyalty in exchange for mine and that's for life, he placed five fingers flat on the table. In or out?" He looked into their eyes. "Death before dishonor" Bea laid her hand on his. "Death before dishonor." Meme put her hand on top of Bea's. Everyone seriously stared into each other's eyes. Justo had lost a brother but gained two sisters in the process. *Justo your'e gone but never forgotten. We lost the battle but not the war, I promise you that.*

Chapter 10

"How can I help you?" the person behind the counter asked. "Ahh yeah let me get a pack of Newports in the box, 2 backwoods, 20 on pump three and a box of condoms", Derrick said to the store clerk.

He paid for his items. The clerk put everything into a plastic bag then handed it over to him. "Good look," Derrick headed towards the exit. He made his way across the store's parking lot to pump three where he was parked. It was late November early December but tonight was one of those nights where it felt like it was still summertime. *I told this nigga to pump the gas*, Derrick opened the driver's door ducked down and threw the plastic bag at his homeboy who was sitting in the passenger's seat with the radio up loud. Joe Joe frowned, "Why you throwing shit?", he turned the volume down. "Nigga didn't I tell yo ass to pump the gas? Youz a lazy ass nigga, damn," Derrick blanked. "I told you we in a rush to meet my uncle!" "What about Keke and her friends?," Joe Joe asked. "See that's your problem right there," Derrick pointed. "M.O.B., nigga money over bitches. You don't listen to nothing I teach you. Make yourself useful and roll some Zaza." Joe Joe looked up to Derrick like a big brother although they were the same age, he hated to upset him. "My bad dog," Joe Joe opened a pack of backwoods then started to roll up. "Silly ass nigga." Derrick walked to the back of his whip to pump the gas.

"8 hundred killa" Derrick heard someone shout. He turned to see where the voice came from. "Oh shit!." His life flashed before his eyes. Derrick reached for his Glock 19, but his efforts were useless. His attacker pulled the trigger, the fully automatic assault rifle came to life. 7.62 rounds chopped Derrick in half. He fell in between the driver's door and the front seat. "What the fuck!," Joe Joe jumped into action seeing the dead stare of his role model. Weed went flying into the air then rained down all over the front interior. The man toting the micro ak-47 stepped on top of Derrick's lifeless body then swung the blick inside the car. Joe Joe opened his door. He tried to jump out so he could get right. But his arm got caught in his seat belt snatching him back into his seat. He dropped his nineteen eleven 45 pistol.

It slid across the pavement. Bullets danced up his torso and finished with a double on top his head. Blood mixed brain fragments and pieces of skull spread all over the windshield. The killer ran off into the night.

****

"You have reached a voice mailbox that has not yet been set up", the automated service said. Omar had been calling his little cousin Derrick for over an hour. "Where the hell this little nigga at?" "If your cousin isn't responsible enough to handle a grown man's business then you should find someone else to take his place". Taliban said with raised eyebrows. "Nah!, my little nigga know better, something not right I can feel it", they were at a stash house Rafiq set up for Omar. The place was filled with kilos of heroin and cocaine. They were waiting on Derrick so that he could drop cash off and re-up. Taliban and his men helped Omar with his operation. Located on the west side of Greensboro. Omar grew up in a neighborhood called 8 hundred block. With Rafiq's drugs and Taliban's fire power Omar was able to put real street niggas and gangsters from his neighborhood in position. Everybody copped from Derrick. Omar felt like he owed Derrick that much because if it wasn't for him Mad Max wouldn't have killed Derrick's little brother Drew. Drew died on Omar's watch. "Have you made contact with the woman from night club?," Taliban changed subject. "Who Kendra? Yeah, we've been texting back and forth. But the bitch is playing hard to get. But since you know I'm something like a pimp I did get her to agree to a lunch date". Omar popped his collar like he was the coolest nigga in the world.

"Fuck'n goofy" Taliban said to himself, staring into Omar's bug eyes.

Although Taliban was from another country it still wasn't hard to know a lame nigga when he saw one. But he still took a liking to Omar.

The night of the shoot out at the club Omar recognized Meme's face as the friend of Kendra although he never got Meme's name. "Do you think Kendra knows that you know her friend was with Justo when we drilled." Taliban spoke slang he loved black urban culture. "I can't say for sure, but if she does know anything she's good at hiding it." "Her friend must die! She's seen too much. Plus, she killed Ali and shot me in the arm. For this she must pay her debt in blood. A life for a life." Meme tried her best efforts to save Justo's life. She killed one man and hit Taliban in the arm breaking a bone. No doubt a lucky shot but Taliban would be wearing a cast for the next 18 months. Before Justo died, he killed a new member of Omar's crew a man named, Peewee just another murder statistic in the city of Greensboro. Their plan was to get Kendra to go on a date, that way they could find out her friend's whereabouts. Omar couldn't take the chance of anybody becoming a possible future witness. He also wanted to find out what Kendra's sex game was like, she looked so exotic he thought about the night he met her.

"Kendra should die as well", Taliban spoke as if they were going to do something as simple as snapping a finger. "Fuck it, if she gotta go, she gotta go" Omar would do anything to keep his plug. That night at the club Omar only saw the end of the fight. He didn't even know who was involved. Only one thing was for sure, Justo had just fallen into Omar's lap. He had to take full advantage he couldn't let him get away. And now that Justo was dead and Mad Max out the picture, Omar had total control of the west side. Better yet the whole city. Justo had other shooters but none of them gave it up like the little demon spawn known as Mad Max. Once he got rid of the girls everything else would-be smooth sailing. The streets belonged to Omar. His phone rang, bringing him out of his thoughts.
"Yo! Dice, what's good?" Omar spoke into the phone. Dice was one of the major distributors for the 8 hundred block boys.

Everybody in the city respected Dice. He would fight you or shoot it out with you point blank, he was with the shits. All his niggas loved him. He showed mad love. He also gangbanged. A well-known Crip. Most of the 8 hundred neighborhood banged Crip because of him. Dice had money way before Omar put him in position. But through Omar Dice was given the opportunity to get his set rich. "What's roll'n cuzz! You talked to Derrick today?" Dice questioned.
Red flags went up when Dice asked about Derrick's whereabouts. "Yeah, I talked to him about an hour ago we was pose to link up but the nigga ain't been picking up the phone. Why what's up?", Omar started to get nervous. He held the phone so tight as though it might break.

"Shiieed cuzz I don't know man I just drove by the Marathon over here on Randleman Road and 12 got this bitch yellow taped up. You can't even pull in if you tried cuzz". Dice parked across the street from the gas station at a closed down strip club called the Cave. He passed the blunt to his little homie Red. Omar knew what dice was getting at, but he needed to make sure. "What you tryna say?" "Maaaan it's like two niggas stretched the fuck out in the middle of the parking lot. There's a black

Audi with both front doors wide open. I see niggas feet, but the sheets got the rest of the bodies covered. Derrick got a black Audi last time I talked to cuzz, him and Joe Joe was together but neither one of them are answering their phones it don't look good, is all I'm saying."

Dice watched another police car pull into the store's parking lot. "Stay on the south I'm on my way." Omar hung up without another word. He didn't want to believe it, but he already knew that was his cousin Derrick's body laid out there dead. He turned to Taliban with a loss of words. But his face said it all. "I'm sorry for you lost, it pays the cost to be the boss my friend. Now you truly understand what that means". "Come on Taliban we gotta go," they locked up the stash house and left.

****

Bigz jumped into his car placed lil nigga in the passenger seat then pulled off. He had just caught two ops lacking. Bigz had been on his way to grab a bite to eat when he pulled alongside Derrick at a red light. "Got cha" Bigz said following Derrick in traffic when the light switched green. He tailed the black Audi for about 15 minutes until Derrick made a pit stop at the hood Marathon gas station on the south side of Greensboro. Bigz kept driving then parked next door at an abandoned *Church's Chicken*. He grabbed lil nigga then got out the car ready to handle business. Justo was dead, Mad Max still in the hospital and Boolaid's somewhere trying to put this whole puzzle together.

Bigz wanted something done now. Fuck waiting, fuck plans, only putting in pain was his thoughts. He was out for blood and just drank a cup full. The night Mad Max got shot Amber showed Bigz a fb post with the other victims. Boolaid asked Bigz did he know anyone and Bigz told his friend a lie, the first lie ever. The truth was he did know someone. *Drew*, Bigz thought. Drew was a young Crip from the 8 hundred. Bigz was from a southside neighborhood called Woodlea Lakes, everyone called it the Lakes for short. Bigz was also part of the Blood Gang Gangstas AKA BGG. BGG originated on the east side of Greensboro in a neighborhood called Cumberland Courts by an OG Blood that moved to the city from New York starting his own Blood chapter. They also went by 3 hundred block. 300 being mostly Blood and 800 majority Crip, their neighborhoods were natural enemies. The Lakes and 800 didn't have beef but 300 and 800 did so, Bigz thought the shooting on Mad Max was because of him but now things were unclear. He was unsure of himself since Justo's murder two weeks ago.

Bigz didn't care though, ever since the funeral he was on straight bullshit. Derrick had had sex with Bigz girlfriend Keke while he did a short bid in the juvenile detention center. She lived on the 800 block. When Bigz got out she invited him to her birthday party. An argument started between him and Derrick. They took it outside where a fight broke out. The 800 block boys jumped Bigz after he got the best of Derrick, Drew being one of the accomplices. Bigz pulled a gun shooting one of the young boys. They'd been beefing ever since. Drew was Derrick's little brother. *Why not kill two birds with one lil nigga*, Bigz thought. If Drew had anything to do with Mad Max getting shot and Justo getting killed, then Derrick was guilty by association simple as that. Bigz phone rang. He looked at the caller ID, Boolaid. He'd been calling on and off for the past few hours. Now that Bigz objective was complete he could answer. He sent the call through Bluetooth. "Yooo!" Bigz said hearing Boolaid come through the radio.

"Nigga I know you seen me calling.
You gonna make me sock yo ass to the flo"
Boolaid threatened. Bigz smiled knowing
his brother was playing but serious at the
same time. A serious joke is what they
called it. Bigz liked to piss off his niggas.
He was a young gangsta and didn't like
hanging with soft niggas. It had been Mad
Max and Boolaid who took him on his first
drill. Mad Max gave Bigz the gun to finish
off the guy they were looking at but at that
time he couldn't bring himself to do it. That
was many years ago when his older brother
was still alive. Times had changed though.
Now Bigz could kill at will. "I been
handling B.I. big homie" Bigz said as he
swerved in and out of traffic. "Yeah aite"
Boolaid talked to Bigz like that when he
knew Bigz was up to something. "Look tho!
We need to talk, but not over the phone.
Meet me at Toya's house in 20 minutes".
"Bet on the way" Bigz disconnected the line.
He defiantly didn't have a problem meeting
up with Boolaid now. He'd just killed two
people and needed somewhere to lay low.
Bigz turned the radio up and headed towards
Toya's.

****

206

"So do you think he took the bait?" Meme asked. "Yeah, I'm sure his ugly ass did. You know niggas think with they're lil head". Bea did a small measurement with her thumb and pointer finger. "I know right," they shared a laugh. "I've been playing cat and mouse games trying to figure out if he's suspicious of me knowing what they did." "Do you think he saw me?" Meme became worried. She wasn't afraid of anybody but just the thought of a random person walking up shooting sent chills through her body. Not knowing where it was coming from was the scary part. Because there was no doubt in her mind that they were dealing with straight killers.

"I can't say for sure if he saw you. But he did ask me how you were doing. A couple times actually. But nothing outta the ordinary. I finally told his goofy ass we can meet for lunch. I was thinking this Friday." "Where at?" "That's what I've been trying to figure out. It has to be a place with people but not too many".

"Because I don't want him to think something's up. Need'm to have his guard down so he won't see the set up. Boolaid and his people gonna be waiting on Omar's ass so they can pull up with the stick and let

it hit", Bea sang pretending to up the pole
and shoot the air. "Good! because this nigga
gotta go. He got a bitch all stressed out"
Meme used her hands to pull down on her
cheeks exposing the forming sandbags.
"And I'm tired of being couped up in this
damn house" Meme frowned.
For the pass couple weeks, the sisters had
been hiding out in their condo. After Justo's
murder they decided to duck off, stay off the
radar just in case they were targets. Kisha
was a dancer at the strip club Bea worked at.
She also was going to school to be a nail
tech. The sisters really liked Kisha. She was
amazing when it came to doing nails, so
they hired her as a manager at their nail
salon. Kisha had been running the business
in their absence. Once a week she would
meet the girls to drop off the weekly
earnings. In return they would really look
out for her. Kisha didn't have a problem
running things. She was just nosey as hell,
asking questions like when they would
return. Bea's excuse was that her and Meme
both had Covid-19 and would be back after
their quarantine was over. She knew Bea
was lying but just kept her thoughts to
herself. "Kisha's a great employee but we
can't just let her run our business forever.

Bea, you know I'm hands on. I like to make sure customers are happy."

Covid-19 had fucked the whole Untied States up, but the virus had died down in North Carolina to the point were everything was open again. A lot of small business owners lost everything they had. Bea and Meme were one of the lucky ones to have a company that thrived within the pandemic. "We do need to show faces, our customers do show hella love. Bea looked into Meme's eyes. She ran a single finger up Bea's thigh. She shivered as the chill creeped up the spine. It was late in the evening. The girls were having a movie night. Both girls were wearing T-shirts with nothing underneath. "Gurl what you doing?" Bea said lust in her voice. "I'm horny" Meme whined we been stuck in this damn house I haven't had any dick in months. She guided her hand in between Bea's legs.

Bea couldn't even flex it really had been a minute. Meme pushed a finger in between Bea's pussy lips and found that she was hot and wet. She softly moaned with her eyes closed. They were best friends but also sometimes lovers. Two females attracted to each other. Having casual sex as long as they weren't in a relationship. Meme and KB agreed she could have fun until he got home.

They embraced with kisses removing each other's shirts. Their nipples became hard from pure arousal. "Ssssshhhh" Meme licked Bea's ear lobe. "Get the stick!" Meme jumped off the bed quickly moving to the dresser. She went into the sock drawer pulling out a 15-inch dildo, a dick head on both ends. Meme rushed back to bed. Bea already waiting in doggy style. Even with it being dark in the room Bea's pussy still glistened with wetness.

Meme massaged Bea's clit with the head of the toy before plugging six inches into her goodness. "Uhmmm you like that baby!" "Yesss," Bea rocked back and forth. Meme turned around then bent over into doggy style. Bea held the dildo in place as she backed up on it like parking a car in the driveway. "Ahhh" both women moaned in unison. Their asses slowly bounce off each other as they threw there booty's backwards. Being careful not to let the dick fall out they took turns catching the pole. "Oh gawd!" They both held on to the sheets with their asses up, face down into their pillows. Their butts wobbled and clapped. "Oh shit! damn baby," they rocked hard making each other holler for joy.

Their asses crashed into one another like two rams in the wild fighting. There pussies swallowing 7 to 8 inches of dick. Digging deep down hitting the G-spot with every stroke. Both women moaned and screamed each others name. "I'm...cu.m.min" "uuwww I'm..bout..to.to nut". The sisters orgasmed at the same time. An explosion filled with ecstasy shot Bea forward. Meme flew in the opposite direction almost falling off the bed. They laid on their stomachs face in the covers breathing hard like they'd just ran a race. Bea's body jolted with after shock of a major climax. "Damn girl that was a good nut." Meme smacked Bea's ass; it jiggled like a bowl of Jello. Then suddenly both girls looked at each other when they heard the loud noise. They were in the bedroom when the sound came from the front of the condo. Then they heard it again this time it sounded like the front door had gotten blown down with c4. " Police! Police! Police!" multiple voices shouted moving through the house. "What the fuck girl," Meme said in a panic. Her heart pounded; she thought it might drum its way through her chest. Bea was nervous as well, good thing they'd left their guns else where she thought. They'd been in police raids a couple of times in their teenage years. "Sis put your hands up!"

They both did. "Were in the back undressed and unarmed" Meme added.

The house became dead silent. The kind of eerie feeling you get whenever in a graveyard at night. "Alright then, I want you two to step out into the hallway. Move very slowly with your hands where we can see them." A voice called out. They obeyed their orders. Stepping out into the hallway. Waiting on them was a small army of men with hard hats bulletproof vest and AR-15s. When the officers saw the girls' beautiful naked bodies some became uneasy while others hungrily licked their lips with lust. The sisters smiled reading each other's minds. Even at gun point men were still men. They all sat in the hallway like a can of sardines having a staring contest.

An older but every handsome man warring a red polo shirt and tan khaki pants stepped forward. "Hello ladies, I'm detective James Ford. I work for the homicide unit, and I need both of you to come with me." Ford couldn't help taking a look at their bodies again. *I ain't got no type, bad bitches is the only thing that I like* he thought but shyly looked away. "Ladies, I will allow you to throw something on. But make it quick and I'll have someone watching". "Thanks, come on sis you heard the man let's get dressed." Bea bit her bottom lip knowing all eyes were on them.

Ford felt himself grow in his pants. Officers began to argue about who would watch the two because they really wanted to holla. The girls took their time getting dressed. Bea took the longest, she always did. But afterwards they were separated, taken in their own squad cars. The sisters stared at one another from their back seat's sadness flooded their eyes. They were not afraid of what one would say to the police. Just sad because days like this were bound to happen. They stayed up late a night many times speaking of this very day. "I love you!" Bea mouthed to her bestie. "I love you more" Meme mouthed back. The officers hit the gas and pulled away from the curb.

"Hey sis", Bigz greeted Toya when she opened the front door. "Hey Bigz" Toya had low energy when she spoke. Bigz could see deep sadness in her eyes. He instantly became flaming hot all over wanting to go spill more blood. "Sis, I swear to God I'ma find out who did this and make them pay" his voice was low but serious. He didn't want Toya's son to hear him speaking about killing people. "Where lil Justo at anyways" Bigz looked around. "He's at my momma's house, I just need a little time to get my shit together you know." "Yeah, I know," "it's like" ... She paused. "After seeing my man laid up in that casket it really got my head messed up. I keep seeing him whenever I close my eyes." Her eyes became watery. Justo's funeral was small and private. You could count on two hands how many people attended. Boolaid, Bigz, 2x, Ghost, and Drama were the only friends invited.

Ghost and drama were Justo's employees as well. They ran the trap houses on the south and north side. Justo didn't have much family. His mother dead, father nonexistent and little brother fighting for his life in coma. But there was a cousin from out of town. He introduced himself to Boolaid as Killah, but Toya knew him as Devonta. Killah and Boolaid spoke a moment after the service was over. The young cousin explained he was down with the murder game. Boolaid had seen killers before, and Justo's cousin was definitely one. They exchanged numbers before departing.

"I understand sis take all the time you need. If I can help with anything just say the word." He put a reassuring hand on her shoulder. "Eye for an eye, tooth for a tooth, life for a life" Toya said now tears falling.

Nat Turner was a slave that was taught how to read the bible. That was the first verse he learned. Then went on a killing spree taking revenge on as many slave masters he could. Justo told Bigz that story, so he knew exactly what Toya was trying to say. "If you take mines, I take yours." He nodded his head in agreement. "Boolaid's in the back" Bigz turned and headed to the back without another word.

"What's good big homie" Bigz stepped into the room then closed the door. Boolaid watched Bigz from the couch. Bigz carried lil nigga in his hand. "What up younger bro what you been up too?" he stared a hole through Bigz. He knew Bigz was a gangsta and was deep in the streets with that gang shit. He'd just did Fed time becoming friends with real big homies of all different kinds of sets. And all in all, they were good people. One thing in common was they all knew what they signed up for. Bigz was a man he had to make his own decisions but that didn't stop Boolaid from giving him good advice. Like getting money staying out the way and not bringing unwanted attention to yourself. "I ain't been doing shit but mining my own business" Bigz sat down on the couch with a heavy sigh.

Putting his gun on the coffee table. "Oh yeah! Minding your own business," Boolaid grabbed the micro-AK-47 by its handle. He instantly could tell the rifle had been fired recently. It didn't weigh its usual weight. In the Army he'd fired his weapon so much, carried it so many miles. You just naturally knew when it wasn't fully loaded. And there weren't any differences holding lil nigga. Bigz watched quietly as his big brother examined the weapon. He knew Boolaid was far from slow. Boolaid put the barrel to his nose then took a good sniff. The smell of used gun powder was strong and evident. For the simple face that the gun was still warm.

"Business! Huh?" He chuckled. "Fuck it, I might as well tell you" Bigz decided. He explained that when Amber showed them the fb post he failed to tell Boolaid he knew Drew; and that he thought the 8 hunnit niggas made a move on Mad Max and maybe even Justo because he had shot one of them at a party over his girlfriend Keke. And instead, just saying what he thought was the issue he kept it all to himself because he felt it was his beef and Blood business; and you never shared Blood business with anyone.

Even though Boolaid was actually like a big homie and big brother rolled all into one he wasn't gang gang. "So, when I saw Derrick tonight, I had to have him. And not because he slept with my girl. For Mad Max, for Justo. And I scored twice because I knocked him and his man off. It is what it is!" He spoke with his chest poked out. Not sure how Boolaid would react. "Yeah, lil bruh, it is what it is!" He answered smoothly. He sparked a blunt of gas he'd just rolled moments before Bigz walked in the room. Ever since Justo's death Boolaid picked up the habit, smoking in his friend's honor.

He took a couple hard pulls then passed the L to Bigz. The brothers sat in silence getting high. Boolaid was in deep thought. Bigz new info gave him a little insight on Omar. Bigz hadn't found out about Omar's involvement. "Well, that's why I called you here tonight to discuss some matters." Omar had a whole hood behind him. This would go from neighborhood beef to an all-out gang war. Boolaid's heart rate went up, even though his eyes were low from the Gelato he'd smoked. Just the thought of war, people dying, made him excited. He missed the thrill of being in the fields not knowing if you would live throughout the day. "I called you here to discuss how to handle Omar and what he did to our family". "Omar!" Bigz looked into Boolaid's eyes, they were blood shot red. "I told Justo that nigga was a snake. I should have done checked that nigga the first time I saw his bitch ass." Bigz shook his head with disgust. "Ain't nothing to discuss, he gotta die", Bigz said as a matter of fact. "Yeah, no doubt but now that I know he's got a hood on his back we might need some soldiers of our own some solid niggas too. Because the shit that's about to pop off carries elbows. Which meant a life sentence in prison if caught. My girls gonna get him to come out in the open that's when we lace his ass". "Fuck it I got a couple homies in mind, they not your homies if they not willing to die for you or do time for you".

The two men stared into each other's eyes showing how serious they were. How important this was to them. "For Justo! For Mad Max". "I'll lose it all for my niggas", "no doubt solider no doubt."

Chapter 11

"Damn little girl where'd you learn to ride a dick like that?" The grown man asked the just barely of age teenage girl. They were parked on Randolph Street. One of the darkest streets off Martin Luther King Jr

219

Drive. He slid the cum filled condom off his penis with one hand, then lifted his ass up off the seat to pull up his pants with the other. He gave Asia a friendly smile as he rolled the window down to get rid of the now used condom. Asia smiled back tirelessly. She'd been walking MLK. Dr. and the surrounding streets all night trying to make money. Only fifteen years old she was darkskin with a nappy afro. Although on the chubby side she had a nice shape. But her body still couldn't compare with the fully developed prostitutes who had been working these streets for months, even years. Tricks would drive right past Asia spending their money with the more experienced hookers. Making it really tough on the little girl to make ends meet. But finally, her hard work paid off because after 8 hours of walking she got a trick to send enough money for her to buy food and get a hotel room to rest her young body. "Can you drop me off on South Eugene Street where the hotels are?" she asked with a shy smile. The man's friendly demeanor quickly changed.

"What the fuck I look like? An Uber? Get the hell outta my car you little slut" the man roared then mean mugged. Asia couldn't believe this guy was really trying to

carry her like this. *Why me?* she thought.
"Pleasse mister the hotels aren't even ten
minutes down the road" she begged the man.
Her feet soar and badly hurting from
walking on concrete all day and night.
Extremely tired, all she wanted was a ride so
she could get something to eat, take a hot
shower, and then go to sleep. "I wouldn't
give a damn if it was 3 minutes away, I said
no!" He flung the used condom. She
flinched as the rubber smacked against her
face. She peeled it off her cheek not noticing
it was upside down. The mans bodily fluids
oozed out onto her hands and down onto her
black leggings. Disgust and hatred filled her
eyes. "What! You fat, black, stank pussy
bitch. I wish you would try something just
so I can break your neck. Now get out my
car before I change my mind" the trick
threatened. Tears filled Asia's eyes then
slowly drizzled down. Not out of fear but
from anger and defeat. She wanted to stay in
the car. She wanted to try and kill him but
knew she didn't have any wins. She
snatched her Family Dollar purse off the
floor, opened the passenger's door then
stepped out into the night. The man pulled
away from the curb so fast he almost took
Asia's arm off as she tried to shut the door.

"Fagot ass bitch!" She screamed at the
fleeing vehicle.

She looked around seeing if anyone
might have been watching. She was really
embarrassed over the whole situation. "I
can't believe my life" she examined herself.
Dry cum in her hair all over her hands with
spots of sperm stained in her leggings. She
sighed, then continued her journey down the
dark street. M.L.K. was a long stretched out
road that led from one of the poorest hoods
straight to the middle of rich downtown
Greensboro. Martin Luther King drive also
divided the east side from the south side.
The many streets that ran along the outside
of M.L.K were drug infested, violent and
run down. This area wasn't called the south
or the east side. Everybody called this place
the dust bowl aka the bowl. People got
robbed or killed in the bowl almost daily.
Most of the streetlights had been knocked
out. So, Asia paid close attention to the
shadows. They seemed to reach out to her
from every direction. She was easy prey in
this concrete jungle filled with predators.
She was from Atlanta, GA. When she was
two years old her father had gotten killed in
a big heroin deal gone bad. Back doored by
his own best friend. Her mother was running
around with some big dope boy from North

Carolina. One day coming from GA to NC they got pulled over by the State Troopers. Simple traffic stop ended with a search and seizure of drugs and money. Asia's mother took the charges for her boyfriend and for her loyalty she was sent to the D.O.C.

Asia's Aunt Beth, her dad's sister took her in as one of her own. Aunt Beth wasn't poor, rather wealthy. With a government job that paid really well. Asia had her own room in a three story four bedroom two and half bath house. Aunt Beth was married to a man named Greg and the two of them had an eight-year-old daughter named Gabby. Asia went to school regularly and was on the AB honor roll every school quarter. Life was good for the 12-year-old child. But all that had changed one day when she had come home from school. She thought she was alone but wasn't. Aunt Beth and Greg shared two cars, but they always carpooled to save money and gas. So, seeing a car in the driveway wasn't anything out of the ordinary. She jumped into the shower like she always did first thing out of school. She walked from the bathroom to her bedroom with a towel wrapped tight around her body. "Oh God!", Asia jumped at the sudden sound of her door being shut closed. With her hand in the air her towel fell to the floor.

She and Greg stared at each other in an awkward silence. She stood at the edge of her bed while he had his back to the door.

"Oh, Iiii didn't know anybody was here!" Asia quickly reached for a towel to cover her naked body. "Hey.. hey" Greg moved in taking her by the hand. "Wait Asia its ok, really just come here for a second." He gently pulled her into him. Asia wasn't a virgin. At 12 she'd had sex before. Only once with a boy named EJ. He was her first true love. But after EJ's parents were offered a really great job opportunity out of state he moved away. Asia was so nervous her body quivered in Greg's grip. He pressed his body against hers. His large hard erection mashed into her stomach. Greg grabbed a hand full of Asia's behind. "Damn girl, that ass fat and soft." He leaned in kissing her on the lips. She didn't want to kiss him back but did away. He pushed her down onto the bed. She landed with a small bounce. Greg's mouth began to water when he saw her private parts. She always thought Greg was fine as hell but what he was doing now wasn't right. She needed to put an end to this right now. "I'm...ima tell my aunt you felt my butt and kissed me", she threatened that's the only thing she could think to say.

Greg started to climb on top of her but stopped when she said something about exposing him. She couldn't believe he was really trying to have sex with her. Greg was like a father to her. "Tell my wife whatever you want. She'll never believe you. With your little fast ass, don't act like you ain't have that boy up here in your room. What you need is a real man, some real dick." He groped himself with a wicked smile. He left the room without another word leaving the door wide open. Asia waited the rest of the day for Aunt Beth to get home so she could tell her what Greg had done. Only to be crushed by Aunt Beth's angry words. "No! Asia you're lying my man would never do such a thing". Greg stood behind Beth with the *see I told you so* face. How could she believe this man, this monster over her own flesh and blood. She looked at her aunt in a whole new light from that moment forward. She no longer felt safe or wanted to be under the roof of her aunt that raised her. Greg stopped carpooling with his wife, so every day that Asia came home from school he would be there to harass and convince her to have sex with him. She started to feel weak, falling for Greg's advances. So, after school she wouldn't come straight home. She'd stay at a friend's house for as long as possible.

And still Greg kept pushing. After months of
Greg's sexual abuse Asia couldn't take it any
longer.

She started not coming home for days
at a time. Trying to be faithful to her aunt.
But Aunt Beth only saw her niece as being a
rebellious child. Greg told Beth that Asia
couldn't be controlled and that she needed to
leave his house. So, Aunt Beth had Asia
placed into a group home. Asia had been
betrayed by the only person in the world she
thought she loved. Someone she thought she
could depend on. But now not only did she
hate Greg she hated Aunt Beth, her own
flesh and blood. Asia felt bad for her little
cousin Gabby because she knew it was only
a matter of time before she became Greg's
victim. Asia's life had been turned upside
down, a mental roller coaster downhill from
that point until now. She bounced from
group home to group home getting into
multiple fights. She disobeyed house rules
like curfew. She started experimenting with
drugs. And then she got arrested for assault.
No group homes wanted her any longer,
there was only one place left to go. Foster
care, Asia was officially a state baby.

A couple of years had gone by. Once,
while on Facebook search, Asia discovered

that her mother had been released from prison and now lived in North Carolina. She stared at the profile picture of her mother and couldn't help but to wonder why she hadn't come looking for her. But none of that mattered now because she'd found her and would make her own way. She stole a credit card from her case workers purse bought a bus ticket round trip from GA to NC. The ride took 12 hours before the bus pulled into downtown Greensboro bus depot. Asia stepped off the bus taking in the new scenery. Happy to finally get away from all her problems back in Georgia. Only to run into another brick wall of disappointments. Her mother was in worst condition's than the teenager. "Hey, my baby look at how big you've grown", Asia's mother embraced her child with a hug. "Hey ma!" Asia said back, now knowing why her mother had never come looking for her. She was strung out on crack. Things were so bad she sold her body to support the habit. Asia had seen pictures of her mother growing up. She was beautiful back then. She couldn't understand how a person could fall so far from God's grace. And that only pissed Asia off more. Nobody loved her in this world. Even though she couldn't remember her father being around she wished he were

Kalub Shipman
PUSH YOU PAY

alive because she felt deep down in her heart if he were alive, he'd be there to help at all costs.

"Fuck it I can do bad by myself ", she never imagined one bus ticket, two states over, and three years later she would be standing on the corner of Randolph and Caldwell Street just getting out of a strangers car selling her body for scraps. The houses in the bowl were close together with small driveways. So, a lot of the people in the community parked on the street, making it easy for prostitutes to make tricks. They would have a John just park in front of random houses and it didn't look out of place. The night was so quiet Asia could hear her own footsteps as she made her way down Caldwell Street. Weaving in between people's front yards ready to make a run for it if anybody jumped out on her. Especially the police. She didn't have time to take an unwanted trip to downtown Edgeworth Street, Greensboro County Jail. She went into her pocketbook taking out her cell phone. 4:49am the screen read. She went to her contacts scrolling until she found the name she was looking for. And hit the call button then placed the phone to her ear. She listened to the ring as she walked through the night. About to hang up when she heard

228

his deep voice. "Yowe!" "Uhmm, hey Raw this is Asia you up?" "Yeah, what you need?" He got straight to the point.

Even though it was almost five in the morning you could tell that Raw was wide awake. Asia had only known him for two weeks. They met at the M.L.K. and Julian Street corner store. This was a hood store that jumped all night long. With anything to do with sex, money, or drugs. She'd bought weed from him that night they exchanged numbers. Raw was a night owl. Everybody knew they could call him on the late night to get straight with the gas. All the other weed men were either sleep or too scared to serve at this hour, afraid to the chance risk of getting robbed. Look I don't need any smoke right now. I really really just need a ride to Eugene Street so I can get a room at the Knights Inn. She waited for him to respond but he stayed silent. "I'll buy some gas from you if I have too. Just please!" She begged on the verge of tears. She called him because he was about his business and the only boy, she knew that hadn't asked her for anything sexual in exchange for anything like something as simple as a ride down the street.

"I gotcha you where you at?" "Thank you Raw" she thanked God. "I'm walking down

Caldwell headed towards Andrews' Street."
"Aite, go to grandma's and I'll meet you
there in 20". He hung up without another
word.

Grandma was an older lady in the
neighborhood that smoked crack. All the
young people in the hood fucked with
grandma to the max. She'd let you post up at
her house. To trap or just chill out. As long
as you paid her in crack or enough money to
buy crack. Asia put her phone up then
continued her walk down the street with a
new purpose. Up ahead she noticed a dark
Avalon, it was rocking back and forth. *Shiit
girl get that money.* This wasn't the first time
she'd walked up on a parked car seeing a
man getting head or seeing a woman getting
hit doggy style in the back seat. But as Asia
neared the rear of the vehicle, she could
have sworn she heard someone cry for help.
"Mind you own business lil girl" she told
herself. She already had enough problems in
her life. Passing the car, she tried her best
efforts to look straight ahead. But what she
heard she could allow herself to ignore. "See
what you made me do?" "Now get up you
little bitch!," the john yelled as he attacked
the woman. He had his back to the window.
Not seeing that Asia was watching. "agh!...

I'm s-s-sorry". "Please Mister don't kill me" the voice begged.

The john was a really big man so big Asia couldn't see over his shoulders to see his victim. Asia could tell by the high pitch of the cry that the women was young probably her age or a little older. She knew deep down she shouldn't get involved. Just gone about her business get her hotel room and get some rest. But her hatred for fuck niggas overpowered her feelings. She thought about Aunt Beth's pedophile husband, and how he had ruined her life all because he couldn't keep his dick in his pants. She thought about the man who had fucked her for money not even fifteen minutes ago and how he just switched up threatening to break her neck for nothing. All because she asked for a ride. "What if that was you in that car" she asked herself. Asia hadn't even answered her own question before she realized what she had done. In a blink of an eye, she had her chubby arms wrapped around the man's neck choking him from behind in a bear hug type clinch. He dropped his chin to lighten the choke. He grabbed at Asia's hands and began to pry them open. "Leave her alone, you punk bitch!" she yelled into his ear as she struggled to hold on for dear life. With the front door wide open the interior light was on lighting up the inside of the car. Asia's eyes opened wide when she saw there was a skinny brown skinned girl folded up on the passenger side floor. Her right eye was swollen completely shut. And her lips looked like two hot dogs that had been put in the microwave for too long.

Fear shot through Asia's body because she knew if this man got loose, he would catch two bodies tonight. Somehow the glove box had been knocked open. Asia noticed that a chrome revolver sat in the corner of the compartment. "Gun! Get the gun!" Asia yelled to the half-conscious girl. But she just laid there like a scared animal. "Get the gun or he gonna kill us!" Asia screamed with tears in her eyes. But the helpless girl still did nothing but watched the fight through the one good eye she had. The john fought that much harder now that the girls knew he had a 357. Asia's arms trembled under the man's grip. She couldn't hold on any longer. He spread her arms wide apart then flung his head backwards. The back of his head connected with the bottom of Asia's chin. Her mouth slammed shut. Top row and bottom row on teeth making a loud chomping noise. The teenage girl's eyes rolled to the back of her head. She fell out of the car onto the pavement. Seeing stars and a bloody mouth. "Now you stay right there and don't move". The crazy man told the petrified little girl on the floor. Asia wanted to get up and just run away but her legs were unresponsive. There was a buzzing sound going off in her ears. The john towered over Asia's body. 6'4" at least 275 pounds. "So, you wanna be captain save a hoe huh?" He kicked her in the stomach. The kick so viscous it stole all the air from her body. Asia's mouth opened wide; a low inhumane sound escaped her throat. She tried to breathe in, but it seemed like forever before her lungs began to work again. "Now ima teach you a lesson for getting into the middle of grown folks' business." He grabbed Asia by the back of her shirt dragging her into the front seat. The top half of her body lay in the driver's seat while her behind and knees hung outside the car. He grabbed a handful of her leggings. He ripped them from her body leaving her in her panties.

He forcefully pulled them to her ankles. He was about to rape her, and she knew it. But she was too weak. He'd knocked all the fight out of her. "Help me!" Asia mouthed to the girl still on the floor. She tried to save her but now she was the one that needed the saving. "Ugh! Ugh!" Asia grunted each time he forced his fingers into both her private parts. "Yeah, get it nice a wet for me!", he dropped his pants getting behind her. "Stop it right now motherfucka," the girl in the floor screamed. She pointed the 357 pistol, it looked so big in her small hands. She couldn't sit back and watch him rape this girl. She risked her life when she didn't have to. The rapist had a sinister sneer. "Stop or what? You ain't gonna do shit you little bit..", the gun barked fired from the barrel. The night lit up for a fraction of a second. Then all went quiet. Asia held her head down with her ears covered. She peeped up. The girl still had the gun pointed like the john might jump up and attack again. Asia turned around to find the giant man stretched out in the street with his pants down. His eyes were wide open even though he no longer could see anything. And he held a crooked smile. He took a doom check straight to the right corner of the forehead. A pool of blood began to fill the street. Dogs barked in the distance. "Are you OK?", the girl with the gun asked. "Yeah, thanks you saved my life" Asia tried to pull her leggings up. They'd been ripped right off her ass leaving threads around the ankles. "Well you saved my life too", both girls looked around

seeing if there were peeping eyes on them.
"I wouldn't have survived much longer if
you hadn't jumped on his back like a mad
woman" she half smiled and finally began to
relax now that danger was gone. She fell
back into her seats with a huge sigh of relief.
Sirens could be heard in the distance. Asia
jumped into action. She ran the dead man's
pockets. "What are you doing?" "What does
it look like", Asia pulled a big wad of cash
from his pants. "You won't be needing this
now nigga." She talked to the corpse. She
hopped into the driver's seat then turned the
key in the ignition. The whip came to life.
The girl with the gun watched with
amazement. Asia moved as if the shit that
just happened was normal. "Who are you?! I
mean what's your name?", the girl with the
gun asked. Asia stopped and looked at her
for a second. "Asia but everyone calls me
Meme. And you?" "Bea!" "Well, nice to
meet you Bea. But we gotta get outta here
before twelve comes. I ain't trying go down
for a body. And you look like you in the
same boat as me. I'm taking this niggas car
are you riding or not?" Meme was right Bea
was in the same boat. She was alone in the
streets with no family. She made her own
decisions. And tonight, Bea made the
decision to ride with a complete stranger. A

stranger that risked their life for her when they didn't have too. "I'm riding" Bea said looking through her good eye.

"Ouch!" Meme laughed cuffing her mouth. She tried to smile but the pain in her jaw was intense. "Good I'm glad you're riding because I could really use the company." The girls slammed their doors. Meme popped her head up from the table at the sound of a door being shut. "Ms. Jones, I'm detective Ford with Greensboro homicide and this is my partner Detective Mcdon" Meme sighed she had been taken to an interview room twelve hours ago and had fallen asleep. *Go to sleep have a nightmare, just to wake up to another nightmare.* "I want a lawyer" Asia rested her head back on the table.

Chapter 12

"I said I want a lawyer!" Meme barked rolling her neck with straight attitude. "I know my rights; I have the right to have an attorney present which I do! And I have the right to remain silent which I am. Now slide." Meme looked away. Slide was a

term she and Bea used when they no longer
wanted to talk on the subject. Ford wanted
so badly to protest but couldn't. He knew she
was right. If he continued to press her
without a lawyer present, he would be
breaking the law. He'd been in law
enforcement for over 30 years always
playing it by the book. No shortcuts. No cut
corners. And he wasn't about to switch up
now. Detective Ford was a very handsome
man who aged very well. In his early fifties
but looked to be in his early thirties. Two
children who were grown living on there
own. He used to be married to a great
woman. A perfect wife. But his marriage
had ended over twelve years ago when she
asked for a divorce. Reluctant at first but he
finally agreed. She felt her husband loved
his career more then he loved his family,
and the truth was he loved her and the kids
to death but when duty called what could he
do? He was bound by an oath to protect and
serve.

Ford was tired from working long
strenuous hours, getting very little sleep in
between. His body was working off extra
black coffee and tons of sugar. In the last six
months the body count in Greensboro was
unbelievable. Eighty percent of the murders
committed were unsolved and the numbers

weren't getting any lower. He stared at this young beautiful dark skinned child hand cuffed to the table and wasn't even sure if he had the right person in custody. But he even knew now a days you couldn't judge a book by its cover because murderers came in all shapes, sizes and genders. She looked so innocent sitting there in her *Marine Serre* leggings, with a print top shirt. On her feet were *Balmain* sandals. Ford turned to leave but stopped just before leaving the interview room. "Oh yeah! FYI that hundred-thousand-dollar car you left at the crime scene a few weeks back. We know it's yours. just can't prove it, yet". Ford kept his back to Meme. "You and your friend seem to be doing real well for yourselves. What is it that you do again?,"
now turning to face her. Wanting to see what type of reaction he could pull out of her. Females wore there feeling all over there faces but not this one. Meme stared back stoned faced her goldish brown eyes seeming to pierce detective Ford's soul. But if he only knew. Her heart was beating at a thousand beats per second. She felt like someone was squeezing her lungs making it difficult to breathe. She thought she just might pass out but none of that mattered because she would not fold, could not fold.

Ford had a license plate and insurance check
ran the i8 BMW. But the names didn't come
back to Meme or Bea. The car legally
belonged to a woman named Olivia
Hightower. She'd been brought down to the
station for questioning. She informed the
detectives that her car had been stolen and
had the police report to prove it.

When she was asked, did she know
anybody by the names of Asia Jones or Bea
Donnell. She'd admitted that she had never
heard of those people. But still Ford wasn't
buying it. *There was definitely something
fishy about this whole thing* he thought. He
finally told the woman he was investigating
a homicide and that if she was lying and he
found out he would come back and lock her
ass up for life. Even still his threats didn't
work Olivia continued to deny knowing
anything about the girls. She's got to be
related some how he thought. Mother, older
sister, or maybe an aunt. He studied Olivia
closely so he could tell she had lived a rough
life. Recovering drug addict, he figured. He
searched through their database and public
records seeing that she'd done seven years in
the department of corrections. But there
weren't any records connecting her with
either girl. At first thought Meme was
worried when she heard the detective bring

up the fact that they had the car but quickly remembered that she was legally adopted by her Aunt Beth so any records before that were sealed away and made private. There was no way of them actually knowing the owner of that vehicle was Meme's mother. Once Meme got her bag all the way up, she went looking for her mother. Even though Olivia had abandoned her when she was young, didn't mean Meme couldn't be the bigger person by taking the first step to make amends.

Meme found her mother then got her off the streets by force, by admitting her into a rehab center. She helped her mother get clean off crack. Once Olivia was out of rehab Meme helped her maintain an apartment until she got a job and could take care of things on her own. Now, Meme and Olivia had finally started to build themselves a real mother daughter relationship and neither one of them was going to allow anybody to ruin that no matter the cost. *Ah bitch! If that's all you got, then you haven't got shit* she thought with a big inward grin. But that inward grin changed to inward panic with the next statement detective Ford said. "Oh yeah, by the way you're being charged with three counts of second-degree murder. Eyewitness positively pointed you out in a photo line up. ID'd you as the shooter. So, you are under arrest, and you are going to jail. You'll be transferred to county whenever we get around to it". Ford looked Meme directly in her eyes, she held a steady gaze. He waited a few more seconds hoping to break her, but she remained intact. "Fine" he shrugged his shoulders. "You'll have plenty of time to think in a cell if you decide to change your mind. Just ask for Detective Ford." Ford left the interview room stepping out into the hallway closing the room behind him. "Shit!" He sighed. He hoped he scared her enough to make her want to talk. Because in his investigation he discovered that two of the men killed at the club were associated with two men.

They were killed in a neighborhood on the east side not even a full month ago. All four men were from Afghanistan. And what was so interesting about it all was that both incidents involved victims that were brothers. One who lived and the other died. Ford believed Meme was with Justo when he died. He tried to get Justo to come clean at the hospital about what he and his little brother had going on. But he took that to the grave because now he was dead, his baby brother in a coma fighting for his life. If he did somehow survive, he most likely would stick to the code of the streets. The code of silence aiming for revenge because he would wake up and find out he was all alone. Ford shook his head at the thought of how young black men just wasted their lives with no meaning and violence. Whatever the case was he needed Meme to spill the beans. She possibly could be the key to solving seven unsolved murders. He looked at the screen on his cell phone to check the time. 2:57pm, he went to his text messages then typed a few lines before putting the phone away. "Where the hell are you Tim?" Ford said, moving down the hall. Mcdon had been the one who found the eyewitness from the club. A man named Jeff Cowan had come forward out of nowhere. He was the owner of the club. Everyone called him Tank. Ford wanted to interview the girls together. They were good at the good cop bad cop role. But Mcdon made it very clear he had a family emergency and needed to leave the office asap!

Ford asked his partner was there anything he could do to help. But Mcdon quickly told him no and that he had everything under control. Ford stopped in front of a door that read interview room E. He opened the door then entered. Staring at him was Bea an amazing looking woman.

She reminded him of someone in his past. Even after sitting and being cuffed to a chair over 18 hours her body still didn't look stiff and there weren't any signs of fatigue, just those chinky eyes. She had a natural beauty like Rhianna the singer.

He shut the door then cleared his voice before speaking. "I'm detective Fo..." Am I being charged with anything" she cut him off getting straight to business. *These some thorough ass women if I ever saw one, he thought to himself.* "Well...um ms. Not at the moment but...". "Slide! I want my attorney present" she cut him off a second time. Ford sat there dumbfounded. In thirty years of all his police work he didn't know what to say. He was used to the average woman crying and praying to God for help but these two were so different. Bea hadn't been identified at the crime scene and she obviously knew her rights like Meme did. There wasn't any evidence against Bea. Ford had no choice but to let her go free. But not without a fight. "Your friend's being charged with murder. If you know anything I'd advise you to come clean so I can help her while I still can", Ford said looking at Bea seriously hoping to get information. The detective saw pain in Bea's eyes from what he'd just told her.

And at that moment he knew he would get the information he needed. "So your'e telling me that I'm free to go?", she asked, like she didn't hear his last statement. "God damn it!" He slammed a fist down on the table losing his temper. He knew she was about to crack but just got let down once again. "Yeah, you're free to go" he sounded defeated. "Handcuffs please", Bea said holding out her cuffed hand. He moved in, taking a small key from his pocket unlocking the shackle, it fell to the table with a loud clunk! Bea massaged her wrist. There was a dark red imprint from where the cuffs still had been digging into her skin. She stood to face the detective, they stared at each other, not trying to size each other up but more of an unknown moment. "Are we gonna just stand here and stare at each other? Or are you going to show me the way outta here?" she asked dryly. Ford wanted to just yell..."Bitch what in the fuck is wrong with you" but instead he opened the door, "ladies first."

****

Mcdon's phone vibrated in his pocket. He already knew who it was without checking but checked it anyway. It was his partner James Ford the message read, *Where you at partner? I really needed you on this one. These bitches are hardcore.*

"Is everything OK? Detective" Rafiq asked in his deep Middle Eastern accent. "Yeah, everything's fine, my partner just wants to know when I'll be back at the office, he said the girls are a handful" Mcdon pushed his phone back into his Levi jeans. "Is this partner of yours going to be a problem? Hmmmm?" Rafiq crossed a leg over his knee sitting up straighter. He, Taliban, and Omar all sat in Detective Mcdon's living room. They sat in silence waiting on Mcdon to answer the boss' question. "Um..ah..well no" he stuttered. "He's just a little worried because I told him I had a family emergency. It's not like me to just up and take off like I did today" Mcdon nervously smiled at the three men who had just popped into his home unannounced. "Hey look you guys! No disrespect but I've done everything you've asked. I convinced the owner of Club Platinum to take fifty thousand to lie and say he saw the Asia Jones girl shoot and kill everyone in the parking lot that night. So, will you just leave me and my family alone?". He pleaded with his hands in prayers position.

Detective Ford and Mcdon were the lead homicide detectives for the Curtis murder and the shooting with Mad Max on the east side. At that point Rafiq had lost a major distributor and two soldiers. Something needed to be done. So, he sent a few henchmen to look into the lives of the officers assigned. He wanted to know if these men were capable of solving the homicides and discovering the identity of the Shirac Cartel in the process. Rafiq couldn't afford that type of heat over such small amounts of drugs. All this hassle over only twenty bricks of heroin. When he was responsible for moving tens of thousands of kilos of heroin and cocaine from the Middle East to the United States of America. In America Rafiq was the king of kings. But compared to the cartel as a whole he was just a runner. A major errand boy. No one was bigger than the Shirac Cartel. Rafiq was well respected but one wrong mistake, and he would easily be replaced by the true boss. And replacement is usually nice words for sudden death. Before he allowed that to happen, he figured he would just buy the police out and put the two detectives on his payroll. Because in the U.S. of A. Everybody had a price. But Rafiq soon found out that detective Ford was a super cop and would not be bribed. He would most likely have to be killed. Mcdon on the other hand was an entirely different story. In his early 30's, married to a beautiful wife who had just recently given birth to his first child. Police officers only got paid $40,000 a year. His wife was a teacher but hadn't been working due to the maternity leave the school placed her on. The couple were trying to buy a house, bills stacked sky high. Rafiq saw this as an opportunity. He told his men to approach and offered him one hundred thousand dollars. In return for the money, he would hide the identity of the dead Shirac Cartel members. And throw a monkey wrench in the whole murder investigation. But Rafiq changed his mind when his men told him what they had discovered about the young cop.

After a few weeks of carefully following the officer, they found out that Mcdon rarely went home to his wife at the end of the nights shift. But instead, made a detour to another house. Detective Mcdon was living a double life. After a very close observation and taking a couple hundred snap shots with a high-powered camera the Cartel found out the detective was doing some undercover work of his own because he was indeed sleeping with a man. Rafiq had the photos spread out across the coffee table for all to see. Mcdon stared at the pictures wide eyed looking at himself kissing and hugging his secret lover. He looked around the room nervously, his wife, just in the next room. If she were to come walking in right now, he would be exposed. She would know about his homosexual activities. And his life would be over as he knew it, his career would be destroyed. He looked back at the pictures and felt like shitting a brick. Rafiq smiled with delight at the sight of Mcdon's fearfulness. "And you should be afraid," Rafiq said coolly. In his country if you were caught doing homosexual acts, Muslim or Christian it was punishable by death. Bottom line was if you had to hide and sneak, whatever it was you were doing then nine times out of ten, you weren't supposed to be doing it nohow.

"Mr. Mcdon, I don't think you understand the severity of our relationship." Rafiq said very smoothly as he held an evil grin. Mcdon looked like he might break down crying at any moment. "You sir are a hoe. And I am a pimp. You are my bitch, now and forever." He laughed gathering the stack of photos then neatly placed them into a brown envelope. He tossed them to Mcdon, he fumbled the package dropping it to the floor but hurriedly picked it back up. Taliban and Omar burst out laughing. Omar had never seen the police being bitched like this. He enjoyed every bit of it.

"Hey honey!" Mcdon almost jumped through the ceiling when his wife came prancing into the room. She was a gorgeous looking white woman. Resembling Paris Hilton in the face but with a country thick black girl body. "Hey baby. What's up?" Mcdon smiled. "I'm sorry to interrupt but I'm heading out to the store. The baby's in the crib sleeping. Can I get you anything while I'm out. Or do I need to get anything extra for your friends? Are they staying for dinner?", she happily asked with excitement in her voice. Everyone just smiled. This was her third time barging in to ask if they needed or wanted something. "No honey, everyone's just fine. And no need for extras they were just about to leave". "Awww" she frowned. "I make a hell of a pasta salad. I'm just happy you boys decided to have a meeting here at the house so my hubby can spend some time at home. I know being with the FBI you don't have the luxury of coming home to your family every night like the other guys on the force. So, I just wanted to personally thank you guys from the bottom of my heart". Tears now in her eyes. "Yes.

Yes! In this line of work, you must be on the
down down low." Rafiq brought out another
brown envelope showing Mcdon he had
copies. "Down low, top secret." He waved
the envelope in the wife's face with a smile.
"Right! Well, I'll let you fellas finish up".
She gave her husband a kiss on the cheek
then lips before leaving. "She is very very
nice. It is too bad you really do not want
her" Taliban said still looking at the door
she'd just came from. Then licked his lips
hungrily. "If you even think about going
anywhere near my wife, I'll kill you."
Mcdon snared in a deadly silent tone all his
teeth showing like a dog really to bite. All
three men chuckled at the detectives' empty
threats. "Fuck you gump!", Omar said.
Mcdon wanted to react but knew better.
They'd probably kill him then the rest of the
house. "Gump? What is this gump? You call
him. I never hear this word before. Oh yes
Forest Gump you mean?" Rafiq said
seriously. Omar and Taliban died laughing.
"What's so funny?" Rafiq wanted to know.
He shrugged his shoulders. "We are not
finished with this Gump secret. You will tell
me what it means. But right now, we must
get back to the business at hand." Rafiq
brought his full attention back to Mcdon.
"So, you do have two women in custody,

correct?" "Yes, they've been at the station for a little over eighteen hours." Mcdons phone vibrated once again. He looked at the screen to read its message. *Asia Jones still in custody. Bea Donnell being released.*

"Oh shit guys, Bea, the friend is about to be released I have to get back to the station asap!" Mcdon jumped to his feet. "Eliminate her no screw ups," Rafiq told Taliban. He nodded his head as he made a phone call. Whoever it was that he called answered on the first ring. They spoke to each other in Pashto, no longer than forty-five seconds before ending the call. "Done" Taliban slid his phone back into its holster. "Good after we deal with this Bea then we see how to handle our jail bird". Rafiq stood to his feet. Omar and Taliban followed his lead. The three moved towards the door. "We will be seeing you later Officer Dragon", they all laughed their way outside. Mcdon closed the door then watched them from his window until he was sure they were gone."Your FBI buddies seem really nice", his wife popped outta no where scaring the shit out of him for the hundredth time today. He wanted to cuss her ass out but held it in. "Maybe one day we could all do a dinner date with their girlfriends or wives," "yeah maybe." Mcdon put on a fake smile. But what he really thought was *No way in hell, no way in hell.*

Chapter 13

"Check up!" Bigz aggressively passed the basketball to his friend Stupid Dude. The ball flew through the air like a missile aiming for his chest. Stupid Dude caught the ball with ease. "Check up then nigga". He released the ball gently. It fell from his hands onto the concrete court, did a light bounce then slowly rolled the rest of its way stopping at Bigz size eleven 1/2 Air Max 95 tennis shoes. He reached down snatching the ball up just as Stupid Dude moved in lightning fast trying to swipe the ball away. He barely missed by an inch. Bigz began to dribble the ball making his way to the goal. He leaned in with his shoulder using straight body. Stupid Dude held his arms out wide blocking Bigz path. He used his chest as a wall. "Yeah, nigga where you going?", Stupid Dude taunted. They both dripped with sweat. Tired from the two previous games they'd already played. Bigz won the first Stupid Dude the second, playing the best out of three. The winner of this game won it all. A simple debate of who's the best baller turned friendly competition into a grand prize of five hundred dollars and bragging rights. Bigz bounced and drove. His shoulder crashed into Stupid Duds chest roughly.

Then he did a spin move going to the left. Stupid Dude stayed with him, pressing hard. Bigz held the ball in his right hand then looked to the goal like he was about to

attempt a shot. Stupid Dude fell for the bait.
He jumped high into the air trying to block a
shot that never would happen. Bigz pushed
the ball in between his legs doing a cross
move right before he sped past his friend.
Stupid Dude wanted to grab Bigz and stop
him but had to wait for gravity to put him
down. Bigz gave the ball one last bounce
then euro stepped. He floated in the air
easily laying the ball into the basket with the
right hand "for the camera!" he shouted with
his left hand holding the back of his head
like he was in a MJ commercial. "Game,
give me my money!" he said with his hand
out and a face full of accomplishment.
"Whooo! I'm tired as hell", Stupid Dude
held his hand out. His and Bigz fingers
interlocked doing their Blood shake. "Good
game" "good game" they walked over to the
picnic table that sat on the sideline of the
court.

They were on the 300 block of
Cumberland Courts. It was a small
neighborhood that was built like a maze.
One two- and three-bedroom apartments ran
through this four-block area. At the bottom
of Cumberland Courts sat the full basketball
court that was filled with trees and bushes.
There was a cul-de-sac that ran next to the
park. That was the only place you could

park a car, otherwise you had to park in someone's parking space, then walk to the playground. The duo grabbed their G star jeans off the table then put them on. Bigz tucked his Glock17 into his waistline. Stupid Dude did the same except he carried a G2 Taurus. Both pistols were nine-millimeter weapons. The brothers made their way through the grass walking to the cul-de-sac where they parked.

They opened the doors to an old school Chevy Impala. The flip flop paint changed from money green to a burnt orange under the sun's reflection. Brand new tires sat on 30-inch chrome rims that looked like giant blade. Bigz jumped into the front seat leaving one foot in the car and the other hanging out. Stupid Dude sat in the seat sideways, both feet hung outside the whip. He was very dark skin with 13 large, wicked dreads tied up into a tight bun. Barely any facial hair on his face except for a super lite mustache. He looked 13 or 14 but was the same age as Bigz. Both were under the command of Mad Max in the blood gang now that Justo was dead. And if Mad Max didn't make it everybody under him would have to flip which meant they would have to find another big homie. Bigz didn't like the idea of that because he already knew what it

was like to be under a fuck nigga. The type
of person that would make you do things
that they wouldn't do themselves. Bigz told
all the younger bloods that they would wait
and see what happens with Mad Max. Until
then he was their commanding officer.
Everybody that was 21 and younger was all
cool with Bigz taking the lead. He was
getting money; he was a thinker and most
important to young gangstas they knew he
wasn't a bitch. All the older bloods that fell
under Mad Max didn't feel Bigz being in
charge. They didn't like the idea of a 17-
year-old telling them what to do. So, they
flipped and got under someone else.

And that was fine by Bigz "it's a
young gangsta world anyway," he would tell
the younger bros. Plus none of the older
blood members had done anything about
Justo or Mad Max and the streets were
talking saying 800 was responsible.
"Straight bitch" Bigz said thinking about
those who betrayed Justo and Mad Max by
flipping. "Hey nigga where my money?"
Bigz checked his cell phone. He had
multiple notifications from FB, IG, and snap
chat. But none of that mattered today he and
Boolaid were supposed to be catching Omar
slipping and making him pay for what he
had done to Justo and Mad Max, the plan

was simple. Boolaid's bad bitches set Omar
up for a lunch date and when the time was
right Bigz would be there to crush Omar,
taking revenge for his fallen comrades. But
Boolaid hadn't sent any messages. "Come on
big homie tighten up", Bigz watched Stupid
Dude go into his jeans then pull out a wad of
cash. They sat in silence as he counted. The
total amount of cash he had was $675, "bruh
let me give you 250 now then give you 250
later", he asked with a silly a face.
"Ooooooo hell naw." Bigz laughed seeing
Stupid Dudes face. "Bro you should have
hella more bread than $675. I tossed you
three pounds of some fire tree there's no
reason why you skint. No, no bruh, hell
no." Bigz shook his head, becoming more
serious. "I still got gas nigga! I just gotta
make some plays." Bigz wasn't falling for no
sob stories. "Nigga shut up yo name Stupid
Dude for a reason."

    "Aite! I fucked the pack up," he
admitted. "But look tho! Let me give you
$250 and two zips of Zaza" Stupid Dude
asked with a big cheesy smile. Him being so
black made his teeth look extra white. Bigz
tried to be serious but couldn't, looking at
his friends' stupid face. He wanted to teach
him a lesson fucking up his money. Boolaid
and Justo taught Bigz that the hardest part

about the hustle was being able to hold on to the money once you made it. Saving money was an art, a skill that everyone couldn't do. At first saving money was difficult. Bigz fucked up a few packs. And Boolaid and Justo didn't cut him off, so he decided he should let his friend slide this time. They'd been friends since they were 12 years old. Stupid Dude was the first person Bigz met when he moved from Florida to North Carolina. "Aite Stupid, $250 and two ounces of za and it better be so official". Bigz climbed fully into the vehicle but left the door wide open. "Nigga what you mean better be some official. It's the same mild pack you fronted me, you need to give that shit back to your uncle". Stupid Dude joked. "Boy stop! You know I got that tight yow!" The brothers laughed until a bullet came flying through the left side windshield.

The bullet blew a gapping hole in the head rest where Stupid Dudes face would have been if he were sitting properly. Stupid Dude fell out the Chevy with a tuck and roll as bullets rained down all around him. When he stood to his feet, he had his G2 pointed at the car trying to kill him. He aimed and fired three rounds but didn't hit anything, he was too busy dodging fire balls that unknown men were sending. He had no choice but to take cover behind a large oak tree. Bark blew off the tree sending splinters everywhere. Bigz jumped out the whip then quickly moved to the rear of the Impala as bullets whizzed past his head. Other bullets hit the wide-open steel doors. He upped his Glock17 and blew smoke at the moving car. Two men hung out their car windows firing nonstop. Bigz saw that his attackers had large extended clips hanging out their weapons. They were easily out gunned. The Glock17 only held 17 in a standard clip while the G2 Taurus held 13. That was 30 rounds total between the friends. Whereas these guys had at least sixty or maybe more. One man fired from the passenger's front while the other unloaded from the back. The four men exchanged gun fire for only 90 seconds, but the gun battle seemed to slow everything down making one minute feel like an eternity. The men in the moving vehicle didn't stop shooting until they bent the corner and were gone just as fast as they'd come.

Bigz saw Stupid Dude posted behind a tree. They gave each other a head nod saying they were good. Then came out from their cover spots. "Got damn Bruh them niggas won't playing" Stupid Dude popped his clip out to check his ammo. "Four left".

He pushed the clip back in. "No doubt, I can't believe them niggas tried us like that." Bigz slid the clip back into his Glock, he had six bullets left. Bigz also recognized one of the shooters. Red was one of the people who jumped him at Keke's birthday party. Red was also Crip and from 800 block. Bigz and Red actually was cool at one time they went to the same middle school, introduced to each other by Stupid Dude. But over time Red chose his side over any friendship. Plus, rumor had it that Bigz was the one who killed Derrick. And mostly likely Red was only trying to even the score for his dead homie. Bigz couldn't do anything but respect it. That's what Red was supposed to do. Bigz just hoped them niggas continued to hold court in the streets when he made his move. Because Bigz was going for the checkmate.

"Boy them niggas was shooting some shit. If them niggas would have doubled back, they might have stretched something." Stupid Dude said excited his adrenaline still pumping. "Factz! Come on bro let's get up outta here before 12 show up, plus people starting to come outside". "Yo Bigz, Stupid," a voice shouted out Bigz and Stupid Dude looked to see who had called their names. "Tre Glockz what's good boy?" Stupid Dude yelled with his arms held in the air. Tre Glockz was the youngest little homie in their gang. Only 13 years old, all the bros loved him. He was the child that the whole village raised. He got the name Tre Glockz because the homies put three Glocks in his book bag one day when the police hit the block. And he held it down by not telling. The little boy rode a ten-speed bike but jumped off it and pointed past his bigger bros. "Look!" He shouted. Bigz and Stupid Dude saw it at the same time. The men who had just made an attempt on there lives were back for a round two. Bigz and Stupid Dude spread out with there poles aimed, firing, and taking cover.

****

Boolaid took a long hard pull from the blunt. Smoking a flavor called real right exotic. The smoke filled up his lungs. He tried to hold it in as long as he could before blowing out a large cloud. He became a little lightheaded and his eye lids became heavy. The room was quiet except for the off and on buzzing sound of 2x's tattoo gun made. Boolaid watched as 2x worked his magic with the small handheld motor. His canvas was a big fat ass of a stripper named Peaches. She laid flat on her stomach as he

finished the shading of his artwork. She
wanted her entire booty tatted into a giant
peach. And that's exactly what he did. From
left to right cheek he turned her behind into
a fruit. The part that amazed Boolaid so
much while he sat there high was that her fat
plump ass really looked like a peach. If she
was to spread, her ass cheeks apart it
actually looked like a peach split in half with
her pussy being the seed in the center.
Boolaid became hungry.

"Oucha" she howled as 2x ran the tatt gun
back and forth making that area darker in
color. "Girl stop all that jumping and shit
before I accidentally tatt that ass hole", he
joked looking at Boolaid with a face full of
mischief. "Here sis hit the blunt." Boolaid
put the blunt to her lips. She took a few
tokes then put her face back down into a
pillow. 2x had a license for tattooing and
piercings. He turned his living room into his
own personal shop. Two booths with
running water to keep the areas sanitized. A
booth for him and one for his little brother
LV, but he was out of town at a tattoo
convention. Everybody who was somebody
went to 2x for tatts. Justo told Boolaid that
2x was holding the last 40 kilo's and if
wanted them to just ask. At the time Boolaid

didn't think that was necessary, but now that Justo was dead and Mad Max still laid up in a coma. Everything had changed. He had almost a million dollars saved up but at what cost? His friends and family weren't worth losing no matter the amount of money. He had only wanted to make money and put his niggas on. He had no intention of jumping headfirst into the drug game. But at this point he felt he had no choice. Omar had forced his hand. And now Boolaid would take over what his best friend had started no matter what the outcome may be. *Life, death, prison it is what it is* he thought.

Justo had six employees, Boolaid didn't trust any of them but Bigz. Once Omar was out of the way he would put Bigz in charge of the operation. His phone rang. The caller's I.D was an unknown number. He was about to ignore it but got a strange feeling, so he answered anyway. "Yo" he said with the phone to his ear. The person on the other end began to speak. He listened as he smoked potent marijuana. "Aite I got you". He hung up then slid his cell into his *Palm Angels*. "Everything good?", 2x asked, seeing stress lines in Boolaid's forehead. "Yeah, everything's good. Just gotta run a few errands." Boolaid stood to his feet. "Check tho, my nigg Ima hit you in a couple hours so we can handle that business you feel me?" "I feel you" 2x held out an elbow Boolaid tapped elbow to elbow. "Peaches tell your sister I said, good look on the rental car hook up again." "OK bruh I got you. Remember she said you owe her a date". Peaches gritted her teeth from the pain. 2x shaded her ass with a 16-pointed needle. "Say no more" He got his Glock 21 off LV's work bench. Tucked it in his waistline then headed towards the door.

****

"Hell yeah, we slid on them dead ass niggas." Pie said with so much excitement he almost lost control of the steering wheel. Dead was a word they used when ever disrespecting someone claiming blood. "Pie shut the fuck up and drive cuz. We ain't do shit!" Blue said pissed off. "We ain't kill nobody, I didn't even see nobody drop." Pie just continued to drive without another word. He was from the west side and an 800 flunky. Older than Red and Blue, they only used him for a ride.

They were cousins who moved to North Carolina from New Jersey Red being down here the longest. Both boys repped Crip although not the same set. Red sixty's, Blue east side gator crip, EGC for short.

Blue was dark skin with a brush cut.
Everybody called him Blue became he had
dark blue eyes with specks of brown. "Man
fuck that cuz!" Red shouted out of nowhere.
He was fuming mad for not catching a body.
"Pie turn this bitch around." Red checked
his 30-round clip then slid it back into his
p80 Ruger. "But Red we-." "Go back nigga"
Red cut him off. Pie saw the seriousness in
Red's eyes and knew better than to protest.
He slowed the whip down then made a u
turn in the middle of the street then pressed
down on the gas. "This time we not leaving
until we slump something." Red looked into
the back seat. Blue gave his cousin a slight
head nod. Red was with Dice when they
drove by the gas station where Derrick and
Joe Joe had been killed, Drew also dead.
And the streets said Bigz did it all or had
something to do with it period. At this point
Red didn't care if the rumors were true or
not. That fact was Red didn't like Bigz
anyway. They all jumped Bigz at Keke's
birthday party. He should of just took that
ass whooping like a man. Why pull a gun?
And, for that reason Red felt like Bigz was a
straight bitch.

They had been cool not too long ago.
But now their gangs were at odds, and they
had to choose sides. And if it was up to Red,

he'd choose 800 every time. Plus, if Bigz did kill Red's homies that meant his team was up three. And was going to make sure this time he scored back. Pie brought the car to a slow creep preparing to turn back on to 300 block Cumberland Courts. "Ready" Red said. "Ready" Blue said with determination in his facial expression. He held his Glock pointed upwards ready to blast someone. They bent the corner immediately noticing the Chevy Impala with the doors still wide open. Their eyes alert searching the scene for there targets. They didn't have to look for long because Bigz stepped out from the rear end of the parked car aimed his pistol and started shooting. Stupid Dude did the same thing coming out from behind the oak tree. Bullets clunked against pies vehicle. One bullet went through the windshield making the entire window crack looked like a giant spiders Webb. "Stop the car!," Red cried out loudly as he ducked down trying his best not to get hit. Pie slammed down on the brake pedal. The car stopped coming to a screeching halt in the middle of the street. Red and Blue exited the car using their doors for protection. They aimed then fired. "Fuck it." Red stepped out into the open and began to walk down on his enemy while busting shots.

Unafraid of death Red emptied his clip
trying to kill. Bigz ducked low having to
take refuge behind the trunk of his car. Blue
jumped from behind his door firing, his gun
nonstop. Stupid Dude's left shoulder rocked
backwards. Blue shot him again making
Stupid Dude do the Harlem shake. Stupid let
off his on rounds refusing to lie down and
die without a fight but tripped on a thick tree
root sticking out of the ground. Stupid
missed his shots except for one. The bullet
ripped through Blues mid section. The force
from the bullet sat him on his ass right in the
middle of the street. "I'm hit" he yelled
holding his stomach while wrenching in
pain. Pie raced to the young boy's aide. Red
knew Blue was off to his left from the sound
of the cry. But he couldn't assist his cousin.
If he turned around, he might get shot in the
back. Something he wasn't willing to afford.
He kept his eye on the prize. "Stop hiding
you bitch ass nigga!," Red shouted as he
continued to pull the trigger over and over.
He walked down puncturing the old school
Chevy with bullets. Sparks went into the air;
he even flattened a couple tires. Red
taunting must have worked because Bigz
came out from behind the car with his pistol
pointed. He shot in Red's direction, bullets
whizzed by Reds face by mere inches. Red

didn't back down, he was determined. He
pulled the trigger and shot Bigz right
through the armpit. Bigz aimed his gun, but
it had de-cocked letting them both know
Bigz was out of ammo.

Red became blood thirsty. He shot again the
bullet entered the top of Bigz right thigh.
His whole body buckled making him fall to
the ground like a rock. "I got yo ass now
son." Red stood over top Bigz pointing the
gun directly at his face, there would be no
missing. He stared into Bigz eyes hoping to
catch a glimpse of fear but saw none. One
thing they both had in common were that
they were gangstas, street soldiers who
respected and honored a worthy death. "For
Drew and Derrick," Red pulled the trigger to
end Bigz life. "Click" the gun de-cocked
instead of blowing Bigz brains all over the
ground like Red expected. "What the
fuck?!" Red shouted furiously. Bigz looked
up from the ground with a weak smile.
"Red, cuz we gotta go, like right now!" Pie
shouted from the driver's seat. He had
already helped Blue into the back seat. He
laid stretched with one knee in the air. Red
looked around. Stupid Dude had his back
against the tree bleeding out. People were
peeping out their windows some even
coming outside. Police sirens screamed in

the distance. "Fuck man! This shit is far from over", Red told Bigz before racing off to his get away car. Pie hit the gas as soon as Red slammed the door shut. Bigz watched the vehicle disappear around the curve. "Big bro, oh shit big bro", Tre Glockz panicked when he saw his homies sprawled out blood everywhere. "Chill'out lil bruh, don't worry. Just get these gun outta here."

He moved into action. He picked up Bigz empty pistol, then ran over to Stupid Dude taking his gun as well. "If you run into twelve don't say nothing", Stupid Dude shouted as the thirteen-year-old fled the scene. "Duh Stupid". He yelled without looking back, he ran behind some apartments and was gone. Police cruisers ambulances and fire trucks swept the neighborhood from all directions. Bigz sat up to look at his friend. They both gave each other, *I'm good* nods. "Yeah, Red this shit is far from over."

Chapter 14

"I've located the girl. She is with a male". Uma spoke into the phone as he spied on Bea getting into a car with Boolaid at the wheel. He listened to the orders Taliban gave him very carefully. Then he hung up without another word. Rafiq had made it very clear he wanted Bea dead along with any associates. Taliban also informed Uma to make the move clean and quiet which meant no guns. And that was fine by him because Uma was Sayad. Sayad was a small group of men that were a part of the Shirac Cartel. Sayad was an Middle Eastern word that meant Hunter. The cartel called a member of Sayad when they needed someone found or killed and disposed of. Uma was responsible for over one hundred deaths. Most of them were due to leaders abusing their authorities or someone betraying the cartel as a whole. Ninety percent of the people killed end with decapitation. Uma sat in a Shell gas station parking lot looking through a pair of high-powered binoculars. He watched Bea exit the McDonalds then jump into the front seat of a cherry red challenger. The car pulled off but stopped at the exit with its left turning signal on. A convoy of police cars, fire trucks, and ambulances flew pass heading towards the Cumberland Courts projects. Once they passed, the challenger shot out making a left turn on to Summit Ave. The driver mashed down on to the gas pedal making the motor roar. The vehicle zoomed by the Shell gas station in a flash. Uma quickly ducked down in his seat as the couple went by. For a second, he actually thought his cover had been blown. The man driving seemed to stare straight at Uma before returning his attention back to the road. Uma waited 30 seconds then pulled out behind them, then began to follow.

****

"Hey" Bea said with a heavy sigh as she got into the car. She swung the seat belt over her chest then locked it in place with a light click. "Hey" Boolaid said watching her closely. He could tell she was exhausted by her sluggish body movements. She had called him 20 minutes ago and told him what had happened to her and Meme. She informed him that Meme was still in police custody, but they had let her go and she needed a ride. The police station was located on Maple Street. A place no street nigga ever wanted to be. She walked three blocks from Maple Street to the corner of Summit Ave, where the McDonalds and Cookout restaurants sat across from one another.

And that's where she'd told Boolaid to meet her. He cruised around the parking lot then stopped at the exit. A group of police cars, ambulances, and fire trucks began

spilling from side streets out into the main
road then made their way towards River
Walk and Cumberland Courts projects. Bea
sat up in her seat at the sounds of the loud
sirens and horns. Boolaid thought about
Bigz. They were supposed to link up today
so they could handle business and get Omar
out of the way once and for all. But due to
the girl's situation things might have just
changed. He snatched his phone out of the
cup holder then sent Bigz a text telling him
to call. Then looked both ways before
shooting out into traffic. He hit the gas
heading for the highway. Boolaid looked to
his right as he raced past a Shell gas station.

His eyes rested on a dark blue charger
and for a second, he thought he saw some
one ducking down trying not to be noticed
but he couldn't be for sure. *Nah, I'm just
trippin* he thought to himself. Putting his
eyes back on the road ahead. He made a
right turn on Textile which led to the
entrance of I-85 south highway. Boolaid
entered the expressway then punched the
gas. A few seconds later the dark blue
charger entered the highway and followed.
The couple rode in silence as they made
their way. Boolaid knew Bea's mind must
have been moving a mile a minute. Her best
friend was locked up for a man she only met

once. But on the token his best friend was dead due to drugs stolen by two women who were basically strangers. "Take me to the house", she broke the silence looking at him awkwardly. He couldn't tell if she wanted to cry or just scream at him. *Maybe both*, he thought. "I don't think that would be a good idea. Twelve probably waiting on you to do that", he said watching her and the road at the same time. She stared off into space thinking, but her mind wouldn't allow her to come up with a solution. "Well where should we go Boolaid? Because I'm tired and frustrated", she folded her arms; her chinky eyes made her look so vulnerable and innocent. She seemed so small and helpless to Boolaid. He wanted to be her strength, protect her, and keep her safe, it felt like it was his natural duty. "I've gotta go outta town tomorrow. So, let's just go to the duck off spot; get you some clothes and a hot shower then will figure everything else out as we go." Boolaid tried to comfort her. She agreed with a simple head nod. "How could there have been any eyewitness when we didn't see anybody in the parking lot?" Bea blurted out loud. "Don't know can't really say for sure." "We need to get my sister a lawyer asap. And not just any

lawyer, I mean a good one." She watched
Boolaid carefully.

"You already know the best money
can buy." They became quiet. Boolaid did
think it was a little odd that Meme had all of
a sudden been identified weeks after the
shooting and not within the first 48 hours.
When he was 17, he and Mad Max got
arrested for murder because of an
eyewitness. But the charges ended up being
dismissed when the eyewitness had a sudden
change of heart and refused to testify in
court. And he had been picked up by the
cops within days of the incident.

The couple had been driving a little
over twenty minutes. The sun was going
down and beginning to get dark. Boolaid
flicked on his right turning signal. Then
merged to the right into existing traffic of
the highway going into the city of
Kernersville. He looked into his rear-view
mirror and saw a dark blue charger. He
instantly thought about the charger at the
Shell gas station. The charger didn't exit, it
kept driving on down the highway. *I hate
feeling like I'm being followed*, he thought,
"are you alright?" Bea looked over her
shoulder out the back window but saw
nothing. She noticed him mean mugging the
rear-view mirror. "Yeah, I'm good." He

stopped at a stop sign, "just a bit paranoid with all that's going on." He made a left turn. "Ain't we all, ain't we all" Bea replied.

****

Uma made a U-turn going back in the opposite direction. He'd been driving around the area for the past three hours. The sun had set long ago and now it was completely dark outside. Uma didn't follow Boolaid when he turned off the Kernersville exit because he didn't want to risk the chance of his tail being made. And now the hunt was on. Uma loved it. The feeling of being alpha made him feel so much more superior than all of mankind. A supreme hunter in the wilderness, searching for its prey, and feigning for his next meal. Uma knew that his natural born killer instincts would guide him exactly where he needed to be. There was no place on earth his targets could hide once he caught a whiff of their senses. He tapped his foot on the brake bringing the car to a slow creep. His eyes grew wide with excitement as he passed a double wide trailer. There was a cherry red Challenger parked in the driveway. This has to be the place he said to himself. A perfect location for death, the nearest neighbor was at least a mile and a half down the road, Uma observed the lay of the land. Uma drove down the street forty more feet, then pulled over to the side of the road. He turned the car off and quickly but quietly stepped out into the night. He didn't have to shut his door completely, with him having the interior lights already disabled. The dark blue color of the vehicle made it near impossible to see in the night.

Plus, someone driving down this road was slim to none with it being the country. Uma took a moment to stretch and limber his well-built body. Standing at 6'3 220 pounds, bald headed, with a short but full beard. He lived most of his life in the Middle East whereas a young child he had to fight over scraps of food just to eat. His family was dirt poor. When he was seventeen, he joined the Shirac Cartel to be able to provide for his mother and baby sister. In just a couple years he advanced in the ranks. Killing was easy to him. Training how to fight hand to hand combat. He'd learned four different Martial arts techniques. The night air was cold and nipped on his dark brown skin. None of that bothered him because his blood pumped lava at the thought of putting in work. In all

black camouflage and military combat
boots, for the soul purpose of fighting and
running. Uma reached for his 1911 pistol,
then pulled it from its leg holster when he
heard a sudden movement. He slid it back in
place when he saw it was only a family of
deer racing through the wood line. Now it
was time for Uma to have a race of his own.
He stealthily made his way towards the
trailer in a light jog. Then stopped with his
back against the wall of the house.

   Just above his head was a window
with the lights on. He closed his eyes
listening, concentrating. Within the wall he
heard running water moving through the
house's pipeline. *Someone was taking a
shower probably the woman* he thought as
he moved around to the back of the house.
He made it to the back yard, where there
was a back patio porch with a glass sliding
door. Uma climbed the steps to the porch to
have a closer look. The glass door had long
white blinds that gently swayed from side to
side. He tried his best to peep inside. There
was a giant LG flat screen television
mounted on the wall. A music video with
two beautiful women dancing in bed as they
sang to each other played on the screen. The
surround sound stereo was loud feeling the
air with *Dojo Cat* and *Saweetie* lyrics. There

279

was a wrap around sofa with a lazy boy
recliner on each end. One of which was
occupied. It was the man Uma saw driving
the challenger. He was watching the
television and smoking a cigar. Uma knew it
was marijuana "hmmm", Uma laughed.
"Like taking candy from a baby" he said
with an evil smile. He went into his pocket
grabbing two small metal pieces in the
shapes of toothpicks with hooks on the end.
He slid the tools into the doors keyhole then
slowly worked his magic. "Click" the locked
popped, "open sesame!"

****

Boolaid and Bea had been in the
house for a few hours when they arrived.
She'd explained that she was physically and
emotionally drained. All she wanted to do at
this point was find something good to eat,
take a bath, and then go straight to sleep.
She went to the kitchen and found a quick
meal to cook. Spaghetti, corn on the cobb,
with garlic bread. Boolaid watched her
move around the kitchen with grace, making
him think of his Aunt Robin. That's where
he would take them in the morning. He'd
never brought a woman to Aunt Robin's

house before. He had nowhere else he could take her and would feel safe. She was a part of the team now. It was only right he thought. She brought him a plate, sitting it down in front of him. His mind drifted back to the night Justo died, then the very next morning the girl's cooked him breakfast. He became flaming hot at the thought of Omar living to see another day. He had to die for his actions. Bea sat at the table with her plate. Over the next thirty minutes the two discussed a lot. How they intended to handle Omar, finding Meme an attorney, and just getting to know each other. After all, they were really strangers to one another. But actually, they had a lot in common. They liked the same foods, music, even liked the same color. They really enjoyed the fact they were the same age, born in the same month only a couple days apart. His February14th and Her's the 16th.

After dinner, Bea washed the dishes then went to take a shower. Boolaid received two unexpected phone calls while Bea bathed. The first was from a young girl named Keke. He knew her as being Bigz girlfriend. She told him that Bigz and his home boy Stupid Dude had been shot in a drive by shooting. Bigz was hit twice, both bullets went in and out. And neither of them

was life threatening. But he was really lucky
to be alive with how the whole situation
went down. The doctor told her that he
should be able to go home in a matter of
days. "I'm on the way" Boolaid told her. But
she stopped him. "No! The police are all
over the place. Bigz told me to tell you not
to come up here. It's too hot he also said he
good and he loves you". "Tell lil bruh I love
him more", Keke disconnected the line. He
walked to the living room and sat down on
the lazy boy, even more stressed out. Bigz
had been shot and he wasn't there for his
younger bro. Boolaid grabbed the remote
control then hit the power button. The 80-
inch TV mounted on the wall came to life.
He channel surfed a while then stopped on
the Yo MTV music video channel, when his
phone rang for a second time. "Oh shit!"
Boolaid cussed out loud.
"Yo!" "What up nigga!" Kb came through
the line, "what's good bigger bro
?", Boolaid said to his mentor. "You already
know another day another bid." KB was still
in segregation but was back online with
another cell phone.
      "You got something you need to tell
me?" KB got straight to the point. "Why you
say that bigger bro?" Boolaid said now
rolling a 3.5 in a back wood. "Shit nigga I

282

know you that's why. Any time you call me bigger bro you hiding something. Plus, Memo haven't answered the phone one time in the last 24 hours and that's not like my baby. So let a nigga know what's up", KB demanded. Damn Boolaid hated being the bearer of bad news but he'd rather tell'm before anybody else.

KB had been out of the loop since being caught with the last cell phone. So, Boolaid gave him the whole rundown on the things that had happened within the last few months. Mad Max in a coma Justo getting killed at the club. And lastly Meme getting locked up for the murders. KB was devastated to hear such things coming out of Boolaid's mouth. But he knew the type of life they were involved in. If you played with fire long enough, you were bound to get burned sooner or later. "I'm sorry big bro. I messed up." "Nah nigga don't do that. I'm proud of you nigga. You came a long way in a short period of time. Never apologize for being solid, shit happens. Hold your head up never down. Stay ten toes down and stay sucka free. Because this is when you find out the boys from the men. Now find a solution," KB said before hanging up. That's why Boolaid fucked with KB like that he always knew what to say and never made excuses. "I will find a solution. Promise you that." Boolaid turned the surround sound up on the TV when he saw *Dojo Cat* and *Saweetie* all hugged up on the screen. "Damn Dojo! You fat as hell", Boolaid said. Lighting the blunt filled with real right exotic. He took a long strong pull that instantly made him relax. "Got damn Saweetie, that's my bestie", Boolaid said blowing out a dark grey cloud, mesmerized by the two super star females on TV.

Suddenly, he felt a cold breeze run across the back of his neck like somebody had opened a window letting a draft in. He looked to his left when the attack happened. Uma moved fast and swiftly trying to drive a ten-inch military hunter's knife through Boolaid's chest but missed by a nose hair. Boolaid rolled dodging the unknown man's strike. The knife plunged deep into the sofa. Boolaid snatched his Glock 21 off the table then raised it to shoot. But Uma moved lighting fast delivering a hard side kick to Boolaid's hand, sending the pistol airborne flying across the room. Boolaid and Uma locked eyes for the first time. *How in the fuck did I let this nigga sneak up on me?* Boolaid thought to himself, seeing the back door ajar. "Because I'm like that!," Uma smiled knowing exactly what Boolaid was

thinking. "Tonight, you die" Uma pointed.
Boolaid couldn't hear what his intruder said
because the music was so loud. He read the
man's lips though and he knew this was
about to be a fight to the death. Uma pulled
the knife out the head rest of the lazy boy.
He flipped the blade in his hand with the tip
pointed downwards.

He lunged in swinging the weapon
left to right then diagonal. Each attack he
attempted would have been life threatening
if he was successful. He hit Boolaid with the
katana blade; but Boolaid was agile on his
feet moving left, dodging right, and side-
stepping diagonally. Uma fell forward.
Boolaid stepped in with a super-fast punch,
catching Uma in the side of the head. He
charged Uma, grabbing the wrist that held
the Rambo knife. Both men fell hard and
fast on to the lazy boy in a struggle over the
weapon. The force from the two grown men
made the lazy boy love seat recline
backwards. Sending them flipping into the
air over the couch on to the floor. Uma lost
control of the knife and it landed in a corner
by the kitchen. Boolaid rolled to a stop on
his hands and knees. So did Uma, *who the
hell is this guy?* Uma thought to himself.
Yeah, nigga I'm like that, this time it was
Boolaid that smiled. They both raced to their

feet. Uma tried to do a round house kick on Boolaid aiming for the chin. Boolaid leaned back just as Uma's foot passed his face. Boolaid jumped into action with a super man punch.

The blow snapped Uma's head back, he lost balance and fell against the wall. Boolaid continued his assault with a series of punches elbows and knees. The mixed combinations were powerful. Uma was definitely caught by surprise by this man's relentlessness to survive. He blocked and ducked most of Boolaid's advances but the blows that did land flush were heavy and painful. Uma intercepted the next two punches then countered with a four-piece combo of his own. Boolaid bobbed and weaved the first three but the fourth was a direct hit to the nose. His eyes instantly filled with tears. Uma finished his combination with a kick to the stomach. Which sent Boolaid tumbling into the kitchen, his back slammed smack into the refrigerator. He fell to the floor. Boxes of cereal and bags of Lays chips rained down on him from the top of the fridge, where Bea had them neatly placed side by side.
Uma a true warrior, looked down at the man in the floor and saw himself. He

could have just ended Boolaid's life with his
1911 but where was the honor in that? When
two warriors had a battle there was a code
you must follow. Allow a man to die
standing on his feet like a man, and not die
on all four like a dog. Boolaid stared up at
Uma waiting for him to do what he had
come to do. But he just stood there waiting.
Uma shuffled his feet back and forth then
stopped in a fighting stance, challenging
Boolaid to another squabble. "The warrior's
code," Boolaid said to himself. He'd
witnessed the code a few times while doing
his tour in the military. If you ever came
across your enemy and a hand-to-hand
combat broke out, you fought to the death
with honor. You never killed your opponent
in a cowardly way. He got to his feet, they
were bare, BBQ chips crunched in between
his toes. He wore a pair of Nike shorts with
a white tank top. He wiped his nose with his
shirt, smearing it with blood he'd lost. The
two men got into fighting positions
preparing for round two. Uma stepped in
with a hard swing, it connected. Boolaid
followed up with his on lick. The two went
hard on one another shooting the fade. They
went toe to toe blow for blow. Wrecking the
entire kitchen. They fought each other like it

was a pay per view UFC championship
fight.

Chapter 15

Bea had taken an hour long hot
steamy shower. She always did when she
needed time to clear her mind. She and
Meme had basically spent every day of their
lives with each other for the past twelve

years and now her bestie was in jail. She felt all alone, just like she did all those years ago when her father died. She wiped the mist from the mirror to examine herself. Her hair was wet from washing it with VO5 shampoo and conditioner. Long, curly, jet-black hair fell past the shoulders. Water dripped from the tips then drizzled down in between her perky breasts. "You do have Boolaid, girl bye you barely even know that man", she said to herself. It was true. She didn't know him but that didn't stop the fact that when she was in his presence, she felt safe and secure. "What in the world?" Bea felt the floor rumble under her feet bringing her out of her thoughts. Then she felt it again, then another hard vibration like someone had tripped and fallen or dropped something really heavy. She thought about her 80-inch TV falling off its mount and got angry.

"Boy what are you doing?" She shouted. But her question went unanswered. Boolaid had the volume up too loud. *This nigga not bout to fuck my house up*. Bea grabbed her *Gucci* robe off the door hanger. She threw her arms in its sleeves, wrapped it tight around her body then tied the strap around her mid section. She reached under the sink where she kept a stack of neatly folded towels. She grabbed one, threw it over her head then stormed out of the bathroom. "This nigga got a bitch fucked up" she said as she marched down the hall into the living room drying her hair as she went. Walking right past Boolaid and Uma. "What in the world." Bea looked around the living room. It was a mess, the recliner looked to be broken in half and the coffee table turned over. She picked the remote up off of the floor then muted the TV. The room became deadly silent. "Boolaid why is my house all fu...", Bea stopped in her tracks turning around seeing Boolaid and an unknown man staring back at her. Both their chest heaved up and down, faces bloody and swollen. They looked like they'd been trying to tear each other apart. Bea wasn't easily shaken, but this guy put fear in her; something about his eyes said death. She looked into Boolaid's and saw the same death stare. They weren't just trying to fight each other off one another, they were trying to kill. The first one to die loses.

Everybody seemed to see it at the same time, the hunting knife on the floor. Boolaid shook his head telling her not to do whatever it was she was thinking. She didn't listen. She went for the knife as fast as her body allowed but Uma was faster kicking the knife away then yoking her up into a chokehold with one arm and then grabbing the 1911 from its leg holster with the other. He pressed the gun roughly up against the side of Bea's head. The moment Uma made his move Boolaid made a move of his own by picking up his Glock 21 that sat nearby on the floor. He pointed the pistol at Uma and Bea's direction. Uma tightened his already vice grip around Bea's neck, she choked struggling to fight for air. Boolaid became flaming hot. Bea looked afraid but ready to die at the same time. "Looks like we're evenly matched." Uma spoke with broken English. "Oh yeah?" Boolaid breathed in and out hard. "If we're evenly matched, then you might as well let her go. Then we can go our way and you go yours." Boolaid suggested, now holding his gun with two hands. "You know I can't let that happen", Uma confessed. Boolaid pulled the trigger. The glizzy fired with a loud roar. The man's head jolted backwards from the direct hit to the forehead then exited the back of his head, which exploded like a grenade. Chucks of meat mixed with blood sprayed the air in a huge mist of clouds.

****

The Muslim woman fell to her knees with a loud cry. Then she jumped back to her feet, racing past Boolaid down the hall and disappearing around the corner. Boolaid and Ranger Battalion Red had been sent on a side mission to apprehend a local terrorist by the name of Yusuf Iman. Intel had informed the squadron that Yusuf was hiding out in a run-down apartment high rise building. The squadron did a three-day stake out trying to figure out how to engage their target.

The building's high rise seemed to be overrun by the Taliban, African rebels, and Cartel members. Just walking through the front entrance was out of the question. Women and children lived in the building. So, capturing Yusuf would have to be strategic. Commanding Officer Captain McRaven saw that the building had a fire escape that stretched from the bottom all the way to the top of the structure. The mission's objective: climb the fire escape undetected then enter the building through a bedroom window once at the top. Halfway up the red squadron had been spotted by a Taliban member, who was keeping watch on the roof of the neighboring building. Trying to kill the entire group of America soldiers, the Middle Eastern man aimed his rocket launcher. Then fired an RPG rocket. The small missile flew through the air with a loud whistle. It crashed into the building instantly killing seven men and obliterating the wall making a hole the size of two cars. The gaping hole also separated Boolaid, Porta Rock, and Johnson from the rest of the team. They were right above the blast when it hit, the three of them at a point of no return; they had to finish the climb up just to get out by going back down within the death trap. Boolaid yelled down to Captain McRaven telling him that they would continue on to complete the mission and for the rest of the team to go back and wait for them at the bottom. The trio made it to the top unharmed. There was a bedroom window. Boolaid pushed upwards and it slid open with ease. They crept into the apartment, where they got into a stand off with a man who took his own wife as a hostage. The three soldiers backed the man out of the apartment into the hallway, where Boolaid took the kill shot dropping the Middle Eastern man dead. They searched up and down the hallways but didn't see a soul. The hallways were small, one way in, one way out; ten apartments on each floor. Five to the left, five to the right. They were at a dead end just finishing the last apartment.

"Nine more to go", Boolaid said to his comrades.

"Joe Papi, we need to split up to cover more ground", Porta Rock said to his brothers. "I second that motion let's find this guy and get the fuck outta here," Johnson joined in on the conversation. They waited on orders from their sergeant, Boolaid, he had the final say. He didn't like the idea of splitting up, but they were right. "Ok we split up." He agreed. Each man took up positions at their own door. Johnson held an open hand in the air then did a slow silent count down "three...two... ONE!" All three soldiers booted their doors wide open. Boolaid entered his apartment with his ARP held high and tight to the shoulder. It didn't take him long to find out he was alone. "Clear!" he shouted. "Clear!" "Clear!" He heard the others call. He stepped back out into the hallway taking position for the next kick door. He super kicked the one-bedroom apartment door inwards then went inside. Immediately he felt a strong presence inside. He walked through the kitchen into the living room which was practically the same room. He stopped and listened, when he heard gunfire, but not live; it sounded like someone was watching an action-packed movie. The bedroom door hung cracked open. Boolaid placed the palm of his hand in the middle of the door then pushed it open all the way. He crept into the room with his rifle aimed. Sitting on the bed was a young man with boyish features. He couldn't have been no more than seventeen.

His skin tone was high yellow, with dark brown hair that was very curly but matted down at the same time. His hair looked like the beginning stages of natural rasta dreads. His neck danced from ten diamond rope chains and bracelets that had red, blue, green, purple, and yellow rubies placed in between each link. And sitting beside him on the bed was a 24-karat gold AK47 with a hundred round drum. The shooting Boolaid heard was from the call of duty video game the boy was playing on his ps3. "Yusuf Iman, I need you to come with me," Boolaid said carefully. "I'm playing call of duty black ops and here you are the black ops." Yusuf smiled like he wasn't wanted by the United States government. His Middle Eastern accent was strong although his English punctuation was near perfect. Someone had definitely taught him the English language at an early age. "I'm not playing lil bruh, this ain't no game. These people want you dead or alive. Boolaid pointed the ARP at the boys chest."

Let me guess, they tell the world that I am a terrorist and that I am very dangerous?" Yusuf put the controller down. But you come to my country and bomb my family and friends from the sky with your airplanes. You kill my mother and my father with your drones," Yusuf spoke with fire on his tongue and hatred in his eyes. His smile replaced with a venomous snare. "You do not even know who you are. Do you? Mr black ops."Yusuf changed the subject. Boolaid didn't have time for all this black history shit. For a second, he thought about crushing the butt of his rifle upside Yusuf's head. But something wouldn't allow him to advance, it was like his feet were glued to the floor. "Who am I?", Boolaid asked. "You see," Yusuf smiled. "You are a black man, and the Black man is Asiatic. I'm a Middle Eastern man, and we Middle East are Asiatic as well. So, you see we are actually one in the same but yet you do all the white man's dirty work. And the white man is not Asiatic, Mr. black ops. He is the one responsible for killing millions of your people during slavery. And you still don't do anything for yourself but do everything he tells you". Yusuf stared Boolaid in the eyes. "Tell me Mr. black ops, how many white people have you killed?" Boolaid couldn't answer. "You sir would be the definition of a modern-day house nigga. Uncle Tom!" Yusuf meant every word. Boolaid stood there in shock. Blown away by the insights of this teenage boy. He'd never heard anybody talk like this before let alone a 17-year-old terrorist. It made him feel a certain type of way. "I'm not a fuckin Uncle Tom!", the only thing Boolaid could think to say.

"Only time will tell Mr. black ops." My name is Yusuf Iman. It means God increase faith, I had just finished my salat, my prayers, before you kicked my door in. Allah told me to send my soldiers away and not to fight today but have faith in him and him alone. So, whatever it is you've come to do then just do it. Because I will not resist, no matter what choice you decide Mr. black ops." Yusuf picked his controller up and began playing the video game. "My name is not black ops. It's Bulak and it means the loyal one", Boolaid said then started to back outta the room. "Well, Bulak ish Allah we'll meet again one day." Yusuf said, just as Boolaid shut the room's door. He turned around a moment before Johnson and Porta Rock entered the living room, guns aimed. "Everything ok Sergeant? Thought I heard someone talking", Johnson said. "Jeah Papi, who ju talking too?" Porta Rock asked.

Boolaid held his hand palm down telling them to lower their weapons. "Everything's all good fellas just a kid in there playing a video game this room is clear!"

Boolaid! Boolaid! Put the gun down, it's over baby", Bea said repeatedly. Snapping him back to reality and out of the shell-shocking episode he'd just had. Boolaid blankly stared down on Uma's slumped body with his pistol still pointed. He hadn't even realized that he almost emptied his entire clip into the man. "It's ok baby", Bea spoke softly, hands held outwards. She moved slowly not knowing if Boolaid might make her the next victim. She laid a hand on his shoulder while gently lowering his hand that held the pistol with her other hand. Bea grabbed the gun by its barrel. She had to tug it a few times before he let the gun go free. She laid it on the floor. "Boolaid! Baby?" Bea held his face with both hands making him look her directly into the eyes. Boolaid was so young and had witnessed so much death while stationed in the Middle East. Once back in the States the military had him see a psychiatrist. He was diagnosed with PTSD and prescribed medication that he couldn't even pronounce. He never took them thinking they wouldn't help anyway. But what he didn't know was without his meds, certain things could trigger him to go shellshock sending him back into the past.

Killing Uma was a for sure trigger putting him into a time machine. Sending him to no man's land. He hadn't fired a weapon in four years, let alone killed someone. This wasn't Boolaid's first episode. He had a few while doing time in prison. No one knew this but him and KB, who was able to bring him back every time. But tonight, it was Bea. "You, ok?" Boolaid finally came back. "You saved my life", Bea said embracing him with a hug. He held her back tight. "Thank you," she talked into his chest, thankful to be alive. Boolaid looked down at the dead man on the floor, not just any dead man this was a trained assassin. Their situation had gone from worst to straight shit. Whoever Bea and Meme had stolen the kilos from wasn't playing and weren't going to stop until everyone was dead. "Whose name is this spot in?" "Meme's momma." "Damn, if she wasn't in a hot spot then she's about to be now. Call her and tell her to get over here now, give no details of our situation, the less she knows the better. We need to grab all your belongings outta here. And tell her not to call twelve until tomorrow morning. Now put some clothes on and we gotta get to work." Bea didn't hesitate.

Chapter 16

The sky was dark and gloomy even though it was in the middle of the day. Nasty looking gray clouds, heavy with rain that had not yet started to fall, whirled around with rumbles of thunder and flashes of lightning. All was quiet except for a large crow cawing in a tree just above an unmarked grave. The dirt was still fresh like someone had just shoveled loose soil over into the hole. All of a sudden, a hand erupted from out of the dirt mound making the crow scared, and it flew away. Slowly but surely the man under the earth clawed his way to the surface. "Eeeeeyyy...Ahhh," Mad Max cried a death screech. Then gasped for air with only the top half of his body pushed above ground. He looked around wide eyed, taking in the scenery as he controlled his breathing. In a rushed panic he began digging his legs out of his grave, then finally stood to his feet once he was done. Mad Max stared down at the blank tombstone. Writing began to appear right before his eyes. When the writing stopped, it read here lays Jason Bryant may he rest in hell.

Mad Max looked around at the hundreds of other tombstones and instantly knew he was standing in the middle of Maplewood cemetery. This was the final resting place of his mother and many other family members. Maplewood was also a Veteran's cemetery. Many of the people buried in this cemetery died violent deaths for fighting in the Vietnam war.

Black people that died at war, who couldn't afford their own funeral would be buried here for free. Mad Max had a great great great grandfather out there somewhere. "Who knew?", Mad Max asked staring at the hole he'd just been birthed from. He had been blessed with a curse because he'd had this same dream as a little boy to a grown man, what seemed like countless times. It would be a little different each time but to Mad Max they were all the same. These were no dreams but premonitions that would come to him. They usually meant that somebody he knew was going to die or that he was going to kill someone. Mad Max felt a cold death chill run up his spine, he shivered. Someone or something stood behind him, breathing down his neck. He slowly turned around to face it. Mad Max stared upwards at a seven-foot-tall demon wearing an all-black raincoat with a pointed hoodie. So blacked out he couldn't make out its face, but only could see the red demonic glow he knew were its eyes. Decaying flesh fell from its hands as it held on to a giant scythe with a razor's edge. "New outfit?", Mad Max said with a smile talking to who he knew as the Grim Reaper. He admired the hoodie because it had *Gucci* prints embedded all over. He and the angel of death had become very acquainted over the past two decades. The reaper had been using Mad Max as a vessel to do the devil's bidding.

The Grim Reaper pointed past Mad Max's head, flesh dangled from the tip of its finger exposing bone and gristle. Mad Max turned to see what the demon was pointing at. And just like that Mad Max no longer stood in the cemetery but in-between two houses. He slowly peeped out into the front of both houses. To his left he saw three men in the front yard, two were standing on the porch and one of those two was sitting on the porch's rail. The third man stood at the bottom of the steps talking up to his friends. Mad Max dipped back in between the houses with his back against the wall. He reached down to his waist fumbling for his pistol, but it was nowhere to be found. "Where my pole at nigga?" Mad Max questioned his demon friend who still stood behind him watching. The reaper pointed to the ground. Mad Max looked. There was a pile of freshly dug dirt that hadn't been there just a second ago. Mad Max fell to his knees and began to dig deep into the earth. Finally, his hands touched something hard. He brushed away at the dirt, discovering a pistol. He grabbed the black and tan F&N pistol by its handle. The gun was grimy and wet with blood and maggots crawling all over the weapon and his hand. He popped the clip of the gun to check his bullet count. "Three bullets? Really Bruh?" Mad Max looked up to death in disbelief.

Although Mad Max couldn't see beyond the darkness of the *Gucci* hood, he could still feel that sinister smile within the abyss. "Fuck it," he shrugged his shoulders nonchalantly. He then walked out into the front of the house with the gun aimed. KALAA! He fired the first shot shooting the man at the bottom of the steps in the side of his head, knocking a crater into his skull. He dropped dead never seeing it coming. Next, he swung his arm aiming at the two men on the porch. KALAA! He fired the second shot. The 7.5 exploded outta the barrel doing flips and cartwheels hitting the man sitting on the rail in the chest, stopping his heart instantly. He fell backwards off the porch, his neck breaking with a loud crunch once hitting the ground. "Last one gotta make it count," Mad Max told himself. He took the gun with both hands aiming at the last man. He stared the man straight in the face but couldn't make out what he looked like, everything was a blur at that moment. KALAA! He fired the third and final round but missed. The bullet hit the house right above the man's head sending pieces of the house everywhere. "Fuck!", Mad Max yelled turning on his heels running away. He raced back in between the houses then sprinted into the backyard. Then he heard the rapid fire of a pistol going off. Boom! Boom! Boom!, ahh!" Mad Max shouted falling to the ground with a bounce and in excruciating pain. He tried to get up and flee but was struck by another blazing shell.

He collapsed into the grass face down. He tried to get up a third time but found that he couldn't move his legs. "Turn yo bitch ass over." The man said kicking Max in the ribs. He slowly flipped over onto his back to face his accuser. Omar stood over top Mad Max with the same bloody F&N. Somehow, he now owned the weapon. Omar put the barrel of the gun to Mad Max's forehead. A couple maggots danced their way down the gun and fell on to his face. "Why?" Max asked, looking Omar in his bug eyes. "Nigga! Why not?" Omar pulled the trigger. Mad Max saw a bright flash then everything went dark. He jolted out of his sleep sitting up in his hospital bed. He stared off into space catching his breath and gathering his thoughts. "Oh shit!" He jumped when he looked to his left, seeing someone seated next to his bed. "I didn't even see you sitting there Bruh." Max smiled at Justo. "What's good, baby brother?" Justo spoke, the room was dark except for the light shining from the crack of the bathroom door. Max got outta bed and met his brother with a warm heartfelt hug. "Bro niggas hit the house hard, I think they might of being trying to rob the trap but..., I already know little bruh everything gonna be aite. You can tell me all about it when we go home. We been waiting on you for a minute," Justo cut his brother off mid sentence. "We?", Max asked with a confused look. The toilet flushed in the bathroom. "Who dat Toya?" Max asked, looking past Justo.

Justo said nothing, just smiled. The bathroom door swung open. Mad Max fell to his knees with tears of disbelief. "My son", his mother said with her hand held out to him she wore an all-white gown, and her body had a gold aura. He was afraid to take her hand. "This can't be real." "It's ok son" she said, gently taking his hand into hers helping him to his feet. "Momma!" He squeezed her tight to his body and she felt extra soft and warm to the touch. Justo got out of his chair to join them. The family of three held each other for a long silent moment. "Ok son, are you ready because we've come to take you home," his mother said. "Home? What is ma taking bout?" He looked at Justo, "we've been waiting on you for a while and now that you're ready me and momma have come to take you home." Justo gestured to Mad Max to look behind him.

"What the..." Mad Max said, seeing himself laying in the hospital bed. I.V's sticking in his arms, tubes ran into his mouth and nostrils. One of his wrists was cuffed to the rail of the bed. Machines and monitors beeped and hummed. At that moment he knew Justo was dead and Omar was the one who he would kill. "Who did it? O? Who killed you bruh?" Mad Max shed tears of anger. "None of that matters anymore Jason. You have a chance to come with me and mommy." Justo happily smiled. "Nah fuck that! Ima not going nowhere. Not until I put that work in on that hoe ass nigga. I need more time send me back," Mad Max demanded. "I can't lil Bruh," Justo looked concerned. "Momma?" Max's face softened. "Ma, I love you and want nothing more than to be with you and Justin. But I can't. Send me back momma." Tears fell down her face as she smiled sadly. "Always remember

your mother loves you more than life itself. I
respect your decision." She pointed a finger.
The tip began to glow, and within an instant
the room was filled with light so bright and
powerful. Mad Max shielded his eyes with
his forearm. Then just like that, darkness.
The only noises that could be heard were
beeps and vibrations of the machines at
work. Mad Max slowly blinked open his
eyes. At first everything was blurry. He sat
in bed blinking a full ten minutes before his
vision adjusted to the dim light coming from
the bathroom. They were blood shot red
from not seeing in over two months.
He raised the right arm, but it snagged due
to being cuffed to the rail. Using the free
hand, he felt around touching tubes and IVs
protruding from his arms and face. Monitors
began to beep singing faster and faster due
to his elevating heart rate. In a panicked rage
he yanked a long tube from outta his nose.
Then did the same with the one in his
mouth. The IVs were the last things to go.
His body bled all over. The machines were
going crazy. He detached the machine
monitoring his heart, it made a loud flat
lining noise. Doctor Allen and a gang of
nurses raced into the room. They rushed the
bed from all sides trying to restrain Mad
Max. "Calm down young man, you're Ok!",

the doctor spoke but Mad Max was being a lunatic. "Gram of fent" Doctor Allen shouted. Not even 20 seconds later a nurse was handing him a syringe filled with liquid. The doctor pushed the needle into Mad Max's neck. His eyes immediately began to flutter then rolled to the back of his head. His body relaxed then the fighting stopped. "Wheeeew! That was a handful. Somebody get Detective Ford on the phone and tell'm Jason Bryant is awake." "Yes Doctor," a nurse said leaving in a flash.

****

Meme had been transported to Greensboro's Guilford County jail located on Edgeworth Street, the heart of the city. She arrived around 5:40 pm after sitting at Maple Street police station for over 24 hours. Now it was somewhere between 2:30 or 3:00 o'clock in the morning, she really couldn't be sure. All she did know was that a correctional officer made their rounds looking in on inmates cells every forty-five minutes. She tried to keep up but lost count over an hour ago. Her body was stressed and super tired. But her mind wide awake, making it nearly impossible to sleep. She lay in her small single cell staring at the ceiling. Her back ached from hours of laying on a steel slab with an extra thin mat that felt like it had no cushion at all. They'd allowed her to make one phone call. She tried Bea but got no answer. She wouldn't dare call her mother knowing her phone call would be recorded. Her life had gone from low to soaring high. Just to hit rock bottom again. She hated not knowing what was going on in the streets. People were trying to kill her and Bea. And now she couldn't even protect her bestie if she wanted to.

Her eyes began to swell with tears. She fought them back with a couple strong sniffs but the thought of losing her freedom for the rest of her life made them drop anyway. Meme heard her cell door unlock with a loud clunk. She quickly sat up whipping away her tears with the sleeve of her orange jump suit. A man wearing a tan and brown sheriff's department uniform stepped into the cell. On the corner of his sleeves were three stripes, letting Meme know he was a sergeant and not a regular officer. "Sssssshhh!" He put his finger to his lips. He reached into his pocket and took out an iPhone. He scrolled through his contacts then hit the face time button. He gave her the phone with a pair of air pods. *What the hell?* She thought, taking the phone, looking at the sergeant unsure. "You've got one hour and don't be loud". He told her before leaving, shutting the cell on his way. It automatically locked. Meme watched the screen waiting for a face to appear. *Who could this be,* she thought. She didn't recognize the number. It seemed like forever before the call was finally answered. It took everything in Meme's whole mind, body, and soul not to scream with joy. "Hey bae!", KB said with a big Kool-Aid smile. She tried to speak back but no words would escape. Instead, she covered her mouth and began to cry. Her emotions were at an all-time high.

"Ssshhh! Baby stop crying. Everything's gonna be alright," he told her in a loving tone. "I know it's overwhelming baby, but I'm here to tell you it's not like it seems. Them people gonna make you think it's over but baby it's never over believe that", KB comforted his woman. Meme nodded her head with understanding as she got herself together. "Listen though baby we don't have long. I talked to Boolaid. He and Bea are together, and they are fine. First thing in the morning they gonna holla at a lawyer then hit the streets and see what they can dig up on the witness. I know this is the last thing you wanna hear, but baby you gonna have to sit in that hell hole until they get everything under control. And whatever you do don't talk to anyone about your case. No one can be trusted." "Ok baby", Meme finally said pulling herself together. "I missss youuuu!", she whined like a baby, "I miss you more." "Bae who was that man that brought me this phone?" "My cousin, anytime you need to relay a message just tell him and I'll make sure Bea gets it. He'll let you use the phone every chance he gets but don't get used to it", KB informed her. "Ok daddy," Meme said lust filling her eyes. "Damn baby, why you looking like that?" He smiled. She posted the phone up on a small steel desk mounted to the wall right beside the bed. KB could see her entire body.

She stood in front of the camera and let her jump suit fall to the floor. KB admired her thick chocolate body. That ass was so fat, shaped like a pumpkin, and big titties to match. He couldn't help but lick his lips hungrily. Meme seductively climbed into bed. She spread her legs wide open giving him a clear eye view of her pussy. She spread her pussy lips apart and started to rub her clit. Her insides were bright pink. "Damn Meme, you so sexy". "Boy shut up and let me see that dick," she demanded pushing two fingers into her wetness and moaning. KB grabbed his jar of petroleum jelly then put that dick all in the camera, so Meme and he could fantasize about fucking each other. "Girl you better stop play'n, you know I'm a jack of all trades."

Chapter 17

Boolaid unlocked the front door then walked into the house. Bea followed close behind with a handbag and rolling suitcase in tow. "Front door," the alarm system said before starting its sixty second count down. He quickly moved through the hallway into the living room so he could punch in the alarm's security code on the keypad mounted on the wall. "Disarmed, ready to arm," the system said once Boolaid typed in its pass code. It was a little bit past five am, the two had been working all night trying to move all Bea's belongings that would be obvious to the police. He couldn't think of any other place to go. Aunt Robin's house was a safe location. Plus, she was out of town visiting a sick friend and he didn't expect her to return for another day or two. Aunt Robin lived in a three-bedroom house on Webb Ave in Burlington, North Carolina. Bea looked around taking in the scenery. "This is a really nice house," she said turning her attention to a wall with a collage of photographs. "Awww look at baby Boolaid," she laughed pointing at a picture of a five-year-old Bulak wearing a suit with a red bow tie. "Yeah, that's kindergarten me. Don't look like that I bet you got some big head baby Bea pics somewhere", he smirked. Bea nodded her head but said nothing. The truth of the matter was her father was a pimp and he never put her in school. She was street smart literally. "Who is this your sister?" She changed the subject.

"Yeah, that's me." He stood beside Bea and looked at the wall. "And that's my baby sister, but she died when I was three." "Oh! I'm sorry. I didn't mean to...", she paused looking at the picture with two babies laying on their backs side by side. Boolaid was wearing a blue onesie and his sister wearing a pink one. "And that's my Aunt Robin, she's the one that raised me." He pointed to a photo of a pretty brown skinned older lady. "That lady right there is my mother, but she also passed away when I was young. I don't really even remember her either". Boolaid admitted. "Oh," was all Bea could think of saying. It surprised her to find out how much loss he'd been through as a child. Like Bea, he didn't know his mother. Bea stared at the picture of Boolaid's mother. She was a younger version of Aunt Robin but more vibrant and so beautiful. Bea began to feel butterflies staring at the picture, it was like the woman on the wall was alive staring a hole through Bea. "Well, come on I'ma give you a little tour of the house," he told Bea snapping her out of her daydream. They smiled at one another. Boolaid grabbed her suitcase by its handle, she followed him. They stopped at the first room in the hallway. "This is the Queen's humble abode", he said allowing Bea to peep in. The first thing she saw was a giant king size bed filled with jumbo pillows.

The bed had four long pillars that had swirl designs on the tips. The theme color in the room was red, gold, and silver. *Fit for a queen,* Bea thought to herself. "And if you'll follow me this way," Boolaid continued on down the hall after shutting Aunt Robin's door.

They stopped at the next room. "And of course, the prince's room," he said coolly. "Yes, I can tell." Bea looked in on what had been the teenage Boolaid's room. There were posters on the wall. 2pac, Kimbo Slice, and Mike Tyson. And to no surprise a ps5 game system hooked up to a 47-inch flat screen TV. His covers and curtains were black and cream in color. "Aite," he said with a hand clap. "You'll be staying in here." He walked directly across the hall. "This is our guest room, but no doubt fit for a Princess." Boolaid led her into the room. Make yourself at home. He tossed her suitcase onto the bed. "Thank you," she sighed finally feeling relaxed after going through so much in such little time. "No prob, I'm sure you woulda done the same for me. But look though a brother is hungry so what I'ma do is cook us some quick breakfast while you get yourself together." "You cook? I gotta see this," Bea laughed at the thought of Boolaid burning the house down. "Girl bye you must not know who I is", Boolaid bolstered before leaving Bea in the room alone.

"It's beautiful", Bea said taking in the room. It was an exact duplicate of Aunt Robin's room except the colors were royal purple with trims of gold and silver. Purple was Bea's favorite color. She walked over to the nightstand then to a huge dresser where there was a mirror cut with three angles. "You can do this", she spoke to her own reflection. If they were going to make it through this situation, she was going to have to be strong. For her and for Meme. She opened a dresser drawer and saw that it was empty. She unzipped her suitcase and began to unpack the neatly folded clothes. Once she was finished, she made her way to the kitchen. "Damn I'm hungry", her stomach growled from the smell of well-seasoned ribeye steaks Boolaid had cooking on a George Foreman grill. He stood in front of the stove whisking his hand back and forth with a fork scrambling eggs in a bowl with cheese, a little salt and pepper, plus a spoon full of milk that helped make the eggs nice

and fluffy. He poured the eggs into an
already hot skillet with melted butter. Bea
stood next to him and watched. The eggs
instantly started to bubble and sizzle. He
slowly worked the fork until the eggs
became whole, fluffy, and extra cheesy.
"OK, you might know a little something."
Bea smiled, measuring a small amount with
the thumb and pointer finger. "Chef
Boyardee," Boolaid said. They shared a
laugh. He moved from the stove to the
kitchen table with frying pan in hand.

There were two plates waiting with
bagels. Taking his time Boolaid evenly
spread the cheesy eggs across the bagels.
Then he topped the sandwiches off with the
steaks. After tossing the pan in the sink he
poured them two ice cold cups of Bright &
Early apple juice. "Finally", he said sitting
down at the table, Bea joined him. "Steak
egg and cheese bagels, I'm impressed", Bea
said with approval at the site of the meal. "If
you think it looks good wait till you taste
that bitch", he assured her taking a giant
bite. "Hmmm!" Bea melted in her seat
taking a small bite. The flavors were perfect
to her taste buds. "Thank you for saving my
life, Boolaid." Bea covered her mouth while
she chewed. "Shit girl, you saved my ass
walking into the room when you did. That

nigga was pumping me drunk for real for real," he joked although he was serious. Bea laughed with a blush then rolled her eyes. The pair finished eating in no time. Boolaid grabbed their plates then took them to the sink. He turned on the faucet to prepare sink water to wash the dishes. "No let me do that! You go take a shower you look whooped", Bea said jumping to her feet to help. He wanted to object but knew he had no wins. "Good look", he sighed then left. Moments later he returned with a towel and wash rag. He sat them in a kitchen chair, "for you." "Thanks," She slightly smiled.

He made it to the bathroom then closed the door and dropped his clothes to the floor. He turned on the shower and jumped in without letting the water heat up. He liked the feeling that cold water gave him. The icy drops hit his skin making all the muscles in his body tense up.

It gave him a sense of being alive. Boolaid thought about his next move as the water became hot, turning his body temperature from cold to steamy. The people that Omar was fucking with were serious and were not to be taken lightly. It was going to take some real strategic planning to get close enough to kill him. Because nine times out of ten he would be

protected by some real hitters. "Damn I miss
my dawg", Boolaid said thinking about
Justo's body laid up in that casket, as he
allowed hot water to rain down over his
head. "And Max, you need to tighten up for
me one time and pull through. I need you
boy", he said soaping up his rag to wash his
body. Boolaid needed to run some errands
and catch up with a couple people like his
young boy Bigz and holla at his gun connect
to buy a new pistol. He left the Glock 21
back at the trailer. But first, he needed to
rest his body for a few hours. He rinsed off
one last time then got out the tub. He
grabbed a towel, dried off, then wrapped the
towel around his body. He stepped out into
the hallway, steam escaped with him as he
made his way through the house.

He stopped in the living room when
he found Bea sitting on the couch. She'd
been patiently waiting her turn holding her
towel wash rag and Olay body wash. They
stared at each other. Bea became shy when
she was always the turned up one. Boolaid
being bashful, "all yours", he told her then
continued his journey to his room. He closed
the door, went to the dresser grabbed a pair
of boxer briefs and polo sweatpants and got
dressed then climbed into bed, closing his
eyes once he hit the pillow. He heard Bea

start the shower. He listened to the constant sound of the water running then started to nod off. He popped open his eyes hearing his door creep open. Bea was standing in the doorway. She had changed her clothes to a pair of balling shorts and a fitted white T. Boolaid hadn't realized he'd been sleep over an hour; he never heard the shower stop. She looked so innocent standing there, but he knew better because at times she could be on straight demon time. "No Bea!" Boolaid said with his face in the pillow. Her innocence turned into a face full of mischief. But the truth was she just didn't want to be alone. She needed a real friend, getting some dick was the furthest thing in her mind, but Boolaid wasn't buying it. *This bitch definitely want some wood,* he thought.

"Ugh! I promise to behave with yo scary self." She rolled her eyes with her arms folded. "Com'on worrisome", Boolaid called from under the cover. Bea smiled with excitement and jumped onto the bed stepping over him. She slid under the covers snuggling up against his back. Then wrapped her arm around his waist taking his hand into hers. Their fingers interlocked. The mixture of Irish spring soap and Olay body wash filled their nose's. She laid her head on his back and closed her eyes in a comfort she'd never felt before. Boolaid was different. She never felt so connected to anyone in her life and it scared the shit out of her. Was she losing her touch? Because over the past 13 years it was men she distrusted, despised, and used only for financial gain. But now she relied on him a man! They laid in silence and warmth. Their breathing became even, their heart's beating together as one drum. Soon after their bodies relaxed. All became quiet, they were sound asleep. "Front door!" Bea opened her eyes when she heard the alarm system speak. She was alone in the bed. *That was either Boolaid coming or leaving,* she thought sleepily.

She climbed outta bed marching into the hallway still drowsy. Her feet stomped on the hard wood floor with every step. "Boolaid hold up..." Bea said in a rush trying to catch him before he left. But it wasn't Boolaid in the doorway.

"Aunt Robin?" Bea said to the pretty old lady, stopping her in her tracks. "Rochelle?" Aunt Robin said in a state of shock like she'd just seen a ghost. "It can't be." She said in disbelief her eyes rolled before passing out in the hallway. Bea raced to her aide in a panic.

****

Detective Ford watched the
paramedics hoist the gurney with Uma's
lifeless body into the back of the ambulance.
He'd been called to the scene after a 911
response team reported a homicide. A
woman had shot and killed an intruder
trying to brake into her home. "Why am I
not surprised?" Ford mumbled to himself
after seeing who the victim was. "Ms.
Hightower this is our second encounter
within the last sixty days. I don't know what
kind of trouble you're in or who it is you
might be trying to protect. But I can't help
you if you do give me anything", he said
with all sincerity. "Help me with what? I
already told you what happened here",
Olivia inhaled her cigarette deeply then blew
out the smoke. "Com'on Ms Hightower.
That was a dead Arab man in your living
room," he pointed at the ambulance just
before the truck pulled away from the curb.
Ford didn't want his left hand knowing what
the right was thinking but he was desperate
for answers, so he had to try something.
"Just like the dead Arabs found by your car
at that night club. Now there's a lot of
craziness going on all around you". He
pointed at her. "And none of it is just a

coincidence, now tell me what's really going on". He piped up praying he would get somewhere with her. "Look detective. All I know is someone tried to break into my home, probably trying to steal my TV to buy some crack as far as I care. But none of that matters because I shot his ass", Olivia said blowing out smoke. Then flicked the butt over into the grass. "You gotta be kidding me", he chuckled like he'd just heard a funny joke. Olivia smiled. "So you're telling me a 5'3 138-pound woman overpowered a 6'3 220-pound all muscle man and shot him with his own Glock 21, while he carried a 1911 on a leg holster?" Ford asked looking at her with the bitch you better not lie face. "Detective, that's exactly what I am telling you." "GOT DAMN IT!" He shouted out of frustration with his hands on his hips. Detective Ford's phone vibrated. "Don't go anywhere", he told Olivia then walked out into the street to check the text.

Jason Bryant has been transported from hospital to Maple Street for questioning.

"We're done here", he told Olivia then headed to his car without another word. Olivia held a silly smirk on her face as he fled. Ford thought about calling his partner but decided against it. Mcdon had just been on the crime scene with Ford but made up some lame excuse as to why he needed to leave. McDon was most definitely up to something, and Ford intended to find out what it was. But first he had a murder investigation he needed to solve. He put the car into drive then headed towards the station.

It took just a little over 45 minutes for him to make it to Maple Street. The detective made his way through the maze-like office. While other detectives made phone calls trying to find clues to solve their cases. They eyed Ford behind their desk. He already knew what they were thinking. *Thank God they didn't have his case*. Too many people dying and not enough arrest being made. "Go get'm James", one detective encouraged. Ford gave his co-worker a slight head nod right before walking into the interrogation room and shutting the door behind him. "Mr Bryant my name is Detective James Ford and I first want to start by personally giving you my condolences for your loss", Ford said to Mad Max trying to break the ice. Mad Max sat in a soft cushion office chair on wheels pulled up to the steel table. His head hung low making his thick bushy rude boy dreads fall over his face hiding his facial expression. With Max being in a coma, it caused Max to lose over twenty pounds of body weight. He appeared to be small and fragile. Both his hands sat flat down on the table. He wore a white tank top. His body was wrapped and taped with medical bandages covering the multiple spots where he'd been shot. "What loss?" Mad Max spoke in a low raspy tone. Ford heard him speak but didn't see his lips move. It seemed like there was some unseen force in the room playing as a ventriloquist using Mad Max as a dummy. Ford couldn't help looking over Mad Max's shoulder knowing nothing was there. But he still felt an unwelcome presence. "Uhmm, Mr. Bryant you do know your brother Justo was murdered while you were away from us". Ford tried his best not to upset Max even though he knew Mad Max had already been informed about his brother's death. Denial wasn't uncommon in these types of situations. *Or maybe it's the medication they're giving him*, Ford thought. "My Brother....is... alive and well I assure you", Mad Max said without moving his body an inch. "Oookay then!" Ford said out loud. He wasn't about to press the man about Justo's death. He'd been in a coma when it happened so it would be impossible for him to know anything about it. "Mr Bryant! I need you too tell me what happened the night you were attacked and almost killed over there on Florida Street". Ford sat down and pulled a chair up. He tried to get close enough to make eye contact, but the man's dreads wouldn't allow him. Mad Max's hair was spellbound, only there for one purpose to hide his identity.

"That...night...that...night!" "Yeah, son that night what?" Ford egged him on. "That night someone shot me then I... I... I don't remember", Max whispered. Ford lowered his head with defeat. He prayed He wouldn't play the Mr. Forgetful role. But he knew anybody in their right mind would. This shit he was involved in was serious and he most likely was guilty in some form or fashion. "So, you don't know who those men were?" Ford questioned. "I don't remember", Mad Max confessed.

Even though all those people died that night. There was no proof of Mad Max committing any crime. As far as anyone could tell he was just a victim. Technically he'd been in police custody while in a coma and no one had yet come forward. And without any witnesses they were going to have to let him go free. "Well young man I guess were done here", Ford sighed. Mad

Max tilted his head to the side. His hair dangled revealing his face. Ford saw pure evil staring back at him. His eyes were still blood shot red. It was as if the gates of hell might spill out of them right into the room. "I need to make a phone call detective Ford". Mad Max brandished a grin so diabolical it made Ford's hand quiver as he passed the cell phone across the table in a trance-like state. He dialed a number then put the phone to his ear. He smiled when the caller picked up. "Hey sis! It's Max. Yeah, it's really me. I'm home". Ford heard the excitement from the woman's voice on the other end. "Yeah, I know sis. But everything's gonna be ok. There letting me go. So, hurry I need a ride".

****

Aunt Robin eyes fluttered open; her vision blurry at first but quickly came into focus. "Are you alright?" Bea asked with a look of concern as she knelt down to help Aunt Robin sit up. The two were still in the hallway but Bea had shut the front door. Aunt Robin looked at Bea and became teary eyed. "It's a miracle. She cupped Bea's smooth face." "Come on let's get you up off this floor", Bea said to her with a smile. She helped her to her feet then escorted Aunt Robin into the living room where they both sat side by side. "You gave me a scare for a second", Bea said softly. "Oh! I'm sorry baby. I didn't mean to scare you honey". Aunt Robin sat her hand gently on Bea's knee.

"It's just. You look so much like your mother it don't make no sense", she said with such astonishment. Bea frowned. Becoming confused. *This lady done went and bumped her head for real.* Bea thought. But even still hearing the words your mother made chills run deep down Bea's spine, then spread all over her whole-body making goosebumps appear up and down her arms. Bea never knew her mother but always wondered who she was. "What do you mean I look like my mother?" Bea questioned Aunt Robin like a child, finding out Santa Clause wasn't real. Aunt Robin saw the uncertainty in Bea's eyes and felt sorry for her. "Oh, bless your heart child. I've been looking for you for over 23 years. Everyone thought you were dead, but I never believed it for one second". She shook her head. "I prayed every night to my Lord Jesus that he would return you to your rightful family and now you have". Aunt Robin spoke like a pastor giving his Sunday's best. Bea heard everything Aunt Robin was saying but it just wouldn't register. How could any of this be possible?, she thought. "I'm sorry but you've been mistaken", Bea insisted.

Aunt Robin took Bea by the hand pulling them to their feet. "Look let me show you". Bea followed close behind in a state of shock. She led them into the guest room. Bea sat on the bed while Aunt Robin went looking through the closet. After a few minutes of digging around she pulled out a large brown box. Then sat it on the floor by Bea's feet. She rambled through the box for only a second. "Here", she handed Bea what she'd been looking for then waited. Bea held a stack of laminated newspaper articles and pictures. The article was a picture of Boolaid's mother. It was the front page. And the headline read *Rachel Rochelle Smith former track star, found dead behind local grocery store. Her three your old child reported missing. Where is she?* Bea covered her mouth and tried to fight back tears. Her middle name was Rochelle. She continued to flip through the articles. One said *have you seen three-year-old Beauty Rochelle Smith*. The next one read *Beauty come home*. Bea thumbed through what seemed like hundreds of amber alert posters.

"This says Beauty Smith. My name is Bea Donnell", Bea said bringing her full attention to Aunt Robin. "No no! Your name is Beauty. We called you Bea for short", Aunt Robin said firmly. "As far as the last name whoever had you must have changed it on your birth certificate somehow", Aunt Robin admitted. Bea flipped through the stack some more then froze when she saw a picture of Rachel wearing a yellow sun dress.

She was holding a little girl's hand looking down into her child's eyes with love and care. And the girl stared up to her mother with happiness and joy. Bea had only taken maybe one baby photo her entire life. But even still looking at this picture she knew without a doubt everything Aunt Robin had just told her was all true. Because this was the image she would see in her mind from time to time, mostly in her dreams. Over the past 23 years she would have thoughts of this very woman and it meant nothing to her but now all of a sudden it meant everything to her. Bea's subconscious had been trying to remind her this whole time. "This is the last time we saw your mother alive and the very day you went missing", Aunt Robin said watching Bea stare a hole into the photo in her hand. Bea's body became hot then she felt dizzy. Her whole life was a lie. She'd had family this whole time. "Why did he lie? Why didn't my father bring me home?" Bea screamed out of frustration, her face burned full of red. Aunt Robin rushed in and held her tight at the sight of her niece's distress. The two of them sat in silence shedding tears for a long moment.

"Now tell me who had you all this time? Was it that damn Pimp God?" Aunt Robin held Bea out looking at her. "Yes! How'd you know?" Bea said surprised. "Baby that good for nothing piece of shit is not your father. That nigga is the devil", she roared. "I went to that man and begged him over and over for him to give you back to me, but he always denied having you. He'd say the john must have kidnapped you after killing your mom and dumping her body. But I felt in my soul that that low down dirty dog was lying. I told your momma he was gone be the death of her. She worshipped the ground he walked." Aunt Robin expressed herself openly. Bea knew she was telling the truth. But her speaking down on Pimp God that way still rubbed her the wrong way and made her a little angry. No matter what it was that he had done it couldn't take away the fact that he had been there for her everyday of her life until he died. Pimp God was the only family she'd ever known. "When your momma would go turn tricks, she would leave you and your brother with me. I had a son of my own at that time, but I was strung out on crack, something serious. I was very irresponsible, leaving y'all kids at home all alone for way too long. So, sometimes my sister would take you with her, and the other prostitutes would look after you, taking turns pulling tricks. Pimp God wouldn't allow them to watch your brother because he was a boy". Bea looked at Aunt Robin not believing the things she was hearing.

"I know me, and your mother should be ashamed of ourselves for living so savagely. But when my sister got killed and you went missing that was my wake-up call. I cleaned up my act and stopped getting high. I tried my damnest to find you. Beauty you gotta believe me", Aunt Robin had pleading eyes. "After seven years of searching the news and police stopped helping me, telling me that you were most likely dead and that I needed to accept it. But I never believed it for one minute. And I was right because it was your own brother that found you and brought you home". She said with pride and joy. "My Brother!" Bea thought out loud. It just hit her like a ton of bricks Boolaid was her brother. "So, that picture of the two babies are me and Boolaid?" Bea questioned. "Yes, Bulak Maquay Smith is your brother". "Bulak and Beauty!" Bea said to herself. "That's why that night at the club he told me I reminded him of someone he knew. I reminded him of our mother. A woman that was a stranger to the both of us", Bea's mind raced. "Did he know about me being missing?" "Yes, I told him when he was old enough to understand", Aunt Robin sighed. "I think that's why he was so rebellious as a child. He knew his other half was still out there in the world lost and he was lost too without you." Aunt Robin shrugged her shoulders. "What you mean other half?" Bea asked with raised eyebrows. "Just like I said Beauty, other half he's not just your brother y'all are twins."

"What!" Bea's jaw dropped. Her entire life she'd had to fend for herself in the streets. All the while she had a family, a twin. "O lord! Y'all two haven't done the nasty?" Aunt Robin looked horrified. "Nooowah!" Bea said loudly like she never had the intention of sleeping with him. "Thank God!" They both said at the same time. Aunt Robin stared at Bea with an evil eye. "Whaaat!?" Bea smiled embarrassed.

"We haven't done anything I swear it". She held up her right hand. "Alright now! Cause if y'all anything like yah momma y'all some freaks". "Aunt Robin!" "Girl I'm for real. I don't got time for none of that mountains have eyes incest mess". She rolled her eyes. "Beauty" Aunt Robin said becoming serious. "Yes ma'am." "I know hearing all of this is a lot to handle. Lord knows I can only image what you're going through. And I understand if you need time to clear your head. Or even if you want to get a DNA test. Just know, I love you. Always have, always will. Besides, I know a Rochelle when I see one." "But how can you be so sure?" Bea asked doubtfully. "Let me tell you a story". Bea gave her her undivided attention. "Your great great great great grandmother's first name was Rochelle. And what she did was help runaway slaves escape the south to up north through the underground railroad. Just like Harriet Tubman. It was said she saved over 85 black people's lives. One day she was captured by the slave masters, they did unspeakable things to that woman before hanging her from a tree for all to see. But for that woman's bravery and courage our family passed down her name to all the female generations after her. Giving her honor and respect because if it were not for

that lady, none of us would be here today.
My mother's middle name was Rochelle. Me
and your mother's middle name was
Rochelle. And lastly but not least you
Beauty Rochelle Smith are the last
generation so one day if you have a little
girl, you can keep the family's name going
through her". Aunt Robin enlightened Bea
with their family's history. "And this is your
room by the way. I've kept it prepared for
the day when you returned. Now I'm not
asking you to move in or anything. Just
know it belongs to you. And you're
welcome here at any time," Aunt Robin said
on the verge of tears. "Damn... I mean dang
I miss Meme." "Who?" "Meme she's my
best frien... No, she's my sister and if it had
not been for her, I wouldn't be here having
this conversation with you right now, she
saved my life", Bea admitted. "Well then
she's more than welcome here". Aunt Robin
patted Bea on the thigh. "So, I have a twin
brother?" Bea said, feeling an overwhelming
wholeness. "Yes, you have a twin. Both of
you came outta yah momma's pooh nah
nahs at the same time! Well not the same
time. Bulak is older by seven minutes."
"But wait, my birth certificate says February
16", Bea said. Aunt Robin went into the box
and quickly handed Bea the original birth

certificate. "I don't know how Pimp God did it but here's my proof."

"You two precious children were born February 14, 1997", Aunt Robin told Bea. *I have an older brother* she thought about it in a daydream. She had always wanted something like this. "Front door!" Speak of the devil. Aunt Robin smiled hearing the alarm system. Bea jumped to her feet with so much excitement and anticipation ready to be the first to break the news. She had returned, the long-lost sister. They'd been missing each other their whole lives. But now she was here. The both of them had been through so much bullshit that a little good news wouldn't hurt. She stepped into the hallway with a wide smile. Her lips made the O shape when she took a hard punch to the stomach. She bent over in real pain. The man standing in the hallway wasn't alone. He grabbed Bea by her hair and the back of her shorts then flung her into her bedroom door. She slammed into the door headfirst, then slid across the hard wood floor unconscious face down ass up. Aunt Robin jumped to her feet in a panic. "Don't move mom!" The Middle Eastern man said with a pistol aimed at her chest. She froze with her hands up in the surrender position. The second man entered the room with a cell phone in his hand. He tossed it on the bed. "Call your son, tell him to hurry home and don't try anything funny or I will kill the girl", he threatened. "O Lord my baby boy what have you gotten yourself into", Aunt Robin said looking at Bea's unconscious body.

Chapter 18

"Damn cuz! That's hella work". Dice said looking into the room from the doorway. "No cap!" Red said standing beside his big homie. "Yeah, that's 325 Ps of Luke Skywalker flown from the west coast

straight to our front doe!" Omar pointed to
the left corner of the room where a small
mountain of marijuana was stacked neatly in
vacuum seals. "And I'm sure you're familiar
with my white girl Hanna". Omar directed
everyone's attention to the pyramid of 50
kilos of cocaine. "Last but not least, the boy,
No R Kells". Omar laughed at his own joke
showing Dice and Red 45 bricks of pure
uncut heroin with a net worth of thirty
million. "That's what's crack'n cuz but I
know you didn't call me over here just to be
a show off". Dice looked at Omar
suspiciously. "Show off!" Omar made a
screw face. "Hell nah nigga. Never, we here
on strictly business", Omar admitted. "Look
man, we from the same neighborhood we
know the same people. Derrick was my
main distributor but now my nigga dead!"
Omar's eyes flashed with anger. "He and
Drew were my nephews; they were your
friends and your little homies". Omar
explained "Ok so, what are you asking?"
Dice talked with interest. "Basically, what
I'm saying is I need a new guy. I don't know
anybody else with the potential to move this
much work", he pointed to the room full of
drugs.

"Somebody as trustworthy and
somebody as solid if shit hits the fan. Plus,

you got the hood on your back. So, can you handle this? Do you accept my offer?" Omar asked. Through Uma and the help of Detective McDon they found out that the man driving Bea was a man named Bulak Smith. And the one who had most likely killed Uma. Through public record McDon located a relative of Bulak's. Taliban told Omar he needed to find a new employee to take Derrick's position because ever since the shooting at the strip club they'd been spending too much time trying to find the girls. And not enough time making money for the Cartel. But now everything seemed to be working itself out. Meme was in jail and wouldn't be going anywhere anytime soon. Taliban sent some goons to what was supposed to be Bulak's aunt's home. Hopefully, they would catch him and Bea there. If not, they would just kidnap the aunt and make them come out from there hiding spots. If he refused, then they would kill her. "Damn right I can handle it cuz!" Dice said seeing dollar signs. He had his own Mexican plug and his own bag, but they weren't giving Dice an opportunity of a lifetime like Omar was trying to give him right now. Omar tossed him a set of house keys. Dice caught them in midair. He looked at Omar with raised eyebrows. "This is your house now. Keep the location unknown to everybody. Call me when you're halfway done with the merchandise. I'll meet you to get the cash hand to hand". Omar gave Dice a handshake and a brotherly hug and gave Red a fist pound. "I'm gone", Omar said before leaving the two alone in the house full of narcotics. "Yooo big cuz that nigga just put you on for real for real". Red jumped up and down like a hype man turning up a crowd. "Nah he put the set on". Dice couldn't help smiling seeing how crazy Red was going. "We bout to take the city over", Dice gave Red dap. Their fingers locked in making the shape of the letter c. "What about that nigga Bigz?" Red wanted to know. He still wanted to get active with his ops. But Dice always told Red you couldn't get money and go to war at the same time. "Don't even worry about that lil cuz. We gonna handle Bigz for what he did to ours. And we gonna kill Stupid Dude for shooting Blue". Dice became pissed thinking about his fallen soldiers. "Matter fact it's up on his whole set fuck Bigz, his big homie all them niggas. We gone get money and get it in blood", Dice promised Red. *That's why I fuck wit this nigga.* Red thought to himself with a proud inward smile. "Yeah, that's my big homie."

341

****

"Yo tango vetta! Un..." "Wait, wait oh
hell no in English", Mad Max said to Porta
Rock. Boolaid had left Bea asleep at his
aunt's house. He made a phone call to his
old army buddy, the Puerto Rican prince. He
wasn't in the Army anymore but still had
connections on the guns. Boolaid was on his
way to meet Porta Rock when he received a
very unexpected phone call from an excited
Toya. Mad Max was awake and wanted to
see him. Boolaid figured he'd kill two birds
with one stone by getting Porta Rock to
meet him at Toya's house. That way he and
Max could shop together. If he knew Mad
Max like he knew he did his friend was
going to want to make a purchase on a few
items.

"I said I have 20 glizzy". Porta Rock
passed out pistols to Boolaid, Mad Max, and
Bigz from a giant handbag. "What else?"
Mad Max asked, breaking down the Glock
then putting it back together. Porta Rock
went into the duffle and pulled out an ARP
rifle. "I have 14 yhoppa's". He spoke with a
heavy Spanish accent. "Choppers, you have
14 choppers", Mad Max joked on the way

he talked. "Hey! Booba what's up wit joe manito? He keeps picking on how I talk. We might gotta shot the one", Porta Rock said seriously. "Listen Papi, I no joe got shot up and everything but I will whoop joe ass and it's not fair for me to take advantage of the handicap". Boolaid, Mad Max and Bigz burst out laughing at Porta Rock's anger management. "Ju no what? I take my guns and go! Ju pendejos are crazy loco". Porta Rock snatched his guns back and started stuffing them in his duffle bag. He was super-hot. "Nah, nah chill out Porta Rock." Boolaid tried his best not to laugh. Thats why he fucked with Porta Rock because even after all this time he was still the same person silly as hell and emotional.

"No no! I drive alllll the way over here just so ju....", "we'll take it all", Mad Max cut him off mid sentence going from all smiles to straight demon mode. "So ju want all my glizzy and all my yhoppa right now?" Mad Max simply nodded. Porta Rock looked to Boolaid for confirmation. He nodded his head the same as Mad Max. "Well why didn't you say so the first time." Porta Rock said instantly becoming super friendly. He shook everyone's hand. Bigz gave him a large stack of blue face hundreds equalling up to 28,000 dollars. "Good doing business wit ju manito's, I appreciate mucho". He told Boolaid before letting himself out. "So, what's the word?" Boolaid asked Mad Max now that the three of them were alone. Mad Max's dreads pulled back into a tight ponytail revealing his face. His dark-skinned complexion was smooth. Even with being in a coma his mustache and goatee had barely grown any. "We get back to work. Resume our normal operations". He said nonchalantly.

"What about Justo's employees? All them niggas is bitches except Gutta, Ghost, and Drama. Get rid of everybody else. This is a reconstruction and only gangstas are welcome. Bigz you really stepped it up by holding this shit down. Most importantly you held me and my brother down when your commanding officers didn't. So, anybody who flipped or wasn't rockin to your beat in my absence are dubs. I'm promoting you to Lt." "Say less I was only doing what you would have done", Bigz said with an inward smile. Proud that his loyalty was being recognized. "2x is holding the last forty birds. Bigz, I want you to get them off his hands for me. Then make a team of soldiers you see fit. Only elite grinders and official steppers. We opening one trap on each side of town. Put ten keyz in each spot.

Tell the homies don't worry about getting paid, just sell the product and I'll make sure everybody eats. That's on gang".

"After all the work is gone, we're not going to have a supplier to reup with. So, what are we gonna do from there." Boolaid became the team's consultant. "We put up the cash and save it for a rainy day. And commit our time and energy towards the war we're about to have with Omar and his hood. Anybody who ain't with us is against us. Agreed!" "Agreed" everyone said in unison. "Oh shit. Big homie your girl Meme is all over the news, fb IG, snap. They saying she smoked everybody at club platinum. She hot as a firecracker". Bigz smiled at the violence. "I already know bruh I'm tryna figure shit out right now you feel me". Boolaid said his face full of frustration. "That's what I'm saying the streets already talking. Word is some nigga named Tank that own the club dropped it off on your sis and got her locked up! Rat nigga's". Bigz became serious. "Word! Thanks for the 411 Ima look more into it". Boolaid said taking his phone from its pocket looking at the screen, it vibrated because someone was calling. "Yes ma'am". He answered immediately seeing it was Aunt Robin. He listened as she told him he needed to get

home as soon as possible. "OK yes ma'am".
He told her then disconnected the line. "Yo
fellas are we done here cause mom dukes
needs a nigga probably ready to cuss me out
for leaving a strange woman in the crib".
They all laughed, everybody knew how
Aunt Robin gave it up, she played no games.
"Yeah, Aunty bound to go upside that doom
piece", Bigz joked.

Giving Boolaid a hug and strong dap,
he and Mad Max embraced with a brotherly
hug and held each other tight for a second.
"I love you bro. And you already know that
bitch ass nigga Omar is dead". Boolaid
whispered. "I love you more my nig". Max
said pulling away from his childhood friend.
"The night I woke up from my coma. I
talked to my moms and my brother. He told
me you stayed with him till the very end.
This shit me and you got". He pointed from
him to Boolaid. "It's forever dog. Until
death and beyond", Mad Max said. "Until
death and beyond", Boolaid repeated. Mad
Max had always been a weird child growing
up knowing unexplained things about death.
How he knew Boolaid witnessed Justo's last
breath when Boolaid never mentioned, it
was just another confirmation that he was
different from the average person. "Tell

Aunty I said what up", "no doubt!" Boolaid said heading for the door.

****

"Hey Jessica! Let me have two lemon filled and a 16 oz cup of decaf roasted bean with ten sugars, Irish Cream and French Vanilla", Detective Ford requested from the young girl behind the counter. "Right away detective", she answered after counting his money then putting it in the cash register. His beverage cost $4.47. He always paid with exact change. Jessica went to fulfill his order with a big smile. It was Sunday afternoon only a few days since he had interrogated Mad Max, with his investigation still leading nowhere but to a dead end. He decided to stop at the local *Krispy Kreme* off Gate City Blvd to get him some coffee and donuts before heading into the office. He stood at the front of the line waiting for Jessica to return. "James?" A woman called from the back of the line. "Ashley! Hey!" He said in a surprised tone when he saw who it was that called him by his first name. She moved to the front of the line with her arms open wide. Her pocketbook dangled from her wrist. Ashley

gave him a big warm friendly hug. "It's so
nice to see you", she said. "Same here.
How's the baby?" He smiled. "Keeping me
up all night. Why didn't anyone warn me,
woah", she joked. The two shared a hard
laugh. "Yeah, being a first-time parent can
be rough. Where's the little bundle of joy at,
by the way? You know things have had me
so busy I haven't had a chance to stop by".
He tried to explain his absence. "Oh, you're
fine, the baby is at the house with Tim and
James. Don't feel bad for not having a
chance to come by. Believe me, I
understand. Tim and the boys are at the
house having a top-secret meeting as we
speak. Said they're working on something
big, but that's all Tim would tell me. You
know how you boys in blue like to play
under cover brother". Ashley gave Ford a
friendly tap on the chest. "Yes, we do," he
played along not knowing what the hell she
was talking about. *I knew you was up to
some fishy shit*, Ford thought to himself.

"Detective your order is ready",
Jessica said, getting his attention. She
handed him his cup of coffee and a small
bag with the donuts. "Well, Ashley it was
really good seeing you." He gave her
another hug. "Oh yeah and remember you
didn't see me, I'm undercover", he winked.

She winked back with a face full of
mischief. Ford left Ashley in the store. He
got in his car and waited. Fifteen minutes
later she exited the donut shop holding a box
of donuts with a cup holder holding three
cups. Ford knew Ashley didn't drink coffee
so that meant only one thing, his partner was
having a top-secret meeting with two
people. And Ford intended to find out who
with. Ashley backed out of her parking
space then pulled away. Detective Ford put
his car in drive then followed.

****

"Front door", the alarm system sang
when Boolaid entered the house. "Momma
where you at?" He called out shutting the
door with his back. The house was spookily
quiet. "I'm in the living room Maquay",
Aunt Robin answered. Boolaid reached for
his newly bought Glock43 nine-millimeter
pistol with a single stack clip holding ten
shots. He aimed the gun straight ahead.
Something wasn't right his aunt never called
him Maqauy. He slowly made his way into
the living room. Aunt Robin and Bea sat
side by side on the couch. "What the fuck?"
Boolaid said seeing their hands and feet

bound with duct tape. There was a man standing behind the couch with a gun to Aunt Robin's head. Boolaid became flaming hot seeing the woman who raised him under so much duress. He tightened his finger on the trigger ready to kill. But stopped when he felt the touch of cold steel on the back of his head. He never checked any of the other rooms allowing him to be snuck up on. *Fuck*, he thought to himself. "Lower your gun or everybody dies", the man said. Boolaid turned the pistol upwards letting it dangle loosely on the pointer finger. Then slowly put it on the floor knowing these unknown men were not playing around.

Boolaid looked into his aunt's eyes. They were filled with tears. Not from fear of being held at gunpoint but from shamefulness of leading her son into a trap. "It's OK ma, you had too", he said reading her mind. He turned his attention to Bea, she had changed. A different woman than the one he'd last seen. He just couldn't tell what it was. All he knew was when he looked into her eyes his blood rushed a little faster. "Don't worry everything's gonna be alright," he ensured his ladies. The man standing behind Boolaid flipped his pistol around then held it high in the air. He then drove it downwards slamming the butt of the gun into the back of Boolaid's head like a hammer does a nail. The girls jumped with shouts, screams, and hollers from the sudden attack. Boolaid dropped to the floor hard. He saw Aunt Robin's and Bea's feet as his eyes rolled to the back of his head. Then there was darkness.

****

"Here you lovely gentlemen are", Ashley said setting on the table a box of a dozen hot and ready glazed donuts. Then she passed everyone their cups of coffee, starting with her husband. "And this one is for you sir", she handed Taliban his cup last. She smiled with lust in her eyes that no one noticed except for them two. "Ok so I guess I'll leave you all to handle your business", Ashley said then headed out the room. She wore pink leggings with a tight white T shirt. Pink, purple, and grey Air Max 95's to match. Ashley's ass was big wide and fat! Taliban watched as it wobbled with every step she made until she was gone. It took everything in McDon's power not to lose his mind. He wanted so badly to kill them both for ruining his life. But he especially wanted to murder Taliban. He felt the vibes between

Kalub Shipman
PUSH YOU PAY

his wife and the Middle Eastern man. Something was definitely going on, he just couldn't prove it. He even thought about confronting her about it but didn't want to come off as insecure. Because at the end of the day he was the one living foul. "Now, now no need for a temper tantrum", Rafiq said seeing McDon still ice grilling Taliban. Taliban smiled praying Mcdon did anything crazy. Putting a bullet in him would be a pleasure.

"Tell me about the Asia girl, is she talking?" Rafiq wanted to know. "She hasn't said one word like we expected. They have her housed on C unit which is the single cell part of the jail for women. She had first appearance in court Friday and was denied bail. If she goes to trial like we're hoping, then she'll lose due to eyewitness testimony". "Good!" Rafiq said with approval. He was glad to finally be getting this situation under control. "And what about the friend and her male partner?" "With the help of Omar and your guy Uma, we identified the man as a childhood friend of Justin and Jason Bryant. Through public record I came up with an address in Burlington. Belonging to a woman named Robin Smith. I gave Taliban the location", McDon said mean mugging Taliban. "I have sent men to the location. I'm waiting on conformation as we speak", Taliban enlightened his higher up. Rafiq dipped a hot glazed donut into his cup of espresso then took a bite. "Oh Jeezus! This is good, holy moley donut shop", he said stuffing his mouth with the sweet desert loving every bite. "You pigs might really be on to something with the coffee and donuts. Mrs. McDon", Rafiq called for the detective's wife grabbing another donut from its box. McDon's eyes went wide with fear not knowing what the Middle Eastern man was trying to pull.

Ashley came flying into the room ready to help please and serve. "Yes, Mr. Rafiq", she smiled happily. "Sooo, you're telling me the donut is hot when you see the red light on?" He asked full of anticipation. "Yes sir, every time you see that red light there's hot donuts", she told him with her hands on her hips like wonder woman saving the day. "DELIGHTFUL!" He shouted with such excitement making Ashley jump and clap with joy from Rafiq's praise. Taliban's phone rang. He answered then listened. "Ten four bring them in0," he tried his best police imitation. "They are in custody", he told the room. "Well Mrs. McDon looks like undercover calls again,"

Rafiq spoke to her very softly. "Awhhhh", she pouted. "Maybe we come by for dinner some time next week?" Taliban offered. "Oh, that would be wonderful". She couldn't help blushing, making McDon's blood boil over. "Baby I'll be home later tonight after work", McDon said then began to kiss his wife like they were about to make a homemade porno, while watching Taliban marking his territory. *Yuck! Straight Gump*, both Middle Eastern men thought making their way to the door. "Where do you go?", Rafiq asked McDon seeing him walking in the opposite direction. "I'm getting in my car so I can follow you guys." "No, no, no, you ride with us", Rafiq said like he had no care in the world. Although he knew this was a demand and not a request. Rafiq jumped into the back seat of his armored G wagon. Taliban at the wheel McDon riding shot gun. They pulled away from the curb then hit the gas. Detective Ford put his car in drive, then followed.

Chapter 19

It took Mcdon and his new friends exactly 53 minutes to drive to their location. Detective Ford followed them the whole way. First, they drove down highway I-85 then merged on to I-68. I-68 was mostly country roads, always busy with passer byers. Until the armored G wagon made a turn on a long stretch of road. Ford had

never been out here before but still knew
this road led to a private air strip used by the
rich and famous. Soon the air strip came into
view. The open area was huge, breaking off
into multiple private runways divided by
fence lines. At the beginning of each runway
there were a number of hangers, so pilots
could land then park their aircraft, or go into
small offices to conduct business. Ford sat
back and observed different types of jets and
planes coming and going. The G wagon
slowed then turned into a gate that read
hanger 56-59. The vehicle headed for a
runway that had three hangers' side by side.
Ford drove straight ahead not wanting to
blow his tail.

He turned into the very next gate
entrance which was at least a half mile from
where his partner had parked. Ford drove all
the way down to the hanger. There was only
one and it was off by itself. He parked and
got out. "Can I help you son?", an old white
man asked as he slid the 40-foot hanger door
closed then locked it in place with a bolt
lock. "What can you tell me about that
hanger over there?" Ford pointed in the
direction of the three hangers off in the
distance. The properties were separated by
fence lines and roads. The old man looked at
detective Ford skeptically ready to protest

his question but quickly changed his mind when Ford show him his badge. "Well, why didn't you just say so son? Anything for a following brother, retired Air Force." He gave a crisp salute, losing all suspiciousness. Ford saluted the veteran back. "All I can really tell you is that most of this place is privately owned. That hanger over yonder is quiet for the most part. Them boys mainly stick to themselves, know what I mean". "Yes sir, I know what you mean. You wouldn't mind if I camped out here for a while, would you?", he asked the retired vet. "No problem son. Just do me one solid would'ja?" "Sure, what is it?" "Before you leave close and lock my gate up front and the entrance. I gotta date with the wife so I can't stick around. Today's our forty second anniversary since she put the ball and chain on the old fella can't miss that". He smiled thinking about his true love.

"Yeah, I know what you mean I had one of those at one time", Ford said referring to his ex-wife. The old man gave Ford a bolt lock then jumped into a 1980 Chevy pick up. Ford watched him drive away. The sun had just begun to set. When it was completely gone, he would make his move. He popped the trunk of his grand mark. He grabbed his Level 2 bullet proof vest. He rubbed his fingers across the writing that said Police in big yellow bold letters. After throwing it over the shoulders he strapped it in place. He checked the rounds in his Glock 19 then sat on the hood of the car patiently awaiting his time to strike.

****

Someone threw a bucket full of water into Boolaid's face waking him up in a jolted flash. Water forced its way down his nostrils making him choke and gag. It was difficult to breath with his mouth duct taped. He tried to attack but found his body couldn't move from the zip ties that bound him to a wooden chair by his wrist and ankles. The back of his head ached, it was busted open and still leaking blood from where he'd been pistol whipped. Then he thought about his Aunt Robin and Bea. Panic began to set in. He looked around then calmed down when he saw them to his right. They too were bound by zip ties. He looked around trying to get his bearings together. They were in a large room with ceilings at least fifty feet high in some sort of warehouse, he thought. *Two rooms,* Boolaid thought one to be an office the other most likely a bathroom. Two men were at a table playing cards. Boolaid ducked his head and shut his eyes trying his best effort to avoid being hit with the empty bucket the man flung at him when he caught Boolaid checking out the surroundings.

His bucket attack didn't hurt Boolaid in any type of way, making him become furious. "Ugh!" Boolaid grunted when the Middle Eastern man smacked the top of his head with an open palm.

Bea's chin hung low into her chest. She slowly looked up when she heard the goon approach. Her breathing became heavy and fast passed preparing her for whatever. She made a loud muffling noise that sounded along the lines of "fuck you bitch". With pure hatred in her eyes. "Yes! yes you like me!", he smiled before smacking her with a powerful blow leaving her dizzy seeing stars. Aunt Robin whimpered with sobs as she watched her niece and nephew being punished. *You monsters,* she thought as he made his way down the line standing in front of her.

She stared at him through horrified eyes. They had bags and were swollen from many hours of nonstop crying. He pulled a knife from his back pocket then rushed in on her pushing the tip of the blade into her

cheek. She jumped screaming with fear. The knife cut into her flesh a little. Boolaid went insane, wide open making his chair lean. He toppled over, crashing to the floor. The men playing cards laughed harder. The man wielding the knife gave Aunt Robin a sinister smile as he gently ran the tip from the the bottom of her chin, down the neck to the collar of her shirt. Then with a sudden rage sliced her shirt straight down the middle then ripped the fabric right off her back. Shirtless sitting in only her bra, outraged, afraid, and embarrassed all at once. She watched the creep closely as he placed the knife in between her breast ready to cut the bra strip leaving her top less. "You ready?" he said in a deep Middle Eastern accent. "3, 2...1". "Enough", a voice called from the back of the hanger. Two Middle Eastern men and a young black man approached. Rafiq said something in Pashto. The soldiers sitting at the table jumped to their feet rushed over to Boolaid sitting him back in a correct position. The man terrorizing Aunt Robin put the knife away and backed off with a kiss.
Rafiq stopped in front of his three captives. His dark almond complexion complemented his three-thousand-dollar Versace suit and fifteen-hundred-dollar pair of Fendi shoes.

His long black shiny hair was pulled back into a tight ponytail and his beard was healthy and well groomed. Although Boolaid was tied and stressed he couldn't help but notice the sandalwood colon the man wore. "Hello! I am Rafiq", he said in a deep Middle Eastern accent and a slight bow, "and this is my second in command Taliban." Taliban watched Boolaid with an unknown interest. Taliban was very light skinned and heavy set, two hundred and seventy pounds with a beard that fell pass chest level. He dressed like a street nigga. Wearing beef and broccoli *Timberland* boots, *G star* jeans, a *BB Simons* belt, and a dark green *champion* hoodie. His forearm still in a cast from where'd he'd been shot by Justo. "And well you shall just call my friend here uhh... Gump. Mr. Forest Gump", Rafiq gestured towards detective McDon. Taliban couldn't help laughing. McDon shook his head angrily but said nothing.

Rafiq smiled. "And you two! the infamous Bea and Boolaid. I really like this name Boolaid. It sounds like the Kool-Aid. Ooooo yeah!" he mimicked the commercial. "Very, very, catchy this Boolaid", he looked around the room making his goons chuckle. *I'ma kill this lame ass nigga* Boolaid thought to himself. Rafiq snatched the duct tape off

Boolaid's mouth. It hurt like hell, but he
concealed his pain well. "You may speak
now," "let them go and keep me", Boolaid
tried to bargain. "Much as I'd like to, I
cannot do this my friend. Your female
companion has cost me much money. Much
time and believe it or not much men". Bea
started to speak but went unheard. Rafiq
snatched her duct tap away. "Ahh!" she
yelped in pain. "Yes ma'am?" Rafiq smiled
with pleasure. "Keep us and let her go", Bea
said looking to Aunt Robin with eyes that
said I'm so sorry for getting you into this
mess.

"Oh, how poetic. Save them, no let
her go, no take me instead." Rafiq
patronized Bea and Boolaid for trying to
save one another. "You and your friend steal
my kilo", he pointed to Bea. "Then you and
your friends sell my kilo. And all of you are
responsible for killing men. Boolaid, you
killed my sayad Uma which is unacceptable.
Your poor Meme will do life in prison. My
police friend will make sure of that", he
pointed to McDon. "And the three of you
will die tonight. I'm going to have your
heads cut off. We will record to show all
employees and enemies an example of what
happens if you cross me," he said becoming
serious. "OK let's get this show on the road",

he told his henchmen. They set a camera up on a tripod then all three soldiers put on ski masks. One went into a dufflo bag and passed out machetes. Detective McDon became uneasy at the sight of a murder in the making. One of the goons focused the camera making sure it showed all three on the film. He turned on some bright lights making their faces come on the video camera clear. He pushed a button and a red light started to blink it was now recording. They tightened the mask one last time then took positions behind their captives. "Kill the older one first," Rafiq ordered. "Noooo motherfucka! Ima fucken kill you bitch." Boolaid went crazy. You could see all the tension in his biceps and triceps trying to escape. But it did no good trying. The zip ties weren't going anywhere.

Aunt Robin's mouth was still duct taped. She didn't even try to put up a fight. She was brave and had accepted her fate. She tried her best to comfort Boolaid and Bea with the look in her eyes. The man standing behind Aunt Robin began loudly shouting in Pashto looking directly into the camera. His aggressiveness telling the world all who crossed Rafiq would pay the ultimate price. He raised the machete high above Aunt Robins head. "ALLAHU

AKBAR!" He screamed at the top of his lungs. Bea closed her eyes looking away. She'd just found her family for it to be ripped away. Gunfire exploded then echoed throughout the hanger making everyone jump with surprise. The man with the machete took a bullet to the middle of the forehead then two more to the chest. He dropped to the floor dead.

"POLICE! FREEZE!" Detective Ford shouted; he had snuck in through a side door undetected. "Don't fucken move", he warned but one of the men with a machete reached for his weapon. Ford gunned him down with a hail of bullets. He dropped the clip out of his Glock 19 and popped a new one in as he walked up. "Don't do it!" Ford said to McDon seeing him attempt to go for his gun. McDon thought wisely. "Robin? Bulak and Ms. Donnell?" Ford said looking at the tied-up people confused. "What in the hell's going on Tim?" Detective Ford asked his partner. Boolaid watched the detective, he'd never met the man in his life. He wondered how he knew his name. But none of that really mattered. He was just happy he showed up when he did. They were still alive because of him. "James, you don't understand", said McDon. "Well help me understand Tim. Who are these people?" He pointed his pistol at Rafiq and Taliban. "And why do they have these innocent people tied up?" "I said don't FUCKEN MOVE!" Ford shouted seeing Taliban take one small step forward. "Tim come on man! I'm your partner for Christ's sake. Talk to me", Ford pleaded to his friend. "Yes, talk to him. Tell him who you really are", Rafiq finally spoke up. McDon looked to be on the brink of tears. "They ruined my LIFE!" He shouted. "Who? Who? Bubby it's Ok, we're in this together", Ford said to his partner.

McDon went for his pistol then put it to the side of his head. "Wait, partner we can fix this. Whatever it is we can fix it," Ford held a handout. "James, I fucked up man. I fucked up big time. Tell my wife I'm sorry", McDon was now crying. "No Don...", but it was too late McDon's mind was made up. He shoved his Glock deep into his mouth then pulled the trigger blowing his brains out. He fell to the floor with half a skull. Everybody in the hanger looked to the sky hearing the sound of a jet engine. It was right above their heads. The entire building trembled with hard vibrations. Someone was landing an aircraft right outside the hanger's doors. "Who is that?" Detective Ford shouted over the loud engine's roar. "What is this?" Rafiq looked to Taliban. He shrugged his shoulders just as clueless. Soon all the noise stopped making everything go quiet. The jets hydraulic pumps could be heard hissing in the night. "Who could this be? There are no shipments scheduled for today," Rafiq said with amusement. Everyone listened to the sound of the dead bolt being unlocked from the outside of the hanger. There was one last bang from someone letting up the latch, then the 30-foot hanger door began to slide open. The bright high beams from the G5 jet lit up the inside of the building like Christmas. Everyone had no choice but to shield their eyes. Ten men dressed in military green uniforms rushed into the hanger with AK-47's surrounding everyone they saw.

"Drop your weapon officer", said a man dressed in an all-white Dolce & Gabbana top to bottom outfit. He came into the hanger once his men had secured all threats. He wore a pair of Prada loafers without socks. The man with the machete dropped his weapon and went into attention position. Rafiq and Taliban did the same thing. "I will not tell you again drop your weapon", he told detective Ford. He didn't want to listen but what choice did he have going against ten men armed with fully automatic weapons. He lowered his pistol to the floor. "Sir! What... What are you doing here?" Rafiq asked with a hint of nervousness. I've come because I was called. Something has been brought to my attention. I'm told you have been abusing your authority as a commander and most importantly as my trusted general. The Middle Eastern man in all white confronted Rafiq, "LIES! I have done no such thing", Rafiq said in outrage.

"Is it not true that you used a sayad without my permission. And you got Uma killed under your watch and didn't report it", the boss questioned. In the Shirac Cartel only the made members could order a sayad like Uma to commit assassination. Otherwise, you had to get it approved. Rafiq went above his bosses' head and ultimately sent Uma to an early grave. Rafiq had confided only to Taliban about sending Uma to apprehend Boolaid and Bea. "You disloyal traitor", Rafiq said with venom and disgust. "My loyalties are not with you. But only with the Cartel's which you have violated", Taliban spoke plainly. "And that you are loyal", the new leader said. Taliban answered with a slight head nod accepting the appraisal. "Yes, I could have easily gotten Taliban to handle such small situations". He referred to having Rafiq killed for his insubordination "but no, I had to come all this way to meet the man responsible for single handily killing one of our best." The boss stepped from the shadows. The first thing Boolaid noticed were the many chains with dancing VVS diamonds accompanied with multiple rubies. Red, green, yellow, and purple. It all glittered in the night. Six long nappy rude dreads fell past the man's chest. And even after all these years Yusuf Iman still had that boyish look.

"Hello, black ops. Looks like Allah is the best of knower's because we have indeed crossed paths again", Yusuf smirked. "You saved my life many years ago and now I have come to return the favor. Let them all free", Yusuf ordered. Three guards moved in and cut their zip ties. "Ooh, thank you Jesus!" Aunt Robin cried breaking free. She rushed Boolaid and Bea yoking them into a vice grip hug. "My babies." They all quietly embraced for a long moment. "Here momma", Boolaid said taking his shirt off putting it over her shoulders. "Baby I know this is going to sound crazy so ima just say it Bea's your sister." Aunt Robin said holding her nephew's chin in both hands. "What?" He looked at the two women. "I said the same, but I think she's right", Bea smiled.

"Y'all trippin my sister is dead". He became angry they were even having this type of conversion at this time. Bea felt like she'd just been kicked in the chest. He didn't believe them. "No baby it's true I'll prove it". "Enough of this! No more kumbaya. An example must be made for our sayad's death". Rafiq broke up their gathering. "This is true someone must pay for shedding sayad's blood", Yusuf acknowledged. Rafiq smiled with approval. "Bulak my old friend you and Rafiq must have a warrior's battle to the death in respect of Uma. We will record this to show all, what happens when a member of the Shirac Cartel abuses their authority." "This is an outrage, I am Rafiq", he said becoming hotter than an oven. "Silence you will do what I say, or you will be slaughtered. You're lucky to even have a chance to live". Yusuf showed Rafiq he was the real boss and much more ruthless. Rafiq quickly calmed down with ten AK-47's jammed in his face. "How does this benefit me? I'm not a member of your cartel", Boolaid asked rubbing his now loose wrist. "Ahh but you will be if you kill Rafiq. You will take his position and I will make you a general directly under me. This will ensure the safety of your family", he pointed to Bea and Aunt Robin. "You will be rich beyond

imagination", Yusuf proposed. "And what if
I respectfully refused", Boolaid asked with
raised eyebrows. "Remember my friend I
owe only one life not three. Besides why
wouldn't you, Taliban informed me all this
is over twenty kilos. You lost a close friend
over nothing. If you don't accept my offer
his death will be in vain. And I take you as a
man of honor". Yusuf gave his personal
opinion of the situation.

"Do it baby kill'm", Aunt Robin urged
him. "Now let's wait a minute Bulak. Think
about what he's wanting you to do. That's
murder and its against the law", Detective
Ford said finally getting a chance to speak.
"Bruh who in the hell are you? And how do
you know my name?" said Boolaid.
Everyone body in the room turned looking
at Ford. "Um... I... I'm a friend of your
mother", he said looking at Aunt Robin for
help. "Well friend of my mother do me a
favor and mind your own fucken business.
You lock black people up for a living I don't
fuck with your kind", "you need to listen to
me!" Ford objected. "James, you heard my
boy now leave him alone". Aunt Robin
helped Boolaid put the icing on the cake.
Boolaid turned to Bea for guidance. They'd
both been through so much in such little
time and somehow while he was with Mad

Max and Bigz she and Aunt Robin had come to the conclusion that they were brother and sister. If this was true, that would be huge for them both. "Do it Boolaid! Kill'm for us... Brother". She held her chest out proud to be part of his family. "Fuck it! I'm doing this for us. for Justo. Let's die nigga". Boolaid said walking up on Rafiq. Rafiq did no talking; he took his suit jacket off handing it to a guard. He unbuttoned his collar shirt tossing it on the floor. His body was chiseled like Bruce Lee's. Then he kicked his shoes off and pulled his socks away preparing for battle barefooted.

The soldiers moved the chairs out of the way creating fighting space. Another person grabbed the camera off the tripod and held it in his hand to record up close and personal. Everybody backed away as the two men squared off. Rafiq stepped in with a punch, Boolaid easily weaved it then countered with a upper cut that landed to Rafiq's mid-section, he gasped for air doubling over to the floor. "You black son of a bitch!" he yelled jumping to his feet changing. He tackled Boolaid by the legs, then lifted him into the air and slammed him on his back hard. Boolaid's flesh made a smack sound against the cement floor. Rafiq moved lighting fast getting on top of

Boolaid while raining down wild and crazy
punches. One punch, two punches, three
punches to Boolaid's face causing blood to
flow from his nose. Boolaid tossed his hip to
the side then slid from under Rafiq with a
side kick. They both got to their feet with
the quickness, looking at each other as they
caught their breath. "Ahhh!" Rafiq rushed
again, him and Boolaid fought heads up.
They squabbled fighting like cats and dogs.
Aunt Robin watched in horror and
amazement at how barbaric her nephew had
become at the drop of a dime. At that
moment she knew he'd been in this type of
situation before. Most women would have
been terrified but not Bea she licked her lips
blood thirsty. She felt strange like she was
watching the male version of herself. "Win,
Brother!" she shouted.

Yusuf smiled at the constant melee,
loving the blood sport. Rafiq threw a two-
piece combo. The first Punch connected to
Boolaid's chin. But he ducked the second
moving in with his own vicious three punch
combination rocking Rafiq's jaw with every
swing. His knees buckled but he didn't fall.
Boolaid did a sidestep then jabbed his hand
in a Y shape up into Rafiq's neck as hard as
he could. Boolaid's hand connected to
Rafiq's Adam's apple crushing the man's

voice box. The blow made a loud cracking noise in the silence of the room. Rafiq fell to his knees defeated. He reached for his neck gasping for air he would never receive. He was slowly suffocating to death. Boolaid looked to Yusuf with triumph. "Finish him", Yusuf ordered coolly. "He's already dead", Boolaid pointed to the helpless man. "Bulak my friend the camera is rolling. Show the world, make an example out of him NOW!" Yusuf demanded. "Yusuf his..." "AHHH!" Bea screamed a hell cry. She swung a machete she'd picked up from the floor. The thick steel blade slashed down hitting Rafiq in between the shoulder blade and neck cutting deep into his flesh severing the spinal cord. Blood erupted into Bea's face. Rafiq's head limped to the side barely attached to the body. "Again" said Yusuf, hungry for more blood. She "AHHHED," with another swing, the machete disconnected Rafiq's head it hit the floor with a thud then rolled to an unsteady stop. The Middle Eastern man's mouth and eyes wide open as if he were still struggling to catch his breath. Bea grabbed the decapitated head by its ponytail. "Don't fuck with us. PERIOD!" she said looking straight into the camera. Then tossed Rafiq's head to the side like it was something as simple as a soda can you throw in the trash. "Very good black ops's sister. I will call you sister ops." Yusuf gave Bea a round of applause. "Didn't I tell you not to call me black ops", Boolaid said seriously. "Yes, yes you did. No disrespect my friend. Bulak you and I have many many things to discuss. I need you to come with me back to Afghanistan." "What about my family?"

Boolaid hugged Aunt Robin. Bea rested her head on his shoulder. "Nothing is more important than family. Do you remember the story I told you about my mother and father?" Yusuf stared off in his own thoughts for only a second. I do remember. "Good because unlike my family yours is free to go". "What about this mess?" Boolaid looked around the hanger, the scene was gruesome. "I'm sure your mother's friend will come up with something", Yusuf said turning to detective Ford with a smirk. Ford observed everybody in the room watching him. Helping criminals was the last thing he wanted to do, especially an international Cartel leader but what other choices did he have? His partner had been tampering with evidence and now there was an innocent woman sitting in jail. "Yeah, I'll come up with something. You guys go ahead and get outta here". "Thank you,

James", Aunt Robin said with a grateful smile. "Boy, where'd you learn to fight like that" Aunt Robin asked, everybody in the room laughed. "Detective thanks", Bea said. "Yeah, I appreciate it. Good look whoever you are", Boolaid joined in. "Alright! Alright! All of you are welcome now leave before I change my mind". Ford meant every word. Although their gratitude secretly made him smile on the inside. It was rare when he was thanked in his line of work. "Taliban make sure those ladies make it home safely," Yusuf ordered. "Yes sir." "Were not going anywhere with him." Bea and Aunt Robin looked hesitant. "It's ok momma. I know this man well enough to know he is a man of his word. I'm gonna be gone for a while but when I get back you two have some explaining to do", he spoke like a parent. He hugged his aunt then Bea. He held her just a little longer. If she was his sister, he didn't want her out of his sight, ever again. He walked them outside to the car and waited until the G wagon was out of sight. When he came back into the hanger, he found Yusuf speaking to his men in Pashto.

"Are you ready my friend?" Yusuf asked Boolaid seeing him approach. "Let's go!" "Very well," Yusuf his ten guards and

Boolaid boarded the G5 jet. The pilot hit the runway. Within minutes they were 50'000 feet in the sky headed for the Middle East. Leaving detective Ford and one of Taliban's soldiers behind. Ford shook his head looking at his partner's lifeless body. "Jesus". He stared down at Rafiq's head. He thought for a long while with his hands on his hips. "Hey what's your name?" Ford asked the Middle Eastern man, "Sosa!" Detective Ford sighed heavily. "OK Sosa, here's the plan".

Chapter 20

Bea smiled so hard you would have
thought her face might get stuck and stay
that way. She watched Meme walk into the
visitation room. She wore a tight fitted
orange county jail jumpsuit; she had gained
a few pounds, but that ass still poked out.
She sat down in a chair across from Bea.
Even though she was in jail she still looked
good. Her dark skin smooth, making her

golden-brown eyes have a glow to them. And her hair was braided in a maze-like design. Bea knew Meme had braided it herself. Bea wanted nothing more than to kiss and hug her bestie and never let her go. But couldn't because they were divided by a twelve-inch piece of thick plexiglass. Meme picked up the phone hanging on the wall so she could speak to her friend. Bea did the same, still smiling. "Bitch! Where you been?," said Meme with the stank face, immediately wiping the smile off Bea's face. "No hold up sis, wait before you cuss me out. I know I been M.I.A, but there's so much shit that's been going on you wouldn't believe it", Bea tried to explain. "Girl bye!" Meme rolled her eyes. "I swear", Bea said now feeling terrible for not being there for her friend. It had been over three months since the last time they'd been in touch with each other. Not because she wanted to but because she had to in order to get their situation certified between Boolaid and Yusuf. Who had just gotten back to the country.

Meme didn't say anything, just continued to stare at Bea with a blank expression. "Meme! I'm sorry, please don't act like this", Bea said, becoming filled with emotions. Both girls turned to mirror images. They pouted, crossed their arms, and sat back in their chairs with their lips poked out. Then grilled each other in an intense staring contest. Neither trying to let up. Suddenly a smirk appeared on Meme's face. Bea saw this and tried to stay upset but couldn't help smiling back. "I miss you biiitttchh!" Meme blurted out with a childish wine. "Awwww, I miss you more BITCH!" Bea said with a sad face. "It's so much I wish I could tell you, but I can't. Just know when you get outta this hell hole we gonna be straight for life". Bea ensured her best friend with a look of pure excitement. The sisters started to rant and rave with loud celebration and showing off their superior ratchetness. "Hey, quiet down Miss Jones or I'm gonna have to escort you back to your cell", a tall handsome correctional officer said coming over to see what all the fuss was about. Bea covered her mouth with both hands full of bashfulness. "Sorry Officer Lewis", Meme said in a sexy flirtatious voice as she reached out and crest his pants leg.

"Alright, Miss Jones stop playing before you get me fired", he said with a smile and eyes full of lust. He walked away going to stand back in his corner. The sisters mischievously smiled knowing men will be men no matter their career choice. "I've been staying in constant contact with KB and he's been keeping my posted with everything. Girl, I know you been out there handling business. I never had one worry of you leaving me out to hang and dry", Meme clarified their long-term relationship. Detective Ford had been trying his damnest to get Meme's charges dropped or at least get her a bond after he'd discovered his partner had been tampering with the investigation. But the judge still denied her saying that although McDon might have broken the law in many ways. It still didn't take away the fact that there was an eyewitness out there still willing to come to court and testify at trial. The judge set the trial date in a year's time. So, Meme was going to have to thug it out and wait until then. The night Boolaid and Yusuf left for Afghanistan, Detective Ford came up with a plan to set the hanger on fire with McDon, Rafiq, and the two soldiers he had killed inside the building while he watched it burn to the ground.

Once he was down at the station for his debriefing. He reported that his partner had called him to the private air strip so they could take a few flying lessons. But in actuality McDon was dealing drugs and had gotten into some trouble. When Ford entered the hanger, he was taking on by gun fire. In the midst of the gun battle he killed two suspects. But McDon didn't make it, being shot and killed in the middle of the action. Somehow a fire started. "All I remember is a huge explosion", Ford told the Chief of Police. He also said he tried his best to get McDon's body to safety, but the fire had become too intense. He had to save his own ass, so he fled the building before it went completely up in smoke. Since the report stated McDon died in the line of duty, they gave his wife 100,000 dollars from the life insurance policy the police department had on all officers. Ford also made sure Ashley and no one else found out about his homosexual activities. It was better that way, Ford thought. "I would never in a million years leave you in here alone. Death before dishonor", Bea said. "Death before dishonor," Meme recited the words back. They pressed their hands against the glass sharing a sisterly moment. "Bitch let me tell you. These niggas is out here killing each other like a mug!" Bea changed the subject. "Yeah, I know I been watching the news seems like somebody dies everyday", Meme agreed. "Gang on gang, neighborhood versus neighborhood beef. It's really dangerous out here. When you get outta here we moving to Miami", Bea said not joking. "I'm down with a new scenery. Anywhere is better than this place", Meme gestured all around her. "It's this girl named Big Moni, she blood gang under Boolaid's friend Mad Max she's good people". "OH BITCH! Fuck that I got to tell you somethin!" Bea cut her friend off. "Give me the tea", Meme put her face closer to the plexiglass lowering her voice to whisper with a childish smile.

"What tea are you talking about girl?" Bea acted clueless. "Bitch don't play! KB already done told me you and Boolaid is brother and sister on some Jerry Springer shit", Meme instigated. "As crazy as it sounds its all true", Bea admitted. Meme's mouth dropped open with shock. "How?" She asked. "His Aunt well our aunt just felt it. She walked through the door, took one look at me then fell out in the floor on some holy ghost stuff". "Bitch stop", Meme laughed. "So serious girl. So, when I helped her up, she was talking about I looked so much like my mother that she knew it had to be". "Oh my gawed". "Right? Thats what I said. Then she started showing me all these different things that couldn't be coincidence. So, we all went to get a DNA test two months ago and it's official. I have a twin brother". "TWINS!" Meme shouted. Other people in the visitation looked in the direction. Officer Lewis mean mugged from his corner. "Sorry!" Meme mouthed too everyone shyly. "Damn sis a twin?" She whispered. "You've finally gotten what you've always wanted, a family. I'm really happy for you". Meme nodded her head with approval. Meme's eyes became sad, and Bea instantly noticed. "Meme! Let me tell you something. If I could change anything in my life I wouldn't. I wouldn't be the person I am today, and I wouldn't have you in my life, which I can't imagine a life without my sister". The two shared a moment of togetherness. "What?" Bea asked seeing Meme's face turn sneaky.

"How does it feel to wanna suck your brother's dick? With yo nasty azz." Meme joked. "Eeewww bitch don't come for me", Bea turned red with embarrassment. "Girl don't act like yo wasn't trying to ride that pole", Meme said with her head cocked to the side. "OK, but that was before I found out we were related. I don't feel like that now. So, let's clear that up right now." Bea became dead serious. "Oookay, Bea if you say so", Meme shrugged her shoulders nonchalantly. "Meme stop", Bea pleaded. "OK girl I'm sorry. I was just joking",

---

Meme said sincerely. They admired each other so much. They'd been through so much. 90 percent of it they endured together. Bea's phone rang in her Gucci bag. She grabbed it and checked the text she had. It simply read. "Ready". "Listen sister I gotta go there's some business that needs attending too", Bea dropped the phone back into the bag. "I'ma come back and see you next week same time". "OK", Meme said with her bottom lip poked out and arms crossed. "I know baby I don't want to go neither but I have to. We will make it through this. I promise everything is in the making", Bea said what she meant. Meme nodded her head with understanding. "I love you!" Bea said. "I love you more", Meme became teary eye. Bea didn't want to get up. It felt like she was ditching her only friend in the world. Meme couldn't take seeing Bea leaving so she got up and left the visitation first. Bea watched the officer escort Meme away. "In due time sis, in due time".

****

"Thanks Robin". Detective Ford accepted a hot steamy cup of coffee Aunt Robin had made for him. They were in the kitchen of her new house in Haw River,

384

North Carolina. "You're welcome, James".
She joined him at the table with her own
cup, she had hot blackberry tea instead of
coffee. "Look James, I know things haven't
always been good between us. Even after all
these years". She paused with a heavy sigh.
"But I just wanted to have a sit down with
you to tell you thank you for covering for
the kids. I know breaking the law was hard
for you", she said seriously. "Yeah, it was.
But you know that's not what bothers me.
What I can't help thinking back on is that
night at the hanger when my son asked me
who I was. Did you tell'm Robin? Did you
tell my son I'm his father?" Ford asked with
a desperate look. "Now why would I do
that? He's already been through so much.
The both of them have". Aunt Robin became
upset. "Well where are they?" Ford
questioned taking a sip of his hot joe. "Now
you listen here. I'm not one of your suspects
and we're not in one of your interrogation
rooms. We are in my house, do you
understand?" She mean mugged "I
understand".

"Good and you don't get to ask where
my children are. They're minding their own
business. Don't try and act like you all of a
sudden so concerned about their well-
being". Aunt Robin spit venom. "GOD

DAMN IT ROBIN. What was I supposed to do, tell my wife I got a hooker pregnant while I was on duty?" He stopped and sighed. "Look I'm sorry, I was married for Christ's sake". "No nigga what you were supposed to do was man up and take care of your responsibilities. Shit, who the hell knows if you would have played your part and took care of your children my sister might still be alive, and Beauty wouldn't have been condemned to the streets her whole life. Lord only knows what that child's been through". Aunt Robin's voice cracked with shamefulness. "How was I supposed to know that my daughter was still out there. They found Rochelle's body behind that store just like so many of the other hookers during that time before we brought that sick son of a bitch to justice," he pointed out. "James you're the detective. But no, you couldn't have known if she was still alive. But a father would never give up until the end. You know what James; I didn't call you over here to fuss and fight. You made your choice to abandon Bulak and Beauty 26 years ago. My sister loved you so much she'd rather raise two kids alone while she sold her pussy for another man than to ruin your little happy marriage and you still somehow fucked that up". Ford wanted to protest but knew he had no wins. Because the truth was whether he was married or not he was wrong. There wasn't any good excuse to the reason why he wasn't there for his own children. Regardless of his relationship between him and Rochelle. Ford's phone beeped. It was a text message. It read *Ready*. "Robin you no what? You're absolutely right. I'm one hundred percent wrong for what I did to Rochelle and my kids, but what's done is done and I can't take it back. But what I can do is promise you that I'll make it up to them both. In whatever way possible", Ford said getting up from the table. He touched her on the shoulder. Robin looked away with tears of frustration. Ford sighed. Make sure you lock up when I leave. He left the kitchen without another word. He closed the front door once outside. "I promise you Robin. In due time, in due time".

****

"Ayo y'all gone head without me I'm sit this one out". Tank spoke into his ps5 headset. On his TV screen there was a lobby full of online players. It was eight o'clock am Sunday morning. One of Tank's off days from running his club. Even though he owned a strip club Tank was truly a geek at heart. Loving video games, his major hobby was being a big call of duty gamer. "Alright bro, bye hurry back. We're gonna need you on when we hit this nuke town", said a fellow gamer with the profile name cuffyochick86. Tank took his headset off then went to peep out his window. Someone had just rung his doorbell. He saw a Camry with a young black lady sitting behind the wheel. *I definitely don't know her*, he thought to himself. There was only a handful of people that knew where he lived. And they all knew to call before showing up. Tank lived in a middle-class neighborhood where everyone kept to themselves. He moved to the front door then looked out the peep hole. There was a dark-skinned boy standing on his porch carrying a book bag. He had neatly braided corn rolls and looked very young. Thirteen, fourteen Tank assumed. "Who is it?" Tank called from his side of the door. "Um, my name is Robert Murphy and I'm selling candy bars for my school, the student that sells the most wins two hundred dollars. I'm going door to door asking people if they would support me", the young boy said with a big grin. "Nah, I'm good lil man try next door". Tank rejected the boy's sales pitch.

The boy's face went from happiness to a wreck of devastation in an instant. His chin dropped into his chest. He then turned to leave. "Damn!" Tank said feeling bad for killing the boy's spirit. He was only trying to get his hustle on. Tank was like that little boy at one time in his life. "Ahh wait... Hold up kid". Tank swung open his front door standing in the doorway. The boy turned still looking upset. "Who's that?" Tank nodded towards the woman seating in the car. "That's my sister, my parents are in jail. She's all I've got". The boy gave more info than he needed to. "So, you just tryna be the man of the house huh? lil man". Tank said respecting the boy's motives. "Yes Sir", the little boy said with his chest poked out showing his bravery. "Aite then. What'cha got on the market", Tank asked. The boy went straight into salesmen mode taking his book bag off with the swiftness. He sat it down on the porch and unzipped it. Tank could see the bag was filled with all types of chocolate bars. "I got goody bars, milk chocolate bars, white chocolate bars, chocolate with almonds, chocolate peanut butter crunch with..." "Oh shit!" Tanks eyes grew with fear. He tried to run but the little black boy was to fast upping the Glock 17 with a 30 round clip he had at the bottom of his book bag hidden by the candy bars. He pumped fourteen bullets into Tank's stomach and chest with one squeeze of the trigger. His pistol was fully automatic.

Everybody body in the streets called this type of weapon a switch. Tank's body seized up then dropped backwards he landed in the door way dead. The killer salesmen stood over Tanks lifeless body aimed the switch at Tank's head pulling the trigger again, the gun exploded with an assault of bullets that Swiss cheesed the already dead mans face in less than four seconds. "You want be needing this". The boy said reaching down into the bloody mess he'd just created taking off the bust down VVS chain that was around Tank's neck. Tank wore a platinum Rolex watch. The boy unclicked it. Then tossed the jeweler along with the pistol into his book bag. He zipped it shut and threw it on his back in one motion. "And my parents are in jail because of rat niggas just like you". He said before racing off to the car with the woman waiting behind the wheel. He got into the car and closed the door. She pulled off and was gone before any neighbors came out.

****

"Baby can you stop at that store so I can get something to eat?" Kisha pointed at the gas station up a head. "Damn lil greedy we just ate," Omar joked. "I know but I want some candy", she whined as she ran a hand up his pants leg then down between his thighs giving him a gentle squeeze. Omar felt heat surge in his groin. His blood rushed, making his manhood grow. Kisha unzipped Omars pants freeing his penis. "What're you doing girl?", he asked with a look of pure lust. "This!" She leaned over the middle console taking him into her wet warm mouth. He almost lost control of the wheel. Due too driving with one hand and holding a blunt in the other. He slowed down then turned his brand-new black on black Lamborghini truck into the gas station. Kisha made slurping sounds as her head bobbed up and down. "Oh... Shit!" He hit the gas then slammed on the brakes making the vehicle skirt to a stop beside a gas pump and almost rear ending a car right in front of them. He paid no attention to the woman at the wheel all he wanted was to bust that nut. He put the truck into park and reclined his seat all the way back so Kisha could finish what she'd started. He wasn't worried about anyone seeing them through the five percent tent windows. Kisha climbed into her seat to get maximum leverage. Omar unbuckled his pants and pulled them down just a little so he could release the rest of him. She worked her mouth fast while using both hands. "Yeah uhm, uhm just like that". Omar had his eyes closed.

She gracefully deep throated all of Omar's pole, then did circular motions when she reached the head's tip. Up and down, she went nonstop suddenly she gripped his penis head choking it and she sucked on the head only. "I... I... I... oh...shit... damn... hold up wait". Omar had never gotten head this good in his life. His hands hovered over the back of Kisha's head; it was as if her hair was a hot stove eye. Because every time he tried to touch the back of her head, she would make him jump with pleasure. She felt his penis beginning to swell. Omar came in her mouth like a volcanic eruption, shooting three heavy loads. She caught every last drop, not wasting even a little. "OK, ok". Omar tapped out but she continued to suck on his wood like a giant straw. "Go..d dam..n shhh.Ki..ssshaa". He fought his best. She gave him one more squeeze making sure he was bone dry. A small droplet of sperm appeared. She seductively kissed it away before sitting back in her chair. Omar's heart was racing in his chest like he'd been running a relay. "What you want from out the store?", he asked, pulling his pants up. Kisha wiped the corners of her mouth with a wet napkin she'd taken from her pocketbook. She looked like she'd just finished a meal. She smiled. Kisha's lips were so damn sexy. She had what you called dick sucking lips and it was not doubt that she was a true eater. A savage when it came down to anything sexual. Her teeth were straight and extra white. Her nose was little and cute, shaped like a button.

Pretty light brown eyes. She kept her hair in a short bob. Today she wore a Prada halter top revealing cleavage of her perky C cup almost D size breasts that made most men drool over. And to put the icing on the cake her ass was big and round sitting up on her back just like a horse. Some people said she was the reincarnation of the porn star Cherokee. "Umm I want a Dr Pepper and some black Forest gummies, and baby you need to drink more water," she instructed. While glamorizing herself in the sun visor mirror. "Drink more water. For what?" "Because your nut tasted too salty you might got high blood pressure. If you drink some grape juice or eat a few Starbursts it's gonna sweeten up", she said seriously. "Girl you are crazy", he said not believing the things she was telling him. "No, I'm the head doctor and I just prescribed your antidote". She took the blunt from the ashtray relighting it.

Omar laughed jumping out the Lambo heading into the store. Kisha watched him until he disappeared out of sight. That's when she made her move. Going into her pocketbook it only took a second finding the military green 40 caliber XD out lined with hot pink. Quickly she slid the pistol under the driver's seat. She almost felt sorry for the man she was about to setup but fuck it. It's a dog-eat-dog world she told herself. Three months ago, Kisha's friend and boss came to her with a proposal she just couldn't refuse. Befriend some nigga named Omar which was easy. Omar jumped on her like a fly to shit the moment he saw her throwing that ass in front of him at the club. Her mission was to plant this gun on Omar at the time Bea told her too. At first though she wasn't with it. Because the only way to get close to a person like Omar, she knew she'd have to be sucking and fucking on him in every type of way. Bea had to give Kisha the full 411 on who he was and what he had done to Meme. Bea also informed Kisha that if she did her this one huge favor, she'd give her the the nail salon. Kisha had already been managing the shop for the sisters almost a whole year now. Making weekly drops of cash never being less than nineteen grand. Originally, they had her managing the nail shop because they told her they both had contracted covid-19. Kisha never believed their story but went along with it anyway. She loved Bea and Meme. They had gotten her outta the strip club, and into a place of business where she could pursue her own career as a real woman of business. Point blank they were good to her. Now Meme was locked up for murder. Kisha knew her friends were deep in the streets. This was her opportunity to help a true friend in need. Kisha had sent Bea a text message over an hour ago while she and Omar shopped at the Four Seasons Mall. Whatever the case may be, her job here was done. This would be the last day fucking with Omar. I'm rich bitch she smiled on the inside as she blew out marijuana smoke. Omar opened his door and climbed into his seat. He gave Kisha a black plastic bag with her items before shutting his door. "Thank you, daddy". She got back into her role like an actress. She passed Omar the blunt and opened her soda taking a swig. "Damn this

bitch still ain't went nowhere." He said
talking about the woman parked in front of
him at the next gas pump. He took a heavy
pull of the blunt then put the Lamborghini in
reverse so he could back out but hit the
brakes when an unmarked police car pulled
into the store directly behind him with its
blue light on. "Fuck". Omar quickly dropped
the blunt into the ashtray. Ever since seeing
the news of Rafiq death at the hanger, he'd
been nervous. Omar was getting major paper
now. Rafiq had placed him in charge of four
stash houses full of narcotics to sell. Omar
put Dice in charge of one of those spots.
While he handled the other three.

Omar had been waiting for Taliban to
contact him for the past three months. So, he
could pay for the consignment he owed. But
when he never showed up, Omar figured he
must have been dead too. Omar had over
seventy-five million dollars' worth of drugs
to play with. It was open season for him
after this he would be set for life.
"Something told me to leave my pistol at the
house". He smiled at Kisha rolling his
window down freeing a cloud of smoke.
"Smoking much?", the officer asked,
fanning the smoke out of his face. "Yeah,
Officer me and my lady been enjoying
ourselves shopping and blowing that Jonny

Blaze", Omar said with a friendly smile. There was no point in lying to the cops, it only made things worse. The officer looked into the vehicle checking out Kisha. She smiled nervously. "Well luckily for you smoking isn't illegal but smoking in the public is, license and registration." Omar slowly reached over Kisha into the glove box. He rambled for a second until he found the correct paperwork. "Wait right here". The officer said going back to his car to check the DMV database.

"It's ok boo. I'm not dirty, everything straight", Omar ensured seeing worry lines on Kisha's face. She nodded her head without a word. "Yeah, yo ass think you not dirty", she said to herself. The officer returned to the car after about ten minutes. "I need the both of you to step out of the car", the officer said giving Omar his license and registration back. Omar wanted to protest but didn't, because the officer had probable cause, the strong stench of weed. Omar got out of the car; Kisha slowly followed suit. They walked with the cop to the back of the Lamborghini and the front of the unmarked police car. "Is there any weapons or drugs or anything you need to tell me about?" The lawman asked Omar. "Nah!", "Ma'am?" He looked at Kisha. "No sir", she said. "Stay

right here". The officer walked to the front
seat of the vehicle to begin his search. He
reached under the seat looking for the pistol
he already knew was there. "Sir I'm going to
need you to put your hands on the top of
your head". Detective Ford spoke with a
strong stern voice with his hand clutching
his holster. "For what?" Omar became upset.
"Look man I'm not going to tell you again
put your FUCKIN HANDS UP. DOWN ON
YOUR KNEES", Ford shouted, making
people stare. Omar was about to buck but
chose wisely not to when Ford upped his
Glock 19 putting it all up in his face. He and
Kisha threw their hands in the air and got
down on their knees. Ford quickly and
professionally cuffed Omar then sat him in
the front seat of his police car. "On your feet
young lady", he told Kisha before retrieving
the XD 40 pistol. She was scared as shit. "Is
this yours?" He popped the clip out de-
cocked the firearm then sat it on the hood of
his car. "No sir". She immediately answered.
"That's not my fucken gun! You tryna set a
nigga up. You fucken pig", Omar screamed
from the passenger's seat going crazy.
Detective Ford and Kisha spoke a few words
that went unheard. She tried her best not to
pay Omar any attention as he went psycho in
the front seat. Ford said something, she

nodded her head in agreement. Kisha looked at Omar one last time then walked away. "Baby! Baby where you going? Don't listen to that nigga he 12 Kisha, he can't be trusted". But his cries fell on deaf ears. He watched her walk to the front of the Lamborghini and get into the passenger seat of the car that had been blocking them in. She closed the door. The car pulled away from the pump then made a U-turn coming around the other side of the same pump. Omar had a look of pure disbelief when he saw who was driving the car. "Kendra! Bitch I'ma kill you". Was all he could think to say. Bea and Kisha locked eyes with him as they passed. They pulled out of the parking lot and sped down the street. Detective Ford watched Omar and felt a little remorse. But he had promised to make things right. "I know she my seed but bitches ain't shit". He shook his head. Detective Ford's phone rang. "James Ford". He answered and listened. It was the office calling. He was needed on scene asap another homicide. They never seemed to stop happening. "10-4, I'll be in route as soon as I transport this detainee to county". He hung up and jumped into the front seat. Omar held his head low, no doubt defeated.

Ford put the vehicle in drive and pulled away. "My work here is done".

Chapter 21

Boolaid blew a larger cloud of Zaza smoke into the air, then passed the back wood to Mad Max. They were at Toya's house in Justo's man cave. The two sat in silence as they smoked and watched the video that played on a 47-inch LG TV. Bea hacked Rafiq's head from his shoulders with a machete then held his decapitated head up to the camera. "Don't fuck wit us, period" she threatened. The video stopped leaving Bea paused with a face full of impoliteness. Boolaid couldn't see Mad Max's facial expression, but he did feel the evil smile he had hidden behind those spell bound dreads. "What nigga? I know you got some ignorant shit to say. So gone head and spit it out". Boolaid broke the silence. "She is a straight demon", Mad Max laughed. He threw his dreads behind his shoulders revealing glossy red eyes dancing with amusement. "And you said that's your sister come to find out?" " yeah, she is. We got a DNA test and everything. She one hundred percent my sibling", Boolaid told his best friend. "Bruh yo sister gangster as hell. How you end up so soft? All in the video like he already dead". Mad Max mimicked Boolaid telling Yusuf, Rafiq was already defeated. "Your sister put in the real work. But that's to be expected", he joked. "Nigga you got me fucked up", Boolaid said with low chinky eyes. The brothers shared a laugh. "Shiid tho my nig you been M.I.A for a while I know you back with some good news for your boy black ops", Mad Max joked seriously.

He and his new crew of men had sold those 40 keys months ago while Boolaid was away with Yusuf in Afghanistan. And

keeping his word with Bigz they popped off
the war with Dice and Red. Things had
gotten really violent, people were dead.
People were in jail. And it didn't look like
shit would calm down any time soon. "I
actually do have good news, great news.
How about a never-ending supplier of
anything we want. We on my nigga I mean
set for life". Boolaid became excited
jumping to his feet giving Mad Max a hard
handshake. "That's what the fuck I'm talking
about," Max said passing the blunt. "Check
though, I knew it's up between three hunnit
and eight hunnit, but is there any way you
and Dice can call some type of truce or
cease fire so we can run this bag up without
interruption of bullets and police? Me, you,
and Dice all went to school together as far as
I can remember y'all niggas was cool".
Boolaid said then choked on the weed
smoke. "For real for real Dice and I are still
tight. I got dude number and everything. But
Boo this shit bigger than me and him. And it
really don't got nothing to do with blood or
crip. Because at this point you got civilians
out here drilling", Max said meaning people
that didn't bang. They were even jumping
into the beef headfirst. "This shit is about
neighborhoods. Some just so happen to gang
bang and some not. They just killed two of

our's bro. And you already know they gunning for Bigz like crazy. Word got out that he smoked Derrick and Joe Joe."

"We already up eight to four on the score board so they trying to line shit up at any cost. I could holla at Dice, but at the end of the day these young niggas ain't trying to squash shit. To many people dead. That's probably why he hasn't reached out to me. He know like I know ain't no friends in war only allies. Out of all the people in the world you should know that Bulak. It's out of my hands doggy. We just gotta let it play itself out. Big bank take little bank you feel me", Mad Max explained. "Yeah, I feel you. Whatever you need I gotcha". Boolaid let his friend know he was down with whatever. "Jason! Devontae's here". Toya called from the front of the house. "Okay sis tell'm we in the back", Max shouted. A few moments later a young dark-skinned boy with corn rolls walked into the room. He wore a bookbag.

He was carrying a six-year-old boy on his shoulders who wore a big smile. "What chall doing? Uncle Jason". The little boy asked even though he already knew they were smoking weed. "We getting high. You wanna get high?" Max asked his nephew. "YEAH!" he shouted climbing down the

dark-skinned boy like a spider monkey. He
raced up to his uncle jumping up and down
in his face. Mad Max took a giant pull of the
Zaza then blew the smoke into the child's
face. Little Justo took the shot gun like a
champ. "Aite Justin get out! We gotta talk
grown folks' business". "Ok uncle Jason.
Uncle Bulak give me a high five nigga."
Boolaid held his hand out, the little boy
smacked Boolaid's hand as hard as he could.
Then punched the dark-skinned teenager in
the stomach before running out the room.
"He looks just like his daddy and just as bad
too", the boy with cornrolls said. "Hell
yeah." Everybody agreed. "Big buzzo
Rifles to Grenades", he said, "Grenades to
Rifles", Max said back. They interlocked
their fingers making the shape of the letter
B. Boolaid assumed they were just on some
gang shit. "Yo Killa, this my nigga Boolaid.
Boolaid, this my lil cousin Killa", Mad Max
introduced the two. They embraced with a
handshake and a back tap. "Yea, we've met,
Toya introduced us to one another at the
funeral", Killa said. "Say no more, but check
Killa did you ever see about that pest control
situation I had?" Mad Max got straight to
business.

Killa swung his book bag off, sitting
it on the floor, he unzipped the bag then

went into it. "Verification", he said giving Mad Max a custom bust down chain with a charm that road Tank in all diamonds. The jewelry was covered with dried blood. "I'm keeping this", he said putting the Rolex around his wrist. Killa had the same blood running through his veins as Mad Max. Mad Max smiled seeing his family member being on demon time like him. He happily gave his cousin a brown paper bag he had sitting on the table. Killa opened it to check the contents. He looked at his big cousin with raised eyebrows. "It's an extra twenty. That's for you and your little girl friend", Mad Max said. "Nigga I told you she not my girl", Killa shot back. "Aite well tell her I'm tryna see what that pussy like", Mad Max declared. "Chill lil daddy". Killa shyly smiled while he held his hands out like he was trying to get someone to slow down, "yeah like I said girlfriend". They all shared a laugh. "Yeah, whateva nigga I got a long ride home, so I'm gone", He said giving everyone dap.

"Boolaid I told you I was down wit the murder game". Killa said with a mischievous smile before leaving the room, shutting the door behind him. "What is he talking about?" Boolaid asked. "Tell Meme I said she's welcome". Mad Max tossed

Boolaid the chain. Boolaid instinctively knew Killa had killed the eyewitness claiming to have seen her that night at the club. "You heard what happen with Omar's bitch ass?" Mad Max asked. "Nah what happened?" "This fuck boy done got caught with a pistol at the store. They say he telling everybody he was set up. It's all-over social media. People making post saying free him. Yeah, free my op". Mad Max clutched his glizzy with a face filled with hatred. "Damn that's some wild shit," said Boolaid. He thought Max was about to say something along the lines of they found the niggas body stretched the fuck out somewhere. While he was away in Afghanistan, Bea told him that she was going to get Omar lined up. He didn't think she meant getting lined up to go to jail. He wouldn't wish that on his worst enemy. *It is what it is,* he thought. But would be sure to address Bea about what she had done.

His phone chimed, a text message from Aunt Robin asking him where he was, he had a dinner date to attend, and he had better not been late. "Yo bro that's moms hitting me I gotta go. The shipment will be in next week". He informed his friend giving him dap. Toya. burst into the room all of sudden with her face full of red. "Hey sis", they both said. "Nah don't hey me with y'all stupid asses. How many times I gotta tell y'all stop getting my son HIGH!" She pouted. Boolaid tried to sneak pass but got punch in the shoulder what seemed like one hundred times before he finally made it through the door. Mad Max couldn't stop laughing. "Yo stay dangerous bro", he called out. "Stay dangerous!", Boolaid shouted back. "AAHHHHHHHH!" Little Justo came running into the room in only a pair of batman underwear. "Stay dangerous Uncle Jason". The boy dived on top of Mad Max. He wrestled with his nephew slamming him on the couch. "Stay dangerous Lil Justo".

****

"Hey, Detective Ford", he said with an extended hand. "Hello! Detective Michelle", she replied. Ford had been reassigned a new partner. This was their first time meeting each other. At the crime scene of yet another murder. "It's so nice to finally meet you. Detective, I've heard so much about you." Michelle appraised him. She was 5'2 with blond hair and light blue and grey eyes. Her body was well shaped with a pretty face to match. *Damn she chosen*, Ford thought to himself. "Nice to meet you as well, so what we got?" He became serious. "Um Jeff Conwon, age 37, multiple gun shots to the mind section and head", Michelle informed him as the forensics team took snap shots of the gruesome carnage left behind by Killa. "Someone really bust this guy's melon", she examined. Tank's face, it was a bloody mess. It looked like someone crushed Tank's head the way you crushed a bug's body under your shoe. His brains lined the floor with a huge blob that turned to specks of meat and bone. One of his eyes were completely gone replaced with a gaping hole, no doubt from a bullet. What was left of his mouth was a jawbone with missing teeth. The man's cheeks ripped and torn open exposing a gum line and tongue. "Any witnesses?" "None sir! Although there was a neighbor who reported seeing a young black male no older then 12 maybe 13 fleeing the the area. But that's it". Michelle read off her notes.

Tank was the eyewitness willing to testify against Meme in court. Bea and Boolaid were tying up loose ends as far as Ford could tell. They wanted Meme home and obviously were willing to do whatever it took. After witnessing all the stuff that went down in that hanger, he knew both his children were well capable. He hated the life that found them. He wished things were different, but they weren't. They were his seeds and no matter what he would see them through this. He'd never give them up. "Looks like we gotta long day ahead of us. They don't need us here. Let's go sit down over a cup of coffee with lots and lots of sugar", Ford said to his new partner. "10-4, sir".

****

One year later...

"Has the jury come up with a verdict?" The judge asked the jury. "Yes, your Honor we have". An older white lady with a head full of grey hair said, standing up to be the representative for the other eleven jurors. Meme sat beside her lawyer at an oak wood table. Her hands were in prayer position and head bowed. The D.A had tried to get Meme to take a plea deal of man slaughter carrying a sentence up to 2 to 5 years. She had already been down a year and some change. One more year didn't sound that bad. Because if she lost at trial, she'd most likely get a life sentence because they would charge her with every count instead of just one. She wanted to take the deal, but her lawyer assured her that they had the case beat so making a deal was unwise. *There was no witness. No one to point her out how could they convict her*; she thought as her stomach turned and twisted into knots. Bea, Aunt Robin, and Meme's mother Olivia all sat in the front row benches directly behind Meme. They were all huddled up in their own prayers hoping for the best outcome. "We the jury, find the defendant.... Not guilty of all charges." Meme burst out with tears of joy giving her attorney a vice grip bear hug. "Thank you, thank you", she cried into his chest. "It's my job". He patted her back. Bea, Aunt Robin, and Olivia jumped up and down with celebration. "Ms. Jones I'm sure this has been a scary experience for you, and I hope an eye opener as well. I never ever want to see you in my court room again. You're now free to go". The judge slammed his gavel. Meme raced to her friends and family. They hugged and kissed each other rejoicing in song like a church choir.

"Damn girl you done got thick", Bea said smacking Meme on the butt. Meme playfully backed that ass up so did all the other women. "I know y'all bought me this little ass dress for trial". "Girl don't act like you would have gotten something any bigger you know you like hoochie momma clothes", Bea joked. Meme had gained over 30 pounds being locked down in a cell with nothing to do but eat soups, chips and honey buns. "You been in there eating all them swolls", Olivia said with a smile giving her daughter another tight squeeze. She was so proud of Meme, being able to stay sane while locked up. Because doing prison time had broken Olivia and if it wasn't for Meme, she would of still been in the streets or somewhere dead. "Ms. Jones I'm sorry to break up the family reunion but you have to go with the deputies so they can process you out the system", the lawyer told the group of ladies. "Ok, Mr. Freeman". Meme smiled at her attorney. "Aite girl gone head. We got to be at the airport in four hours", Bea said. "Airport?" Meme questioned. "Yes bitch. We going on a 30 day girl's trip", Bea smiled. "Just a little vacation baby", added Olivia. "OK, where we going?" Meme said with raised eyebrows. "MIAMI!" All three women shouted excitedly.

****

"Hey Boolaid!" Keke said with a big smile when she opened the door to let him

in. "Sup girl what y'all got going on?" He
stepped into Bigz's three-bedroom condo,
he'd bought paid in full with his share of the
money Mad Max had given him after selling
the forty kilos. "Nothing, we just chill'n in
the living room. I'm twist'n his nappy head
for his birthday", she said as Boolaid
followed her. Keke was dark-skinned and
very, very pretty. She was a young high
schooler with a nice shape like a track
runner. Keke was 17, she and Bigz had been
together since they were 12 or 13. The two
had been through a lot with each other. She
was there when Bigz mother died. Boolaid
walked into the living room and found Bigz
sitting on the floor with his back up against
the couch. Keke sat down on the couch with
Bigz in between her legs. He had a comb
dug in his hair separating the new growth
from the freshly twisted locks she'd already
done. "Damn that shit look like it hurt",
Boolaid said seeing the man's scalp bulging.
"Nah this shit ain't bout nothing. What's
poppin though big homie?" Bigz spoke with
a backwood dangling in the corner of his
mouth all the while playing 2K on ps5.

"Nigga don't play dumb you already
know what's Poppin. Happy born day my
young boy". "Preciate it. What's that?" Bigz
noticed Boolaid carrying some sort of

412

suitcase. "What do you think it is?," Boolaid smiled, so did Keke. "A present? Forrr mee?" Bigz sounded surprised with a hug cheesy smile. He dropped the controller no longer thinking about the game. "Hold up bae". He stood to his feet and gave his mentor a hard dap then hug. He took the case from Boolaid and sat it on the coffee table. Quickly he unlocked the latches then looked inside. "Oooooh snap. For real dog, Baby look," Bigz said picking up the 24k all gold micro drako with monkey nuts. "Big bro she's beautiful". Bigz held the weapon like a newborn child. "Everybody say hello to Baby Girl". Bigz told the whole room.

Boolaid and Keke shared a hard laugh knowing how much Bigz loved his guns. "Nah thanks for real big bruh, you really out did yourself this time", Bigz said placing Baby Girl back into the case like he was putting his own child into a babies play pen.

"Aye I'm glad you liked that. I just came by to give you your present before I slide out". "Word, where you going?" "Miami with my girls. I gotta make sure they stay out of trouble". "Factz, them some wild girls", Bigz joked. "Tell Meme congrats. Its all-over social media she took them people to trial and smacked they ass", Bigz said walking Boolaid to the door. They

gave one another a firm handshake. "Aye
bro, do you think you can do me a solid?"
Bigz brought his voice down to a whisper.
"Yeah, anything lil bruh, what up?" "While
you down there in Miami can you make a
quick visit to my mom's gravesite and put
some fresh flowers on her grave? It's been a
minute since I've been back home". "No
question bruh, I got you. Anything for
momma CC", Boolaid said remembering the
times he was with Bigz moms. She was
really cool to him when she was alive.
Boolaid wished things could have been
different with how her life had turned out.
"How's your investments with Stupid Dude
and the music shit going?" Boolaid wanted
to know. "Shit, to be honest a little rocky
Stupid Dude got a buzz throughout the city,
but we need just a bigger push, its so many
rappers in the Town you feel me?"

"Yeah, I feel you. So, check this when
I get back me and you gonna take that trip
down to the ATL., we gonna build on some
little bruh big bruh shit. And while we're
down there I'll introduce you to some good
people I've networked with in the industry".
"No doubt big homie I love you bro", Bigz
said meaning every word. "Love you more".
Boolaid turned to leave. Bigz closed the
door and went back to the living room.

Keke's phone was ringing but she just ignored it. Bigz got back in position in-between her legs. He held his head back with his eyes closed as he caressed Keke's feet and ankles. "Happy birthday baby, I love you". She said massaging his scalp and going back to twisting his hair. "Love you too boo". Keke's phone chimed letting her know she had a FB notification. She rolled the screen down to see the message. It was from Red, and it read *where you at?* She replied *at home* then sat the phone face down on the couch. "Who dat?" Bigz asked with his eyes still closed as she twisted away. "Nobody baby just somebody sharing a post". She lied as her phone chimed once again. This time when she checked the message it said, *on the way.*

Omar stared up at the ceiling. He'd been doing this for over an hour. He was in disbelief. "How could such a thing like this have happened to me?" He spoke out loud to himself. Omar was at the top of the food chain the alpha and omega just to be tricked off the streets by some ratchet ass bitches. Framed for a pistol that wasn't his. And what made things even worse, only a few months after being arrested he was brought up on more charges. Murder? "This can't be life", he said to the detectives. Apparently, the

gun had been used at the strip club the night
Justo was killed. Meme had killed one of the
Middle Eastern men with a shot to the face.
Omar had already figured he'd been set up
on the club shooting which was bad enough
but what blew his mind was when the
detectives indicted him for Curtis's death.
Again, that gun had killed another one of his
associates. At that moment Omar knew Bea
and Meme were the masterminds behind the
whole situation from the beginning. Luckily
for Omar there wasn't enough evidence to
convict him of any of the murders. He just
couldn't get around the fact that the weapon
was found under the front seat of his car. He
had to wear that although he swore to his
lawyer that Kisha had set him up while he
shopped for her in the store. But that's not
what the police report stated. According to
the officer on the scene Omar was the only
occupant in the vehicle. Omar didn't want to
risk the chance of losing at trial and getting
a ten-year sentence.

Because of his criminal history, he
signed a plea deal for two to four years. In a
couple months he'd been transferred to a
federal penitentiary somewhere out in
Kentucky. Fifteen months down with good
time and a few classes he could be home in
the next 8 months. "I'll be home soon

enough and when I do, I'ma kill them bitches. Then I'm run that bag all the way up". He talked to himself and the four walls in his cell. Dice had been holding shit down like a true nigga. Plus, Omar still had two stash houses no one knew about. He'd be back to his old self in no time. He just needed to tough this shit out. Omar sat up on his bunk, when he heard a loud double tap on his cell's door. "Visit", the C.O said looking through the small window in the middle of the door. Omar jumped out of bed and put on his fresh icy white new balance 95's. Then he stood in front of the cell door. The C.O put a key into the chuck hole to open the slider. "Turn around and give me your hands," he ordered. Omar obeyed by turning around and holding his hands out backwards. The officer reached into the cell through the small slider hole in the steel door cuffing Omar's hands. Omar continued to stand with his back to the officer. That was a prison protocol to ensure the safety of the staff working the facility.

"Turn around", the C.O said. Omar turned on his heels and was caught by surprise when an unknown man grabbed him by the throat snatching him up off his feet. The man brought Omar down on his back with a bone crushing choke slam knocking out all the wind in Omar's chest and body. The back of Omar's head cracked against the cement busting it wide open. He tried to scream for help, but nothing escaped but a low growl. "Three minutes", the officer told KB before closing the cell door locking the two men in there alone. "More than enough time", KB snared reaching into his waistline brandishing a long home-made ice pick. KB squeezed as hard as he possibly could around Omar's neck. Omar fought wildly, flopping like a fish out of water. But with his hands cuffed behind his back there was nothing more he could do. KB rammed the ice pick deep into Omar's chest. Once, twice, then again. He pulled it out then jammed it in again. Over and over again like this was a *Friday the 13th* horror movie.

"Shut the fuck up!" KB covered Omar's nose and mouth with his hand smothering all sounds. Omar never thought there could be pain this real. "Yeah, I know", KB agreed seeing Omar's facial expression. "You tried to kill my lil nigga? Huh?" KB rammed the ice pick into Omar's body. The tip of the blade blew a hole into the man's lung. Blood began to flood the organ. Omar could taste the metallic flavor of his own DNA. He gagged drowning in his own blood. "Then you tried to kill my

BABY!" He questioned Omar who wasn't listening but only fighting to stay alive. "Nigga you got life fucked up", KB evilly whispered into Omar's ear.

KB held the ice pick high into the air one last time before driving it down at top speed. The makeshift metal broke through Omar's breast plate piercing the heart. All fighting ceased. Omar coughed blood. It jolted from his mouth and nose like a volcano. Tears streamed down the sides of his eyes as he looked into KB's eyes. "Shhhhh!" KB pushed the blade, but it wouldn't good any deeper. "Go to sleep hoe!" He coached Omar into his approaching death. Omar's feet became numb, then icy cold. The coldness and numbness crept up his legs into his stomach, then arms. Finally, it rose up through the chest and neck. Omar looked up at KB in a dreamy stare. No more hurt, no more pain he felt, only sleepiness. His mouth hung slightly open. He looked passed KB no longer seeing him. Instead, he saw a tall shadow hooded figure pointing directly at him. Omar blinked his eyes a few more times, then he saw nothing. KB saw the blank stare of a dead man and knew he was gone to a place nobody on this side knew. The C.O opened the door. "We need to hurry", he said peeking inside. "Right on time we're done here". KB pulled the knife out of Omar's body then stood to his feet. He walked to the door but stopped and turned around to look at Omar one last time. "If you push you pay. Pussy."

TO BE CONTINUED.......

**Like what you just read? Take a sneak peek into
PUSH YOU PAY: BIG 6 Head Crack
"only the strong survive"**

Chapter 1

Dallas TX
2030, present day

I took a long hard pull of the grape
backwood filled with a 3.5 of Zaza. My
lungs filled up with smoke that tasted like
Fruity Pebbles. The marijuana was strong
and very potent, making my body relax
instantly. I held in the cloud of gas for as

long as I could before blowing it out with a hard cough. I took one more pull then passed the blunt to my nigga Blaze. He followed suit by doing the same thing I did. This was the ritual we did before we popped shit off. Tonight, we were in Dallas, Texas about to hit a quick lick for fifty thousand. Even though the blunt helped calm my nerves, my body still felt wired like I had been plugged into a wall socket.

Electricity surged all through my body making me feel super charged. "JA'Doe are you ready?" My manager Shampoo asked me and Blaze. She wore a mic head set with an all-black shirt that read UMG Manager in white bold letters. I nodded my head, letting her know I was ready. Blaze did the same by giving her the go. "Ok then. Three... two... one! we're on". She talked into her headset as she did her countdown holding up one finger. The beat dropped; music began to play through the speakers filling the building with loud sounds. Me and Blaze rushed out on stage making the crowd jump to their feet going crazy. "Dallas, Texas whatz poppin?" I shouted into the mic as I looked down into the masses of gangstas, street niggas, hoes, thots, college kids and normal working people.

Tonight, they all had one thing in common. They paid money to watch me, and Blaze put on. Our DJ started to mix and master multiple singles we'd dropped. The fans whooped and hollered. Then the DJ stopped on my latest song. That's when I showed my ass. "All of my niggas on go. None of my niggas on froze. Catch a case keep my mouth close. Head shot watch his brains explode". Thousands of people rapped along with me as I performed. It still amazed me that people all across the world actually learned the lyrics to my songs. So many people out there that thought like I thought, felt like I felt and even in some cases really lived like I lived. "UMG we gonna slide through, big homie still get them pounds through". Blaze jumped on the chorus making the bitches lose their minds. It was the way he harmonized and rode the beat that made their pussies moist. It wasn't rapping or singing but a mixture of both. A God's gift that made him different from the rest of the artist. A straight gangsta but from the outside looking in you would have thought he was just a pretty boy. Very dark-skinned complexion. The type of black skin that looked extra smooth. He had a straight line of white teeth with a neatly trimmed mustache and goatee. Eight wicked dreads

that fell waist length but tonight they were
tied up in a tight bun. Lights of all types of
colors danced all around the stage following
wherever we went. Both of us had on
enough jewelry to buy fifty bricks of heroin
a piece.

Our fingers, wrists, and necks were lit
with multiple iced out rings, bracelets, and
chains. We both wore matching UMG
chains that glittered with crushed bust down
vvs diamonds that shined like a night sky
full of stars without a cloud in sight. We
looked like modern day kings from the
motherland of Africa. Outfits, top of the line
designer. And I'm not even gonna lie, before
all this rap shit, I wasn't even into all the
new fashion. Give me a pair of jays and
some sweatpants and I was straight. Blaze
on the other hand had to be fly at all times.
So, most of the time I just let him style my
clothes for the shows. Because I knew with
him you couldn't go wrong. Blaze walked
over to the left side of the stage where a
group of women were. They reached
upwards grabbing at his feet praising him
like a God. He looked directly into one of
the screaming fans' eyes pointing to her as
he performed. "Oooh my God, he's talking
to me!" She shouted with hands
uncontrollably shaking in front of her

425

mouth. Her eyes rolled to the back of her head right before passing out.

I laughed to myself shaking my head, he made at least one woman pass out every show. Security standing at the corner of the stage moved through the crowd of people then carried the unconscious lady away. Blaze knelt down at the edge of the stage to get closer to his followers of groupies. One reached up; he took hold of her hand. The sexy women jumped up and down crying out with pure joy and excitement as he sang sweet nothings to her. When out of nowhere, a hand grabbed Blaze by his UMG chain yanking the 30-thousand-dollar pendant. It didn't pop, the solid gold locket wouldn't allow it to break. If a nigga ever said they snatched a rapper's chain from around their neck, them niggas was capping or either the chain was cheap ass a bitch or just fake as hell. You really had to put in some work and earn a bust down chain like mine. The only way to win my trophy was to rob me at gun point or beating my ass then removing the necklace from around my neck yourself. You wasn't about to do some easy shit like snatch and run. Oh, hell naw I'd rather die than give a thief anything. I'm hardheaded by the way! You was gonna have to show me. Whoop me! Shoot me straight up! If a

nigga let somebody beat them for their chain
and didn't have to go to the hospital
afterwards, they were a straight bitch, I
mean goofy, at least in my eyes.

Blaze fell off the stage headfirst into
the sea of people. And I was right behind'm
I jumped off the stage drop kicking the man
that tried Blaze right in his face with both
feet. The force from my air attack made his
body fold inward like a lawn chair. All three
of us hit the ground hard. Blaze and I got to
our feet quickly. Men and women patted us
on the back and tried to cop fills. The chain
bandit still laid on the cement floor, I'm sure
still dizzy from the blow he'd just taken.
Blaze booted the man directly in the mouth
knocking him out cold along with some
teeth. He stomped the man in the head one
more time for good measure. We thought the
guy was alone until I got hit with a blind
punch from a nigga standing to the side of
me. Another man squared up with Blaze,
they wasted no time ganging it out. I threw a
wild punch that hit nothing but air. He came
back with an upper cut to my chin, my knees
buckled but I kept my balance staying on my
feet instead of hitting the ground. If I hadn't
been as big as I was and been in as many
fights as I'd been in, this nigga probably
would have knocked me out. I dropped my

chin into my chest and crouched low in my fighting stance. We went hard on each other going toe to toe. Tonight, went from a music concert to a double boxing prize fight as people yelled wanting to see blood instead of hearing songs.

"Yeah nigga!" I said moving in crushing this nigga with a powerful two-piece combo. My diamond rings slit his face open like razors with each blow. There was a piece of meat dangling from his cheek, and he had a big ass gash right above the eyebrow. Blood rushed down his face dripping into his eyes knocking all the fight outta his hoe ass. He kept his guard up as he slowly backed away then disappeared into the ocean of people making a get away. I looked around for Blaze "Dammnnn!", I said finding him and about ten bitches beating the shit out of the chain bandit and another nigga. Real police officers and security were now pushing people out of the way trying to get to us so they could break up battle royale.

They turned the lights on, the DJ stopped playing music. I rushed over to Blaze. "Bruh, we need to get back on stage". I yelled into his ear over the loud crowd of people. One thing I've learned over the years in the music industry is that you honored your contacts. We still had more songs to perform. I didn't have time for any lawsuits, or rumors spreading that me and my camp didn't finish our jobs. Blaze and I didn't care about this weak as fight. We used to fight just for fun back in the hood. We climbed back on stage looking out on the thousands in attendance. People were cheering, some booing. Other fights had broken out in different sections of the arena. Local hood beef, no doubt in my mind. "JA'Doe, Blaze come on let's get outta here! The show's over!" My manager Shampoo screamed in my ear. I didn't pay her no mind; Shampoo was scary as hell. Any sign of drama she was ready to get on that bike. "Nah poo! get us a mic". She looked like she wanted to protest but knew better. She was the manager and great at her job but when it came to shit like this, I made the final decisions. I wasn't about to miss out and lose this easy fifty bandz. A brother needed that cash. She ran off stage then returned with two microphones. "YOOOO, YOOOO!" My voice roared out the speakers echoing through the building. All the mayhem and melee' stopped just like that. The entire building went quiet, all eyes on me. "They just told me and the blood we gotta go the shows over. Is the show over?"

I held the mic out to the audience.
"Hell no, the show ain't over!" The crowd
answered then started booing and cussing.
"The show must go on, right?" I said turn't
up. "Go, Go, Go, Go" the people chanted.
There was a one hundred-thousand-dollar
bounty for anyone that could get their hands
on my, or Blaze's UMG chain. The
challenge came from a rap artist named B
Hooks. All because of a bitch. I didn't know
she belonged to him. She didn't tell me that
while I was beating that pussy down.
Anyway, a year ago me and B Hooks did a
show together, he pressed me backstage
about the damn girl. One thing led to
another, a fight broke out and I knocked his
ass out. We been beef'n ever since. I
already had beef back home in my own city,
now this. Now let me explain how rap beef
goes. You don't just beef with the rapper
you beef with the nigga's fans too. I had ops
worldwide because of this guy. Anybody
that fucked with B Hooks was an enemy of
mines. I really didn't give no fucks, but for
real for real that shit was sad. I thought
music was gonna be my way out the streets,
it just got me in more streets. I mean a nigga
couldn't even go legit without still having to
drop his nutz. Tonight, a nigga tried to get
that hunnit bandz but came up empty handed

and left toothless. Blaze allowed the women that helped him fight get onto the stage. I can't even front all them bitches was bad. Different shapes, sizes, colors, and got damn phat asses. I already knew they were coming back to our private penthouse in downtown Dallas.

The crowd waited in a stunned silence not knowing what was about to happen next. Was the show going to continue? Or would they lose out on the money they spent? For one I'm a real nigga. I wouldn't even feel right if I'd left and didn't put on like I knew I could. Plus, I just beat the shit out of a nigga in front of thousands. I was pumped the fuck up. And you already know, ain't no telling how many phones done recorded the brawl. It was going viral right now. So, I said the first thing that came to my mind. "Let a nigga take my chain, I bet not". There was an instant uproar of cheers, from fans and the haters all agreeing with the *Money Bagg* punch line. You fought for yours at all costs. The DJ dropped the beat right on cue. Blaze and I killed that shit.

****

I woke up the next day to the sound of my iPhone vibrating against the nightstand. I

431

went to reach for the phone but had a hard time trying to move. I was trapped, lying in the middle of a super big king-sized bed. My body intertwined with five beautiful naked women, two on my left, two more on my right. Each one holding on to one another while they held on to me. They all were trying to rest their heads on my chest and stomach like I was a life size pillow. Arms and legs everywhere keeping me locked in place. Then to top it off, there was a chick actually asleep under the covers in between my thighs. I could feel her warm breath blowing heat on my nuts. To this day I still don't know how in the hell she was able to sleep in those harsh conditions. Her parents must have been scuba divers. After the show was finished, we brought the ladies my nigga hand pick for us back to the hotel suite. He took five with him to his room, I took five with me. I popped two perc's, tens off the gate I already knew shit was about to get real. Me and my niggas liked to take the pill before sex. It kept the dick up and hard. I called it giving a bitch the numb dick. After about an hour of smoking hella blunts of gas and running through a few bottles of Henny and Pink Champagne the pill had kicked in and was riding me hard. I could tell by the warm sensation that started in my stomach then crept up into my chest. We all got naked and went crazy on each other. I made sure I passed around a fair share of dick. The girls sucked, licked, and ate on one another while I took turns having fun with them back shots. Ass and pussy, everywhere. After the sixth nut it hurt to get the wood up. They were like a pack of wild Piranha wanting blood after waiting days without food. I was their prey because they savagely ate me alive. I slowly untangled myself by peeling away arms, gently lifting legs to the side. Some moaned and mumbled words in their sleep too low for me to hear. One girl that told me her name was Lil Bit opened her eyes and gave me a sleepy smile. She was the baddest of all the others. Not because she looked better, because all five were fine ass hell. She was just that type of female I was attracted too. I loved dark skinned women, but she was different. Her complexion wasn't dark black or brown. She was a dark red with eyes along the color of grey and green I really couldn't tell. But what made shit official was the long jet-black hair that fell well past her little bubble butt. And she had perky B cup breasts, the ones I like. She couldn't have weighed no more than a buck 40 and didn't look to be

over five feet tall, my guess 4'9. I called
that fun size.

I was a real giant compared to Lil Bit.
I stood 6'4, 247 pounds with a thick pole,
dreads that dropped waist length. I've been
growing them since a teenager. Straight up I
was big nigga. Not fat, or diesel, I was in
shape, I just like to eat. My chest was big
and burly with shoulders and arms to match.
My stomach wasn't flat, but it didn't poke
over my belt or jiggled when I walked. My
beard was full and thick. I kept it well
maintained.

People said I resembled the rapper *J. Cole*
who is definitely in my top five favorite
rappers alive. Hopefully, I could get a
feature in the near future. All in all, I see
myself as the black lumber jack. "Good
morning", Lil Bit yawned. "You mean good
afternoon", I climbed out of bed grabbing
my phone just as I missed the call. The
screen saver read 1:57 pm. Lil Bit slid outta
the bed and came to stand in front of me.
She stood so close that her nipples brushed
up against my skin, they were hard. We sat
in silence admiring each other's nakedness.
Her hand gently moved from the top of my
chest down to my semi hard penis. She
massaged me in her hands. I used my facial
recognition to log into my phone to see who

had been calling me. Missed call from Blaze, one from Shampoo, and a few from the homies back home in Greensboro, North Carolina; twenty missed calls from my baby momma Keke. I'm sure only checking to make sure I was good from the fight that happened last night. Because Dallas police, will lock your black ass up.

By the time I made it to the hotel last night the fight was all over social media. FB, IG, Snap Chat, World Star you name it, it was up there. Once again, I proved to the world me and mines ain't no bitches. Lil Bit had a nigga hard as a brick. She was so short I could damn near put it in her mouth while she stood straight up. She took hold of my dick with both hands. Hands so tiny she barely could wrap her fingers around the whole thing. She put the head in her mouth then moaned with her eyes closed like she'd just tasted the best food in the world. "Com'on". I put the phone down, taking her by the hand. I wanted to fuck this one down low.

She followed close behind in a dream-like state probably still in shock that she was really getting dicked down by a superstar. We ended up in the bathroom with the shower shooting hot steamy water making the room fogged out with mist. But we weren't in the water although Lil Bit was super wet in between her legs. I sat her up on the sink crushing the pussy with her back pressed up against the mirror. She swung her arms around my neck and wrapped her legs around my waist. I lifted her off the sink "mmmmm" she moaned as I ran my man hood deep into her goodies fucking her in the air. She used my shoulders for leverage bouncing up and down on the dick like a pogo stick as I stood tall. "Oh yes daddy. Fuck my pussy daddy!", she cried biting my neck. "Oooowwwa you gone make me cum already. I'm...cum.min on your dick". Her whines made me become more ruff pinning her to the wall. "Ahh", her back hit the wall hard. I went to work pumping ten inches all up in them guts. Her pussy walls squeezed gripping me like someone trying to ring the water out of a washcloth. Cum gushed from her pussy hole running down my nuts and legs. I let her down to her feet. Her legs shook and wobbled. I had to hold her up to keep her balance just so she wouldn't fall.

"Turn around!" I demanded. She turned her back to me and we stared into the mirror watching our reflections. She was slightly bent over giving herself to me as she held on to the sink waiting to be punished. She was so short I had to bend at the knees just to get up in her. "Damn Lil Bit." I couldn't help myself; her pussy was really that good I couldn't even play that shit off. She moaned wildly then looked down at the floor filled with ecstasy biting her bottom lip. "Nah look at me while I'm fucking you". I grabbed a hand full of her long jet black hair giving it a strong tug like I was riding a horse. Her head lifted backwards, she tried her best to look at me through the mirror but struggled, closing her eyes from my magic stick.

I smacked her ass it, wobbled. I palmed her cheeks open, ramming her, our skin made slapping sounds. "Ugh! Ugh!... shit". Was all she managed to get out. "Yeah, watch me fuck that pussy". I took hold of her hips banging her out. "Fuck me, fuck me yeesss, just like a dog fuck me just like a dog!" she yelled. "Daddy my pussy is sooo hot," she said as we stared at each other in the mirror. My vision started to get blurry feeling the nut coming. I know I was supposed to be wearing a condom, but I wasn't. And I know I was supposed to pull out, but I couldn't. In the heat of the moment a brother's pull-out game was weak as hell," ahhh shidd". I shot a whole hunnit rounds in the pussy. I'm talking straight monkey nutz. It took a full five minutes before we caught our breath. Someone knocked on the door, then entered before I could even answer. "So that's where you two been hiding", a yellow bone chick named Emoni said with raised eyebrows and a face full of mischief and lust. She was super thick with a short hair style. Her face was really cute, and she had a tattoo of a broken heart under her right eye. She stood in the doorway. I noticed the rest of the gang all trying to take a peep in.

They stared at our nakedness. None of them had put on any clothes either. "Damn I'm need another perc", I said. Because I knew I was about to be taken advantage of. "Let's take a shower", I told them all. After about two more hours of them sucking and fucken the soul out of me we bathed, got dressed, and ordered food service. I allowed them to have whatever they wanted on the menu. It ain't tricking if you got it. While the ladies enjoyed their meal, they were laughing and giggling amongst each other with their phones out. I'm sure expressing to the world how much fun they had last night being thots. I stepped out onto the balcony to call the mother of my children.

The view I had on the balcony was something crazy you could see all of downtown. "Hey Bae, is everything ok", my BM asked as soon as our face time

connected. "I been calling you for hours",
she admitted with a face full of concern.
"Yes, BM I'm good", I ensured her as I lit a
blunt of some Zaza called Dragon's Milk.
"You know niggas been trying us ever since
that shit wit B Hooks popped off". I took a
toke of the blunt kicking myself in the ass
for even mentioning B Hooks name. Keke
knew just like the rest of the world that this
lame assed beef was all because I fucked his
girl that he didn't even go with anymore.
"Uhmm and I saw you and Blaze help'n
them girls on stage. That's probably why yo
ass ain't been answering the phone". Keke
had the stank face and suddenly changing
the whole subject from the fight to the
bitches. "Bae don't do that", I said seriously.
I mean for real. A nigga could be in a
burning down house with flames
everywhere. We'd have nowhere to go. The
only chance of survival would be to call
911. She'd hear a female operator and would
be like who is that operator's bitch you was
talking to. Bitch we bout to die. I couldn't
help smiling at my own thought. "Whatever,
JaQuan. When you coming home? I miss
you and so do the kids".

"We gonna be down here in Texas
one more day. Miami's the next stop. After
that I'm shoot'n straight to the hizouse". I did

a dance for my baby. "And don't try and put everything on the kids. I know what's really going on Keke. You tryna keep tabs on this dick". I pulled my sweatpants down letting her have a quick sneak peek. "I miss you and so does he. Neither one of us will ever get enough of that big, fat, wet kootie kat". Keke tried but couldn't keep a straight face. She cracked that beautiful smile. She loved the sound of her man singing his love for her. That's all she really wanted to know, she's still my number one. I still had her, and she had me. Us two had been missing around over the past 14 years. We had two children. An eight-year-old girl named Khiah and a two-year-old boy named Kobe. When I first got my rap deal things had gotten rocky between us. I was always on the road, spending most of my time in the stu. Stu was short for studio. While I was out getting money trying to make shit stable for us, she was at the house, being insecure. Worrying about all the wrong shit. She knew how serious the beef was with them eight hunnit niggas. Shit! Her own cousin almost smoked my boots bout his hood. Luckily, he ran out of bullets. People were really out in the streets dying and it seemed like all she thought about was me fucking bitches that meant nothing to me. I sat her down and told her what it was. If I had sex on the road I wouldn't catch feelings, fall in love, bring any babies home or STDs, most importantly secret relationships.

She was reluctant at first but finally agreed, even though she didn't like it. And it wasn't necessarily because I was having sex. It really was because she didn't trust other females and their unknown motives. Sometimes I only feel like Keke fucks with me because when I was younger, I did a little jail time. And while behind bars she did some not so loyal shit to me if you know what I mean. So now that were back together, she's only trying to prove to me that she's truly sorry for how she did a nigga. Probably that and a little guilt rolled up in one. I really could give two fucks; Keyona is and forever always will be my first true love.

I sat on the balcony talking to my love for over an hour. I always gave her phone time when on the road. That was one of my ways of showing her she could keep my attention. And that I loved her nonetheless than I did fourteen years ago. Shampoo stepped out onto the balcony. I held a finger up telling her to hold on. "Look baby, Poo just popped up". "Hey Keke!" Shampoo said jumping into the camera. "Hey girl, make sure he behaving", Keke said becoming excited seeing my manager. She liked Shampoo, they'd became good friends over the past few years. Shampoo knew all about the rap game. She always knew the right words to use on Keke when ever she fell into one of her crazy bitch moods. Plus, her being gay didn't hurt. At least she knew Shampoo wasn't fucking her man behind her back. "I gotcha girl", Shampoo said acting like she was about to take off her belt and beat a nigga. "Aite boo I love you but I gotta go". "Ok. I love you more". She looked sad with her sexy lips poked out like a baby. I ended the call then gave my full attention to my manager.

I liked Shampoo a lot, a really good friend everything she did for me was always in my best interest. And yes, she was very intelligent. My brother Boolaid introduced us some time before he fled the country. "I take it the families doing well?" "Families well", I answered. "What's on the roster for the day?" She tapped the screen on her tablet looking through it. Shampoo kept that tablet at all times. "Photo shoot, then rest". She looked back into the hotel room where my favorite fans lounged and laughed. "Aite sis. Get rid of them. Make sure everybody gets rides to where they want to go, but that one right there!" I gestured towards Lil Bit. "Get her contact info. I needed to feel them insides on more time". Shampoo gave me the evil eye not liking my request but knew better, so she just let it go. "Where's Blaze?" "Do you really have to ask". Shampoo said searching through her tablet. "Spending money as usual". I shook my head with a sigh. There was nothing wrong with enjoying yourself have fun by all means, but my nigga had a spending habit. He needed to learn how to invest paper and not give it away. When we were trapping that work in the street's he was doing the same thing, some people just never learn. I just started to figure stacking money was a gift, everybody couldn't do it.

This life, the rap life, famous life, could be here today and gone tomorrow. "OK well when he's finish fuckin that check up, come back to the room. We're all gonna have a sit down and discuss a few things about how we can further our brand". I was always thinking of ways to expand. "But right now, I need a lil time to myself". "Will do boss". Shampoo went inside without another word. Before the girls left, I took a single selfie with each one of them then took a group pic tossing it on my IG. My following was growing more and more by the day. After last night's events my page would soar. Soon I was all alone in my penthouse suite. I loved to have moments of solitude, bathing in my own silence. It helped me put my master plan together. I rolled yet another blunt. Went into my phone uploading an instrumental that a popular DJ named DJ K sent me. Anybody he gave a beat to, song went platinum. I pressed play and closed my eyes listening. I bobbed my head and began to think back on my life.

About the Author:
Kalub Shipman

Currently serving a life sentence in a federal penitentiary, during incarceration he discovered the talent of writing. Creating stories in the genre of fictional realism. Just like his situation, the characters in his novels go through real life situations that readers can grasp and relate to. Not only that, but his novels are also filled with action and adventure causing his characters to express real emotions and thoughts, leaving you sitting on the edge of your seat wondering what's going to happen next. The storylines are one of a kind and if you look closely there are jewels and messages that can be learned from each one of his characters.

What's Poppin? I just want to thank everyone who stood by my side in the midst of adversity and the struggles I've endured. Following the characters I've created. I love to make people dig deep into their imagination making their emotions run wild. It's my way of giving back. God blessed me with a gift and I'm humbly thankful that he showed me my gift when he did. Because it got me through hard times when I didn't think I would make it. It's never too late to get it right. No matter where your home is. In the streets or behind that wall. When one door closes another one will open. Always have faith. A mind is a terrible thing to waste. So, use it before it's useless. Get it right before you get left.

I have two beautiful daughters that love me to death. Khiah and Khaileah And that's who I do it for, Peace Almighty.